D1666584

European Yearbook of International Economic Law

EYIEL Monographs - Studies in European and International Economic Law

Volume 31

Series Editors

Marc Bungenberg, Saarbrücken, Germany

Christoph Herrmann, Passau, Germany

Markus Krajewski, Erlangen, Germany

Jörg Philipp Terhechte, Lüneburg, Germany

Andreas R. Ziegler, Lausanne, Switzerland

EYIEL Monographs is a subseries of the European Yearbook of International Economic Law (EYIEL). It contains scholarly works in the fields of European and international economic law, in particular WTO law, international investment law, international monetary law, law of regional economic integration, external trade law of the EU and EU internal market law. The series does not include edited volumes. EYIEL Monographs are peer-reviewed by the series editors and external reviewers.

Pieter Van Vaerenbergh

Greening Trade Remedies

Environmental Considerations in the Law
and Practice of WTO Trade Remedies

 Springer

Pieter Van Vaerenbergh
Brussels, Belgium

Dissertation zur Erlangung eines Grades einer Doktorin/eines Doktors des Rechts der Rechtswissenschaftlichen Fakultät der Universität des Saarlandes vorgelegt von Pieter Van Vaerenbergh

Tag der Disputation: 10. Oktober 2022
Dekan: Prof. Dr. Annemarie Matusche-Beckmann
Erstberichterstatter: Prof. Dr. Marc Bungenberg
Zweitberichterstatter: Prof. Dr. Reinhard Quick

ISSN 2364-8392   ISSN 2364-8406   (electronic)
European Yearbook of International Economic Law
ISSN 2524-6658   ISSN 2524-6666 (electronic)
EYIEL Monographs - Studies in European and International Economic Law
ISBN 978-3-031-38171-3   ISBN 978-3-031-38172-0   (eBook)
https://doi.org/10.1007/978-3-031-38172-0

This Springer imprint is published by the registered company Springer Nature Switzerland AG
The registered company address is: Gewerbestrasse 11, 6330 Cham, Switzerland

Preface

This monograph was submitted as my doctoral thesis, which was written during my time as a research associate at the Europa-Institut of Saarland University. My thesis was supervised by Prof. Dr. Marc Bungenberg, who offered me the opportunity to explore an academic career when I was an LL.M. student at the Europa-Institut. I am grateful for the freedom and opportunities he granted me throughout my time as a research associate at his Chair. I am also indebted to him for flagging the importance of environmental concerns in the law of trade remedies.

The public defence of my thesis took place in October 2022, before a doctoral committee of legal experts, authorities in their respective fields and my academic role models. I thank Prof. Dr. Thomas Giegerich, director of the Europa-Institut, for chairing the committee and guiding the pleasant discussions. I thank Prof. Marc Bungenberg for organising the defence, his feedback and thoughtful questions. I thank Prof. Dr. Reinhard Quick for accepting to be the second supervisor and for the challenging and insightful discussions at the defence. I thank Prof. Dr. Helmut Rüßmann to complete the committee and for the years of working together on the successes of the Vis Moot team of Saarland University.

This book would not have been possible without the company and support of my wonderful friends and colleagues. Their support has made my PhD process and my time as a researcher a pleasant and enriching experience. I wish to thank all my colleagues at the Chair and the Europa-Institut over the years, and especially Angshuman Hazarika, Andrés Alvarado Garzón and Bianca Böhme. I should also extend my gratefulness to Andrés and Bianca for proofreading my manuscript and providing honest feedback for improvement—you are right, the law of trade remedies is a complex and technical matter!

On a personal note, this thesis would not have been possible without the continued and unconditional support of Konstantina, who has been by my side throughout the whole journey, and of my parents and family in Belgium, who had to miss me a little longer than anticipated during my extended stay in Saarbrücken.

Last but not least, I am thankful to Saarland University, the Europa-Institut, and everyone who has been a part of my journey in Saarbrücken, which has been an incredibly pleasant and fascinating experience.

Brussels, Belgium   Pieter Van Vaerenbergh
May 2023

Contents

1	**Introduction**.	1
	References.	5
2	**A Role for Trade Remedies in Greening International Trade?**.	7
	2.1 Introduction	7
	2.2 Global Policy Objectives of Sustainable Development and Environmental Protection Applicable to World Trade Disciplines. . .	8
	2.2.1 WTO Commitment to Sustainable Development and Environmental Protection	8
	2.2.2 Legal Status of the Preamble of the WTO Agreement.	10
	2.3 Trade and Environment: From Conventional Beliefs to a New Generation of Cases Featuring Trade Remedy Challenges	11
	2.4 Dual Role of Trade Remedies in Achieving Environmental Protection Through Trade Measures	16
	2.4.1 Lowering the Trade Remedy Burden on Green Industries with Positive Spill-Overs.	17
	2.4.2 Application of Trade Remedy Duties to Level the Environmental Playing Field	19
	2.5 Chapter Summary	21
	References.	22
3	**WTO Rules for Greening Trade Remedies**.	25
	3.1 Introduction	25
	3.2 Regulation of Trade Remedies in the WTO.	26
	3.2.1 History and Emergence of the WTO Trade Remedy Rules	26
	3.2.2 The Foundations Underlying the ADA, ASCM and SGA . .	27
	3.2.3 Policy Discretion in the Rules of the ADA and ASCM	30
	3.2.4 Trade Remedy Rules in WTO Accession Protocols.	37
	3.2.5 Trade Remedy Rules in RTAs	39

3.3   Domestic Legislation on Trade Remedies in Selected WTO
       Members   40
       3.3.1   Overview   40
       3.3.2   Case-Study: EU Trade Defence Instruments Regulations . .   42
3.4   Chapter Summary   46
References...   47

4   The Use of Trade Remedies on Green Goods   49
4.1   Introduction   49
4.2   The Case for Liberalising the Environmental Goods Market   50
4.3   Defining Environmental Goods   51
       4.3.1   Tariff Lines for Environmental Goods   52
       4.3.2   Environmental Goods: Impossible to Define or
               Impossible to Negotiate?   53
       4.3.3   WTO Compatibility of Environmental Tariff Lines.   58
4.4   Restrictions on the Use of Trade Remedies on
       Environmental Goods   64
       4.4.1   Abolishing the Imposition of Trade Remedies on
               Environmental Goods   65
       4.4.2   Disciplining Trade Remedies on Environmental Goods ...   66
4.5   Options for Implementation...............................   74
       4.5.1   Amendments to the ADA, ASCM and SGA   75
       4.5.2   Environmental Goods Agreement   78
       4.5.3   Regional Trade Agreements........................   79
       4.5.4   Unilateral Policy Choices: Who Sets the Right Example? . .   82
4.6   Chapter Summary   86
References...   87

5   Low Environmental Standards and the ASCM Rules   91
5.1   Introduction   91
5.2   Low Environmental Standards as Subsidies   92
       5.2.1   The 'Invisible' Subsidy of Low Environmental
               Standards   92
       5.2.2   Low Environmental Standards as Actionable Subsidies
               Under the ASCM   94
       5.2.3   Rethinking the Scope of WTO Subsidies Disciplines   101
5.3   Dual Pricing Schemes as Actionable Subsidies Under the ASCM . .   104
       5.3.1   Environmental Impacts of Dual Pricing Schemes   105
       5.3.2   Dual Pricing Schemes as Input Subsidies Under the
               ASCM   107
       5.3.3   Strengthening WTO Subsidy Disciplines for Dual Pricing . .   115
5.4   Benefit Calculation and Environmental Costs of Production   117
       5.4.1   ASCM Rules on Benefit Calculation (Art. 14 ASCM)   118
       5.4.2   China-Specific Methodology (Sect. 15 CAP)   125
       5.4.3   Remodelling ASCM Benchmarking Rules   126
5.5   Chapter Summary   128
References...   129

6 Low Environmental Standards and the ADA Rules 133
6.1 Introduction 133
6.2 Environmental Regulation and Government-Distorted
Costs and Prices.. 134
6.3 Environmental Cost Distortions and Normal Value Calculations .. 136
6.3.1 Market Economies: Standard Methodology
(Art. 2.1 ADA)..................................... 136
6.3.2 Market Economies: Alternative Methodologies
(Art. 2.2 ADA)..................................... 137
6.3.3 Non-Market Economies: Alternative Methodologies
(Art. 2.7 ADA + Second *Ad* Note)................... 154
6.4 Fair Comparison and Environmentally Motivated Adjustments
to the Dumping Margin 162
6.4.1 Price Comparability, Fair Comparison, and Adjustments
(Art. VI:1 GATT and Art. 2.4 ADA) 162
6.4.2 Environmentally Motivated Adjustments to the
Dumping Margin 165
6.5 Reform of the Anti-Dumping Regime 168
6.5.1 Expanding the Concept of 'Dumping'................. 169
6.5.2 Interpreting the Existing ADA Rules................. 171
6.6 Chapter Summary 172
References... 173

7 Low Environmental Standards and the SGA Rules 177
7.1 Introduction 177
7.2 Environmental Considerations in Safeguards Investigations...... 177
7.3 Expanding the Scope of Safeguards Measures 180
7.4 Chapter Summary 181
References... 182

8 Environmental Injury and Trade Remedy Rules................. 183
8.1 Introduction 183
8.2 Environmental Harm and the Injury Rules: State of Play 184
8.2.1 Environmental Harm in Trade Remedy Injury
Determinations.................................... 184
8.2.2 Environmental Costs in the Calculation of the Injury
Margin 185
8.3 Expanding the Scope of Trade Remedies: Recent Developments
and Legislative Proposals................................. 188
8.3.1 US Environmental CVD Proposal 189
8.3.2 Regulating Environmentally Harmful Subsidies 189
8.3.3 Rebalancing Measures in the EU-UK TCA.............. 194
8.3.4 Proposals for Social Safeguard Measures 195
8.4 Designing Trade Remedy Calculation Methods to Remove
Environmental Injury..................................... 196
8.4.1 Applicable Environmental Standard 196

		8.4.2	Violation and Evidence	201
		8.4.3	Remedies	203
		8.4.4	Enforcement Mechanisms	204
	8.5		Chapter Summary	205
	References.			205
9	**Concluding Remarks**			209
	9.1		A Dual Role for Trade Remedies in Greening World Trade	209
	9.2		Limiting the Use of Trade Remedies on Green Goods	210
	9.3		Calculating Environmental Costs of Production in Trade Remedy Calculations	211
	9.4		Designing an Instrument to Remedy Environmental Injury Based on Trade Remedy Calculation Methods	213

Cited Case Law 215

Abbreviations

ACCTS	Agreement on Climate Change, Trade and Sustainability
ADA	Anti-Dumping Agreement, Agreement on the Implementation of Article VI of the GATT
ADD	Anti-Dumping Duty
AoA	Agreement on Agriculture
APEC	Asia Pacific Economic Cooperation
ASCM	Agreement on Subsidies and Countervailing Measures
BADR	EU Basic Anti-Dumping Regulation
BASR	EU Basic Anti-Subsidy Regulation
CAFTA-DR	Dominican Republic-Central America Free Trade Agreement
CAP	China's Accession Protocol to the WTO
CBD	Convention on Biological Diversity
CIS countries	Countries of the Commonwealth of Independent States
CITES	Convention on International Trade in Endangered Species of Wild Fauna and Flora
CJEU	Court of Justice of the European Union
CNR	WTO Committee on Rules Negotiations
CNV	Constructed Normal Value
CPTPP	Comprehensive and Progressive Agreement for Trans-Pacific Partnership
CTE	WTO Committee on Trade and the Environment
CTE-SS	WTO Committee on Trade and Environment in Special Session
CVD	Countervailing Duty
DDA	Doha Development Agenda
DDG	Deputy Director-General
DG	Director(ate)-General
DSB	Dispute Settlement Body
DSU	Dispute Settlement Understanding
ECJ	European Court of Justice
EGA	Environmental Goods Agreement
EGS	Environmental Goods and Services

EITE industries	Energy-Intensive Trade-Exposed industries
EPPs	Environmentally Preferable Products
ETS	Emission Trading Scheme
EU	European Union
EU-UK TCA	EU-UK Trade and Cooperation Agreement
FIT	Feed-In Tariffs
FTA	Free Trade Agreement
GAAP	Generally Accepted Accounting Principles
GATT	General Agreement on Tariffs and Trade
GC	EU General Court
GHG	Greenhouse Gas
HS Convention	International Convention on the Harmonized Commodity Description and Coding System
ICTSD	International Centre for Trade and Sustainable Development
ILO	International Labour Organisation
IPPC	International Plant Protection Convention
ITTA	International Tropical Timber Agreement
IUU fishing	Illegal, Unreported and Unregulated fishing
LDCs	Least-Developed Countries
LDR	Lesser-Duty Rule
MEA	Multilateral Environmental Agreement
MFN	Most-Favourite Nation
NAFTA	North American Free Trade Agreement
NME	Non-Market Economy
NTB	Non-Tariff Barrier
OECD	Organisation for Economic Cooperation and Development
OTC	Ordinary Course of Trade
PAGE	Partnership for Action on Green Economy
PMS	Particular Market Situation
PPM	Process and Production Method
PPP	Polluter-Pays Principle
PSMA	Agreement on Port State Measures
R&D	Research and Development
RTA	Regional Trade Agreement
SDGs	Sustainable Development Goals
SG&A costs	Selling, General and Administrative Costs
SGA	Safeguards Agreement
SM	Safeguard Measure
SOEs	State-Owned Enterprise
TDI	Trade Defence Instruments
TESSD	Trade and Environmental Sustainability Structured Discussions
TFEU	Treaty on the Functioning of the European Union
TiSA	Trade in Services Agreement
TPEA	US Trade Preference Extension Act
TPRM	Trade Policy Report Mechanism

TPSSM	Transitional Product-Specific Safeguard Mechanism
TRA	UK Trade Remedies Authority
TRQ	Tariff Rate Quota
TSD chapter	Trade and Sustainable Development chapter
TTIP	Transatlantic Trade and Investment Partnership
UK	United Kingdom
UN	United Nations
UNCTAD	United Nations Conference on Trade and Development
UNFCCC	United Nations Framework Convention on Climate Change
UNFSA	United Nations Fish Stocks Agreement
US	United States
USDOC	United States Department of Commerce
VCLT	Vienna Convention on the Law of Treaties
WCO	World Customs Organisation
WTO	World Trade Organisation

List of Figures

Fig. 3.1   The Lesser-Duty Rule. Source: Author's own creation 35
Fig. 4.1   Example of the hierarchical structure of the Harmonized System.
           Source: Author's own creation. 52
Fig. 5.1   Subsidy pass-through. Source: WTO Negotiating Group on
           Rules, Benefit Pass-Through, Communication from Canada,
           TN/RL/GEN/7, 14 July 2004. 110
Fig. 5.2   Including environmental costs in amount of subsidy calculations.
           Source: Author's own creation. 119
Fig. 6.1   Including environmental costs in dumping margin calculations.
           Source: Author's own creation. 135
Fig. 8.1   Target price determination in the EU. Source: Author's own
           creation. 187

List of Tables

Table 2.1   WTO challenges of trade remedies on green goods 14
Table 8.1   WTO matrix on trade-related measures pursuant to selected
            multilateral environmental agreements (MEAs) 198

Chapter 1
Introduction

In December 2020, former Deputy Director-General (DDG) *Wolff* observed that "the WTO is at the dawn of a new era of addressing deepened and broadened environmental concerns of its Members."[1] Underscoring the fact that trade policies, pursued in accordance with the WTO agreements, have the potential to support environmental sustainability, he highlighted the role of the WTO in advancing global policy objectives of environmental protection levels and climate change mitigation.[2] The WTO has moved beyond the traditional conception of its role in world trade by embarking into two new roles closely related to the achievement of sustainable development:

- liberalising environmental trade, and
- disciplining environmentally harmful trade.

Supported by the Preamble of the WTO Agreement, which foresees that all trade instruments shall contribute—albeit in different manners—to the achievement of the goals of sustainable development and environmental protection,[3] the WTO recognises that world trade disciplines are intrinsically linked to environmental protection and sustainability considerations. Therefore, sustainability considerations appear in all fields of WTO law, even those fields where, on the face of it, it may not be expected—such as the law of trade remedies.

The WTO rules on trade remedies—the Anti-Dumping Agreement (ADA), the Agreement on Subsidies and Countervailing Measures (ASCM), and the Safeguards

---

[1] Deputy Director-General Alan Wm. Wolff, The WTO must not continue as it is, 10 December 2020, WTO Newsroom, 10 December 2020, available at https://www.wto.org/english/news_e/news20_e/ddgaw_10dec20_e.htm (last accessed 26 June 2023).

[2] *Ibid.*

[3] Preamble to the WTO Agreement, first recital.

Agreement (SGA)[4]—comprise a highly technical and regulated legal framework which is largely vested on economic considerations. The trade remedy rules are based on economic criteria, market benchmarks and corresponding calculation methodologies, as well as a detailed procedures for the conduct of the investigation by domestic authorities. Accordingly, it has been argued that trade remedies do not constitute a suitable instrument for WTO Members to exert wider import policy objectives in a manner consistent with WTO legal framework.[5] Nonetheless, there are multiple intersections between the law of trade remedies and environmental protection and sustainability. Each of the traditional trade remedies under WTO law present different challenges to sustainability considerations and the development of renewable energy.[6]

A major discussion is that differences in environmental regulation impacts the cost of goods and whether charges of "unfair trade" are justified in that regard. Many countries have increased their environmental regulations in response to environmental degradation, the depletion of natural resources and the uncertainties surrounding climate change. A frustration exists among these (mostly developed) countries that they see their efforts to regulate environmental protection within their territory nullified through the importation of sub-standard goods from foreign countries where environmental costs for domestic firms are low compared to international markets, or even completely inexistent. This situation has been coined as "eco-dumping",[7] although it refers to a situation of alleged unfair trade under both the anti-dumping as well as the anti-subsidy rules. The argument holds that producers obtain hidden 'subsidies' in terms of low pollution abatement requirements, and they can consequently engage in dumping practices by placing their products in international markets at prices that do not reflect the true cost of production.[8] Developed countries therefore advocate for trade measures that equal out substandard imports from countries with low environmental standards. These countries refer to a danger of transboundary externalities or threats to the global commons (for instance climate change) from these low environmental standards, which is a concern in some, but not necessarily all cases.

However, for developing countries, the level of regulatory intervention on the market constitutes a legitimate source of comparative advantage. They posit that, although some governments may willingly set low environmental standards to attract investments, many others may simply not have the capacity or funds

---

[4] See Agreement on Implementation of Article VI of the General Agreement on Tariffs and Trade 1994, LT/UR/A-1A/3, 15 April 1994; Agreement on Subsidies and Countervailing Measures, LT/UR/A-1A/9, 15 April 1994; Agreement on Safeguards, LT/UR/A-1A/8, 15 April 1994.

[5] See, for instance, Müller et al. (2009), para. I.04.

[6] Meléndez-Ortiz (2016), p. 11.

[7] See, for instance, Sands and Peel (2018), p. 899; Charnovitz (1993), pp. 31–32; Esty (1994), p. 163, fn. 13; Rauscher (1994), pp. 823–825; Lothe (2001), pp. 197 ff; Pauwelyn (2013), pp. 465 ff.

[8] Rauscher (1994).

available to imposed adequate protection levels.[9] This position is also supported by the GATT Secretariat, which has historically rejected competitiveness concerns for environmental trade measures and underlined that differences in environmental standards are a legitimate source of comparative advantage.[10] Equally, the Appellate Body acknowledged this principle in its early GATT jurisprudence.[11] Therefore, not every insufficient environmental standard shall be labelled as an unfair competitive strategy.

To reconcile these two seemingly opposing views on the North-South axe, it is important for the legislator to strike a balance between the positions of developed and developing countries. This balance can be expressed in terms of two conflicting environmental principles which have been codified for instance in the Rio Declaration. On the one hand, the Polluter Pays-Principle (PPP) prescribes that "national authorities should endeavour to promote the internalisation of environmental costs."[12] The PPP intends to ensure that the cost of environmentally harmful measures is reflected in the cost of goods and services which cause pollution in their production or consumption.[13] As such, developed countries argue that a consideration of eco-dumping under the trade remedy rules would be in line with the PPP. On the other hand lies the acknowledgement that environmental standards should reflect the environmental and developmental context they apply in and that standards applied by some countries may be inappropriate and of unwarranted social cost to other countries.[14] This principle of differentiated harmonisation takes into consideration the capacity of each country.[15] Developing countries raise that the trade remedy rules are inapt to address alleged situations of eco-dumping. Striking a balance between developed and developing countries regarding comparative advantages on account of low environmental standards is therefore a challenging task.

Against that background, this study aims to reconcile goals of environmental protection with the rules of trade remedies under the law of the WTO. The objective is to examine all aspects of trade remedy law and policy to identify manners in which trade remedy practice can contribute to the achievement of the objectives of environmental protection and sustainable development.

---

[9] Esty (1994), pp. 156–157. The author argues that punitive measures do not work when the standards of trade partners are low because of lack of information or lack of capacity to adopt environmental protection measures. In such cases, the policy recommendation must be to work together. This might well be different when low standards are a strategic choice, which cannot be seen as legitimate because of specific circumstances including climate, weather, population, economic needs, risk preferences, existing pollution levels, or other local influences. Trade penalties or trade duties may only be allowed in such cases.

[10] See GATT Secretariat, International Trade 1990-1991, Vol. 1, GATT Secretariat (Geneva 1992).

[11] Appellate Body report, *United States – Import Prohibition of Certain Shrimp and Shrimp Products*, WT/DS58/AB/R, adopted 6 November 1998, para. 167–169.

[12] See, for instance, Rio Declaration, Principle 16.

[13] Sands and Peel (2018), p. 894.

[14] See, for instance, Rio Declaration, Principle 11.

[15] Kunz (2015), pp. 311–323.

The first chapters of this study deal with the industrial policy options and the legal framework for greening trade remedies respectively. Chapter 2 sets out a double role for trade remedies to contribute to new policy strategies in the pursuit of the objectives of liberalising environmental trade on the one hand and disciplining environmentally harmful trade on the other hand. Trade remedies may contribute to advancing environmental protection, mitigating the effects of climate change and thereby contributing to the attainment of the Sustainable Development Goals (SDGs). To achieve these goals, the WTO legal framework governing trade remedies must be assessed. To that extent, Chap. 3 sets out the flexibilities and policy space for competent domestic authorities in WTO Agreements on trade remedies. The chapter reveals that the scope of manoeuvre for legislators and investigating authorities is limited but not inexistent.

The study then proceeds with a discussion of the first role, namely the liberalisation of trade in green goods, which can be achieved by preventing or at least disciplining the use of trade remedies on such green goods. Chapter 4 elaborates on the thesis that the use of trade remedies shall be limited in sectors relating to green goods, particularly renewable energy goods. Trade remedies are a market access measure that may render goods less competitive by raising their price.[16] Relieving green goods from additional burdens to trade can therefore be a pathway for trade remedies to support development and innovation in the green goods sectors. This may be a unilateral policy choice of an individual WTO Member to reduce or abolish trade remedies on green goods or take the form of an agreement between willing trade partners.

The second role for trade remedies relates to the calculation of environmental costs of production in the trade remedy duty. The aim is to set out whether and how trade remedies can be used as level playing field measures to ensure environmental cost internalisation. Three chapters are dedicated to each of the three trade remedies. Chapter 5 explores possibilities to resort to subsidies disciplines to counteract imports from low-standard countries where environmental legislation does not ensure full internalisation of environmental costs in the price of goods, which entails an investigation of the width of the subsidy concept to encapsulate environmental regulation in foreign countries as a subsidy, as well as an investigation in the calculation methods to determine the level of countervailing duty (CVD). Chapter 6 turns to the anti-dumping rules and the possibility to calculate environmental costs in the benchmarks for anti-dumping duties (ADDs) by exploring both the concept of normal value as well as price comparability. Chapter 7 examines the limited practice of considering environmental policies in the law and practice of safeguard measures (SMs). Given the restrictive notion of the disciplines of the WTO agreements, the rules do not foresee the possibility to take an activist approach and include environmental costs. Therefore, novel approaches to expand the notion of contingent protection in bilateral or regional trade between strategic economic powers must be

---

[16] Matsushita et al. (2015), pp. 215–216.

developed—which may serve as a catalyst for change on the multilateral level in the long term.

Focusing on several recent developments, Chap. 8 then turns to the injury determination and the rules governing the calculation of injury margin values. Shifting the looking glass to the production costs incurred by domestic industry instead of the exporters, it analyses the potential to include environmental harm in the injury notion and explores the flexibilities of the Lesser Duty-Rule (LDR). It forms the basis for the development of new mechanisms in trade agreements inspired by the trade remedy disciplines which evolve in the direction of combining sustainability considerations with level playing field approaches.

This study starts from the rules and jurisprudence of the WTO trade remedy agreements. It also analyses the interpretation of the basic concepts and provisions of the ADA, ASCM and SGA by the WTO Dispute Settlement Body (DSB) to reveal the possibilities, obstacles, and pitfalls of using trade remedy rules to pursue green objectives. A narrow definition of trade remedies is adopted by only focusing on the three tradition trade remedy agreements and not on other instruments which may be labelled as trade defence instruments. Furthermore, this study is fuelled by existing research on certain relevant aspects, legislative changes in certain domestic jurisdictions and negotiations between trade partners pursuing similar goals of sustainability. It develops on the treatment of non-market economies (NMEs) in trade remedy investigations and state capitalist policies affecting prices of exported goods, which represents one of the most contentious discussions in trade remedy law on which much of the debate on environmental protection can be hinged.

In a novel approach of combining two potential roles for trade remedies to contribute to green international trade, this study is the first all-encompassing analysis of the trade remedy rules in relation to sustainable development and environmental protection. Moreover, it sheds light on how recent legislative developments, including the recent amendments of the EU trade remedy laws, the multilateral negotiations on fisheries subsidies and the conclusion of the EU-UK trade agreement, progress and influence the importance of sustainability and environmental protection in the law of trade remedies. As such, the objective of this study is to advance to the scientific debate on sustainable world trade and to highlight the role of trade remedies.

References

Charnovitz S (1993) A taxonomy of environmental trade measures. Georgetown Int Environ Law Rev 6(1):1–46

Esty DC (1994) Greening the GATT. Trade, environment, and the future. Institute for International Economics, Washington

Kunz M (2015) Principle 11: environmental legislation. In: Viñuales JE (ed) The Rio Declaration on Environment and Development. A commentary. Oxford University Press, Oxford, pp 311–323

Lothe S (2001) Contradictions between WTO and sustainable development? The case of environmental dumping. Sustain Dev 9:197–203

Matsushita M, Schoenbaum T, Mavroidis P, Hahn M (2015) The World Trade Organization, law, practice, and policy, 3rd edn. Oxford University Press, Oxford

Meléndez-Ortiz R (2016) Enabling the energy transition and scale-up of clean energy technologies: options for the global trade system. E15 Expert Group on Clean Energy Technologies and the Trade System, Policy Options Paper

Müller W, Khan N, Scharf T (2009) EC and WTO anti-dumping law. A handbook, 2nd edn. Oxford University Press, Oxford

Pauwelyn J (2013) Carbon leakage measures and border tax adjustments under WTO law. In: Prévost D, Van Calster G (eds) Research handbook on environment, health and the WTO. Edward Elgar Publishing, Cheltenham/Northampton, pp 448–506

Rauscher M (1994) On ecological dumping. Oxf Econ Pap 46(Suppl 1):822–840

Sands P, Peel J (2018) Principles of international environmental law, 4th edn. Cambridge University Press, Cambridge

Chapter 2
A Role for Trade Remedies in Greening International Trade?

2.1 Introduction

International trade and commerce play a focal role in the achievement of global policy goals of sustainable development. The currently widely accepted definition of sustainable development is contained in the 1987 report of the World Commission on Environment and Development titled "Our Common Future"—better known as the *Brundtland* report, after the chair of the Commission, *Gro Harlem Brundtland*. The report defines the concept of sustainable development as:

> [...] development that meets the needs of the present without compromising the ability of future generations to meet their own needs.[1]

It further foresees that sustainable development "is not a fixed state of harmony, but rather a process of change in which the exploitation of resources, the direction of investments, the orientation of technological development, and institutional change are made consistent with future as well as present needs."[2] One common understanding is that sustainable development comprises three pillars—an economic, social, and environmental pillar—which, together, must affect real change to ensure development that can last.[3]

The importance of putting trade in the service of sustainable development goals and environmental protection has been recognised in several forums such as the 1992 Rio Summit, 2002 Johannesburg Summit, the 2005 UN World Summit, and the UN 2030 Agenda for Sustainable Development.[4] Accordingly, the WTO has

---

[1] World Commission on the Environment and Development, Our Common Future, 1987, para. 27.

[2] *Ibid.*

[3] Gehring (2005), p. 368.

[4] See UN General Assembly, Report of the United Nations conference on Environment and Development, Rio de Janeiro, 3–14 June 1992, Annex I: Rio Declaration on Environment and

© The Author(s), under exclusive license to Springer Nature Switzerland AG 2023
P. Van Vaerenbergh, *Greening Trade Remedies*, EYIEL Monographs - Studies in European and International Economic Law 31,
https://doi.org/10.1007/978-3-031-38172-0_2

embraced its position as the international forum for trade law and policy and committed to achieving objectives of sustainable development and environmental protection through trade regulation.

Traditionally, the WTO has ensured environmental protection through application of general exceptions mandating deviation from free trade rules for *inter alia* environmental reasons. How the WTO can implement its pledge for environmental protection and sustainability in the law of trade remedies is yet to be fully explored. Accordingly, this chapter fleshes out the obligation of the WTO and its Members to pursue these goals of sustainability and environmental protection considering the language and legal status of the Preamble to the WTO Agreement (Sect. 2.2). A new line of WTO case law at the WTO level shifted the trade and environment focus from environmental exceptions to the role of the trade remedy agreements (Sect. 2.3). Against that background, this chapter identifies a dual role for trade remedies in the achievement of environmental protection and climate change mitigation: liberalising environmental trade and disciplining environmentally harmful trade (Sect. 2.4). This chapter concludes by defining concrete issues that may help to 'green' trade remedies (Sect. 2.5).

2.2 Global Policy Objectives of Sustainable Development and Environmental Protection Applicable to World Trade Disciplines

2.2.1 WTO Commitment to Sustainable Development and Environmental Protection

As the global organisation regulating and facilitating international trade, the WTO recognises its role in allowing for the optimal use of the world's resources in accordance with the objective of sustainable development. Hence, the protection and preservation of the environment are fundamental to the WTO. The Preamble to the WTO Agreement opens with the following statement:

> The Parties to this Agreement,
> Recognizing that their relations in the field of trade and economic endeavour should be
> conducted with a view to [...] allowing for the optimal use of the world's resources in

---

Development, A/CONF.151/26 (Vol. I), 12 August 1992; World Summit on Sustainable Development, Johannesburg Declaration on Sustainable Development and Plan of Implementation of the World Summit on Sustainable Development: The final text of agreements negotiated by governments at the World Summit on Sustainable Development, 26 August–4 September 2002, Johannesburg; UN General Assembly, 2005 World Summit Outcome, Resolution adopted by the General Assembly on 16 September 2005, A/RES/60/1, 24 October 2005; UN General Assembly, Transforming Our World: the 2030 Agenda for Sustainable Development, Resolution adopted by the General Assembly on 25 September 2015, A/RES/70/1, 21 October 2015, SDG17.

accordance with the <u>objective of sustainable development</u>, seeking both to <u>protect and preserve the environment</u> [...].[5]

This first recital of the Preamble underlines the fundamental importance of the goals of sustainable development and protection and preservation of the environment throughout all WTO agreements. The fact that the two central objectives of free trade—reduction of tariffs and other barriers to trade (market access) and the elimination of discriminatory treatment (non-discrimination)—are only found in the *third* recital of the Preamble puts this commitment even more in perspective.[6]

By elaborating on the importance of sustainable development and the environment in the Preamble, the WTO took a stance on sustainability and environmental protection in world trade and reinforced the recognition of environmental concerns and sustainable use of the world's resources in the WTO as opposed to the focus on resource extraction under the GATT.[7] The GATT 1947 Preamble opened by recognising that the GATT aims at "raising standards of living, ensuring full employment and a large and steadily volume of real income and effective demand, developing the full use of the resources of the world and expanding the production and exchange of goods," before the free trade objectives of market access and non-discrimination treatment. This was in line with the Havana Charter, which already contained a social clause, recognising that unfair labour conditions create difficulties in international trade and that Members should eliminate such conditions in their own territory.[8]

As an expression of its commitment to sustainable development and environmental protection in the Preamble, the WTO recognises and embraces its role in achieving the SDGs.[9] The SDGs, formulated in 2015 at the level of the United Nations (UN), are the latest centrepiece on sustainability and underline the interdependence of the economic, social, environmental, and cultural objectives included in the goals.[10] The SDGs put significant emphasis on the role that trade plays in promoting sustainable development and recognise the contribution that the WTO can make to the 2030 Agenda. Although the SDGs are not legally binding, governments are expected to establish implementing measures in the national frameworks for their achievement. Topical issues in trade and environment at the WTO include working on trade and climate change measures, trade and green economy, and

---

[5] Preamble to the WTO Agreement, recital 1 (emphasis added).

[6] *Ibid*, recital 3.

[7] Hestermeyer and Grotto (2008), Preamble WTO Agreement, para 23.

[8] This clause did not appear in the GATT, nor in the WTO. See Kaufmann (2014) para 7–9.

[9] See United Nations, The Sustainable Development Goals Report 2019, available at https://unstats.un.org/sdgs/report/2019/The-Sustainable-Development-Goals-Report-2019.pdf (last accessed 24 June 2023). See, in detail, Bellmann and Tipping (2015).

[10] UN General Assembly, Transforming Our World: the 2030 Agenda for Sustainable Development, Resolution adopted by the General Assembly on 25 September 2015, A/RES/70/1, 21 October 2015. See *United Nations*, The Sustainable Development Goals Report 2019, available at https://unstats.un.org/sdgs/report/2019/The-Sustainable-Development-Goals-Report-2019.pdf   (last accessed 24 June 2023).

cooperation with multilateral environmental agreements (MEAs). Several WTO legal instruments have directly contributed to the SDGs: The elimination of agricultural export subsidies contributed to achieving Zero Hunger (SDG 2.B), the TRIPs Agreement ensures access to medicine in developing countries, thereby contributing to good health and well-being (SDG 3.B), the WTO gender initiatives are new (SDG 5), the Aid for Trade programme supports economic growth (SDG 8.A), the Fisheries Subsidies negotiations aim to achieve SDG goals too (SDG 14.6). More generally, also the WTO plays a role in the promotion of renewable energy (SDG 7.2), technology transfers (SDG 9) and SDT treatment (SDG 10.A). Moreover, the need for global partnerships is included in the 17th and last goal (SDG 17) to ensure policy coherence for development. As such, the WTO contributes to the achievement of the SDGs on a substantive level as well as a procedural forum for cooperation and exchange.

2.2.2 Legal Status of the Preamble of the WTO Agreement

Preambular language has no immediate power within the WTO legal framework. Its legal significance is limited under public international law because the preamble does not create legal obligations by itself[11]—it only does so when incorporated in the operative parts of the WTO agreements by reference. Although the objectives of the WTO Agreement are referenced further in one article,[12] the actual impact of it remains very limited. Consequently, commentators have described this commitment "wholly theoretical" or "essentially hollow", with reference to the fact that in practice the development aspect has been ignored entirely at the expense of the Global South countries.[13]

Nonetheless, preambular commitments to agreements in the WTO framework may become relevant for the interpretation of the text of certain provisions. Art. 3.2 DSU instructs Panels and the Appellate Body to interpret the WTO covered agreements, in accordance with customary rules of interpretation of public international law, *i.e.* by relying on their text, context, and object and purpose pursuant to Art. 31 of the Vienna Convention on the Law of Treaties (VCLT).[14] The Appellate Body has addressed the legal value of this notion of sustainable development and environmental protection in the Preamble. In *US – Gasoline*, the Appellate Body emphasised the importance of the Preamble for environmental issues.[15] It confirmed that WTO Members have a great autonomy in designing domestic environmental

---

[11] *Mbengue* (2008) Preamble to the WTO Agreement, para. 11.

[12] Art. III:1 WTO Agreement.

[13] See Eliason (2019), p. 557.

[14] See Appellate Body report, *United States – Import Prohibition of Certain Shrimp and Shrimp Products*, WT/DS58/AB/R, 12 October 1998, para. 153.

[15] Appellate Body report, *United States – Standards for Reformulated and Conventional Gasoline*, WT/DS2/AB/R, adopted 20 May 1996, p. 30.

policies, which are only circumscribed by the need to respect the requirements of the WTO covered agreements. [16] In *US – Shrimp/Turtle*, the Appellate Body relied on the objective of sustainable development for the interpretation of the term "exhaustible natural resources" under Art. XX(g) GATT.[17] The Appellate Body combined an acknowledgement of contemporary concerns of the community of nations about the protection and conservation of the environment with the explicit recognition of the objective of sustainable development to interpret broadly the exception under Art. XX(g) GATT. In addition, the Appellate Body held:

> As the preambular language reflects the intentions of negotiators of the WTO Agreement, we believe that it must add colour, texture and shading to our interpretation of the agreements annexed to the WTO Agreement […].[18]

Consequently, the Appellate Body held that the pursuance of non-trade objectives in the Preamble may be achieved through application of the exceptions to the GATT.[19] As such, jurisprudence confirmed the influence of the objectives of sustainable development in relation to Art. XX(g) GATT[20] and Art. XX(j) GATT.[21] Beyond environment-specific exceptions to the basic GATT disciplines, the interpretation standard set out in *US – Shrimp* requires the principle of sustainable development to be taken into account, as far as the specific circumstances of the case allow it, not only for the GATT 1994 but also for the other covered agreements.

2.3   Trade and Environment: From Conventional Beliefs to a New Generation of Cases Featuring Trade Remedy Challenges

Traditionally, the WTO has relied on the exceptions to the GATT to ensure that environmental values are taken into consideration in the pursuance of free trade. Indeed, while pursuing the removal of trade barriers, GATT rules did not intend to restrict countries from taking legitimate action to protect societal values and

---

[16] *Ibid.*

[17] Appellate Body report, *United States – Import Prohibition of Certain Shrimp and Shrimp Products*, WT/DS58/AB/R, 12 October 1998, para. 129–131.

[18] *Ibid*, para. 153 (emphasis added).

[19] Appellate Body report, *European Communities – Conditions for the Granting of Tariff Preferences to Developing Countries*, WT/DS246/AB/R, adopted 1 December 2003, para. 94.

[20] See, for instance, Panel report, *China – Measures related to the Exportation of Various Raw Materials*, WT/DS394/R, WT/DS395/R, WT/DS398/R, adopted 22 February 2012, para. 7.374–7.375; Appellate Body report, *China – Measures related to the Exportation of Various Raw Materials*, WT/DS394/AB/R, WT/DS395/AB/R, WT/DS398/AB/R, adopted 22 February 2012, para. 306; Panel report, *China – Measures Related to the Exportation of Rare Earths, Tungsten and Molybdenum*, WT/DS431/R, adopted 29 August 2014, para. 7.259–7.261.

[21] Appellate Body report, *India – Certain Measures Relating to Solar Cells and Solar Modules*, WT/DS456/AB/R, adopted 14 October 2016, para. 5.72.

interests, including environmental protection.[22] The trade and environment debate emerged already in the 1970s, but gained traction in the early days of the WTO in the verge of several landmark decisions in GATT/WTO dispute settlement procedures. Challenges of restrictive government policies underpinned by environmental considerations have shaped the discourse of GATT jurisprudence on environmental protection and environmental exceptions under the WTO rules.

These cases share a joined narrative where developed countries enacted domestic environmental measures coupled with trade restrictions on imported products that did not meet similar environmental standards, to level the playing field and not put their domestic producers in a disadvantageous competitive position.[23] As a response, developing exporting countries challenged these policies before the GATT/WTO, for violating *inter alia* Art. III:2, III:3 and XI:1 of the GATT.[24] On their turn, the defending countries relied on the general exceptions of Art. XX GATT which allow WTO Members to take restrictive measures in pursuit of important societal values and interests.[25] Environmental values are included *inter alia* in the recognition of measures "necessary to protect human, animal or plant life or health" or measures "relating to the conservation of exhaustible natural resources".[26] In recognising these exceptions, an important balance must be struck between the need of countries to enact environmental legislation and the need to avoid protectionism and discriminatory practices.[27] The traditional nexus in the trade and environment debate is how to balance off in the framework of the WTO the encouragement of national environmental policies with the removal of protectionist barriers, which will spur

---

[22] Van den Bossche and Zdouc (2017), p. 545.

[23] Wu and Salzman (2014), p. 408.

[24] See, *inter alia*, GATT Panel Report, *United States – Restrictions on Imports of Tuna*, 3 September 1991, unadopted, BISD 39S/155; GATT Panel Report, *United States – Restrictions on Imports of Tuna*, DS29/R, 16 June 1994, unadopted; Appellate Body report, *United States – Standards for Reformulated and Conventional Gasoline*, WT/DS2/AB/R, adopted 29 May 1996; Appellate Body report, *United States – Import Prohibition of Certain Shrimp and Shrimp Products*, WT/DS58/AB/R, adopted 12 October 1998; Appellate Body report, *European Communities – Measures Affecting Asbestos and Products Containing Asbestos*, WT/DS135/AB/R, adopted 5 April 2001; Appellate Body report, *European Communities – Measures Prohibiting the Importation and Marketing of Seal Products*, WT/DS401/AB/R, adopted 22 May 2014.

[25] WTO Members can rely on environmental exceptions to pursue the WTO objectives of sustainable development and environmental protection. See Art. XX GATT, but also Art. XIV GATS, the TBT Agreement, the SPS Agreement, Art. 27.2 and 27.3 TRIPS, Art. 8 ASCM, Annex 2 of the Agreement on Agriculture, the Decision on Trade and Environment and the Decision on Trade in Services and the Environment.

[26] Art. XX(b) and (g) GATT. Six out of the 10 subparagraphs of Art. XX GATT may be considered for sustainability purposes: Paragraph (e) on prison labour is the only PPM example of justification for aspects that are not found back in the physical characteristics is explicitly mentioned, paragraphs (a), (b) and (g) are the classic grounds invoked for sustainability, paragraph (d) on compliance with national laws and regulation could be invoked for national labelling requirements, and paragraph (h) allows PPM measures contained in commodity agreements.

[27] Gustafsson and Crochet (2020), p. 188.

environmental protection too.[28] In its case law of the last decades, the DSB has struck a balance between these legitimate regulatory policies and discrimination against or among foreign importers.[29]

In recent years, a shift in the landscape of environmental measures can be observed. Government policies enacted across the globe to support renewable energy and clean energy technology have included renewable energy support schemes, carbon taxes and Emission Trading Schemes (ETS). The imposition of trade remedy measures also plays a role in this new approach in industrial policy-making. Several WTO Members, including the US, EU, China, and India, have adopted trade remedy measures on green goods imports to protect their domestic industries, particularly in the renewable energy sector (solar energy, biofuels, wind energy).[30] Consequently, WTO Members have reported a rising number of ADDs and CVDs in the last years at the WTO.[31] This has led in parallel to a surge in challenges of these measures at the WTO judiciary. These trade remedy disputes are different than the classic WTO environmental protection disputes which challenge illegitimate use of protectionist measures and the non-discrimination principle, whereas in the case of trade remedies, a legitimate protectionist tool may be employed in case of unfair trade practices. Spurred by this new generation of cases, discussions on the balance between free trade and environmental protection have now shifted to the ASCM and the ADA.[32] Accordingly, government measures supporting renewable energy is steering the 20-year-old trade and environment debate at the WTO towards those areas of WTO law that deal with unfair trade.[33]

All three types of trade remedies that have been imposed on imports of renewable energy goods have been challenged at the WTO. Table 2.1 below provides an overview of these cases in chronological order.

First, under the ASCM, only one case concerned a challenge of CVDs on environmental goods. *US – Countervailing Measures (China)* concerns a challenge by China of CVDs on imports into the US of *inter alia* solar panels and wind turbine products for violation of Art. VI GATT, the ASCM and Sect. 15 CAP.[34] Although China based its complaint on the provisions of Sect. 15 CAP, the Panels, Appellate Body, and arbitrators refrained from addressing the provision in their respective reports. The Appellate Body decided on the benchmark determination by the US Department of Commerce for CVD calculations regarding Chinese imports, including solar power and wind power equipment.

---

[28] Wu and Salzman (2014), p. 404.

[29] See Quick (2013), p. 969; Mavroidis (2015), pp. 303–328.

[30] PAGE (2017), p. 38.

[31] See also Sect. 2.4.1.1 below.

[32] See, for instance, Wu and Salzman (2014).

[33] Kulovesi (2014), pp. 342 and 352.

[34] Appellate Body report, *United States – Countervailing Duty Measures on Certain Products from China*, WT/DS437/AB/R, adopted 16 January 2015.

Table 2.1 WTO challenges of trade remedies on green goods

DS-number	Year	Name of the case	Type	Product concerned
DS437	2014 2014	*US – Countervailing Measures (China)*	CVD	Solar panels, wind power equipment
DS473	2016 2016	*EU – Biodiesel (Argentina)*	ADD	Biofuels (Biodiesel)
DS480	2018	*EU – Biodiesel (Indonesia)*	ADD	Biofuels (Biodiesel)
DS545	(2018)	*US – Safeguards on PV Products (Korea)*	SM	Solar power products
DS562	2021	*US – Safeguards on PV Products (China)*	SM	Solar power products
DS572	(2018)	*Peru – ADD and CVD on Biodiesel (Argentina)*	ADD + CVD	Biofuels (Biodiesel)

Source: Author's own creation

Second, under the ADA, two important cases concerned renewable energy inputs.[35] In *EU – Biodiesel (Argentina)* and *EU – Biodiesel (Indonesia),* the Panels and Appellate Body faced challenges of ADDs imposed by the EU on biodiesel from Argentina and Indonesia.[36] In 2013, the Commission used the price adjustment mechanism in investigations on imports of biodiesel from Argentina and Indonesia to offset the differential export tax system of soybeans, which, according to the Commission, as raw material inputs, depressed the price of biodiesel.[37] The findings by the Panel and Appellate Body dealt predominantly with the situation of input dumping, where the price of the main raw material for the production of a good is distorted. The Appellate Body considered that this rule violated the conditions for disregarding costs in the records kept by exporters or producers under Article 2.2.1.1 ADA. It ruled that the 'reasonableness' test in the second condition of Article 2.2.1.1 ADA is one whether the costs are reasonably captured, not if the costs are reasonable as compared to hypothetical costs that should have been incurred.[38] Therefore, the EU did not have sufficient basis to disregard the domestic prices solely based on the finding that those prices were lower than international prices due to the tax system.[39]

---

[35] For an overview, see Vermulst and Meng (2017), pp. 348–352.

[36] Appellate Body report, *European Union – Anti-Dumping Measures on Biodiesel from Argentina*, WT/DS473/AB/R, adopted 6 October 2016. The Panel in Indonesia followed this decision. See Panel report, *European Union – Anti-Dumping Measures on Biodiesel from Indonesia*, WT/ DS480/R, adopted 25 January 2018. See also *EU – Cost Adjustment Methodologies (Russia)*, WT/ DS474 (pending).

[37] See Council Implementing Regulation (EU) No 1194/2013 of 19 November 2013 imposing a definitive anti-dumping duty and collecting definitively the provisional duty imposed on imports of biodiesel originating in Argentina and Indonesia, OJ 2013 L 315/2.

[38] Appellate Body report, *European Union – Anti-Dumping Measures on Biodiesel from Argentina*, WT/DS473/AB/R, adopted 6 October 2016, para. 6.41.

[39] *Ibid*, para. 7.2.

In addition, since 2018, trade remedies both in the form of ADDs and CVDs on biodiesel are being challenged at the WTO in *Peru – ADD and CVD on Biodiesel (Argentina).*[40] The ADDs in case are applied by Peru against imports of biodiesel from Argentina since October 2016.

Third, under the Safeguards Agreement, one challenge of a measure in the renewable sector was launched recently.[41] *US – Safeguard Measure on PV Products* pertains a complaint by China against definitive safeguard measures on imports of crystalline silicon photovoltaic products imposed by the US in November 2017 for alleged violations of the Safeguards Agreement and the GATT. Korea and China challenged the imposition of safeguards imposed by the "Proclamation 9693 of January 23, 2018".[42] The Panel report rendered in the case is notable, because it is the first time that a global safeguard measure challenged at the WTO has fully survived the panel review.[43] Safeguards measures that have been challenged at the WTO had so far never survived the assessment of the Panels and Appellate Body. One commentator foresaw a break in this tradition and held that the challenge may be successful in law.[44] The legislation has already been repealed in the US.[45]

The analysis of trade remedies case law is relative, because of the slowness of WTO review. Countries may apply CVDs or ADDs, await reaction by any WTO Member in the form of a WTO challenge (a tit-for-tat reaction of imposing domestic trade remedies on other products is also possible), await a decision by the Appellate Body, and retract the duties afterwards without the threat of penalties or obligations to refund.[46] Especially in the renewable energy sector, this accounts even more, where fast developments in the renewable energy technology make that a product cycle is no longer than a couple years—the same timeframe for a WTO challenge.[47]

Although many parallels can be drawn with the classic cases, the complex relationship between cheap renewable energy goods, anti-dumping/anti-subsidy rules and climate change objectives pertains to a novel aspect of the trade and environment discussions in the WTO.[48] On the one hand, the burden of trade remedies can

---

[40] Request for consultations by Argentina, *Peru – Anti-Dumping and Countervailing Measures on Biodiesel from Argentina*, WT/DS572/1, 5 December 2018.

[41] Constitution of the Panel at the request of China, *United States – Safeguard Measure on Imports of Crystalline Silicon Photovoltaic Products*, WT/DS562/9, 25 October 2019.

[42] Proclamation 9693 of January 23, 2018 – To Facilitate Positive Adjustment to Competition from Imports of Certain Crystalline Silicon Photovoltaic Cells (Whether or Not Partially or Fully Assembled Into Other Products) and for Other Purposes, 83 FR 3541.

[43] Panel report, *United States – Safeguard Measure on Imports of Crystalline Silicon Photovoltaic Products*, WT/DS562/R, circulated 2 September 2021. See Kreier (2021).

[44] Dawson (2020), p. 370.

[45] Inside US Trade, Senators introduce bill to repeal Section 201 restrictions on solar products, 12 June 2018, available at https://insidetrade.com/daily-news/senators-introduce-bill-repeal-section-201-restrictions-solar-products (last accessed 24 June 2023).

[46] Brewster et al. (2016), p. 335.

[47] *Ibid*, p. 336.

[48] See, for instance, the Chinese solar panels trade war.

be relieved or lowered on environmental goods, thus fostering the development of environmentally friendly goods sectors. On the other hand, trade remedies may ensure the inclusion of environmental costs in production costs of imported goods. Both aspects will be developed further in the next sections.

2.4 Dual Role of Trade Remedies in Achieving Environmental Protection Through Trade Measures

Trade remedies are an important example of border measures, which can be made part of a green industrial policy strategy promoting green industry development, climate change mitigation and environmental protection. The Partnership for Action on Green Economy (PAGE) has formulated several ways in which border measures may advance green goals by boosting green industries.[49] The application of border measures may serve to boost the competitive position of certain producers or sectors which have a lot of benefits for the environment. Policy rationales pursued in relation to border measures and sustainability goals include:

- **Protection of infant industries**: The infant industry theory holds that nascent (*in casu* green) industries need protection against competitive pressure until they mature. Tariffs may be an instrument to achieve that protection, as they will raise the price of competing products in the domestic market and thereby make them less competitive as compared to products not subject to the tariff.
- **Promotion of green industries with positive spill-overs**: Tariff levels may be distinguished between environmentally friendly and environmentally unfriendly industries, instead of between domestic and foreign products. In such case, increased tariffs are applied on certain goods because of their higher environmental footprint as compared to other similar but less harmful goods or, conversely, decreased tariff level are applied on the latter goods to make them more competitive.
- **Levelling the playing field by reflecting the negative externalities of competitors**: The competitive position of green industries may also be boosted when the competitive disadvantage arising from lower environmental requirements abroad is corrected upon importation at the border. Whereas carbon adjustment measures have received a lot of attention in the context of climate change, a similar role can be played by trade remedy duties in levelling the carbon/environmental playing field.
- **Raising the cost of exporting products**: Export restrictions and duties may benefit the environment and domestic industries. By raising the cost of export products such as raw materials or other inputs, their environmental footprint in production may reduce.

---

[49] PAGE is an initiative by UNEP, ILO, UNDP, UNIDO and UNITAR in cooperation with partners and external experts. See PAGE (2017), pp. 28 ff. and p. 30, Box 1.

Trade remedies may play a role in advancing at least two of these roles. First, green industries with positive spill-overs may be promoted by reducing the burden of trade remedies on environmental goods (Sect. 2.4.1). Second, trade remedies may level the environmental playing field by addressing the lack of incorporation of environmental externalities in the price of competing products (Sect. 2.4.2).

2.4.1   Lowering the Trade Remedy Burden on Green Industries with Positive Spill-Overs

2.4.1.1   The Burden of Trade Remedies on Environmental Goods

A first role for trade remedies in the achievement of environmental protection and climate change is to reduce the burden of trade remedies on environmental goods. Trade remedies are an additional tariff imposed in response to low prices due to dumping practices or foreign government subsidies.[50] The imposition of trade remedies on environmentally friendly goods may therefore become an obstacle in the development of the market and hinder innovation in the sector.

The renewable energy goods market can be used as an illustration for the burden of trade remedies on environmental goods. Generally, tariffs levels on renewable energy goods are low, ranging between less than 5% for developed countries and 5–20% for developing countries.[51] Quite in contrast to these low tariff levels, renewable energy goods are a prime target of the imposition of trade remedy duties. An analysis of the targeted goods in trade remedy investigations on energy-related goods has revealed the problem that trade remedy action increasingly targets the renewable energy market.[52] Up to two-thirds of CVDs and three quarters of ADDs on energy-related goods are imposed in the renewable energy sector, as compared to the traditional energy sector.[53] Accordingly, the imposition of trade remedies puts the renewable energy market in a disadvantaged position compared to the market for traditional energy and energy goods. The UN Conference on Trade and Development (UNCTAD) outlined that various renewable energy sectors are affected by massive imposition of ADDs: biofuels (biodiesel and bioethanol), solar energy including crystalline silicon photovoltaic cells and modules, solar grade polysilicon, and solar glass including wind energy, wind turbine blades and wind turbines.[54] CVDs are mostly targeted on biofuels and solar panels. This tendency is

---

[50] See Art. II:2(b) GATT.

[51] Frey (2016), p. 453; Vikhlyaev (2004), p. 101.

[52] UNCTAD (2014); Kampel (2017); Kasteng (2013); Lester and Watson (2013); Dhanania and Chantramitra (2014).

[53] Espa and Rolland (2015), p. 9.

[54] UNCTAD (2014), p. 10.

not only noticed in the practice of the EU, but is equally observed in the US, India, and China.[55]

Commentators have observed the trade-restrictive effects resulting from the application of excessively high trade remedy duties in the clean energy sector. The seminal work of *Wu/Salzman*, for instance, labels the rising phenomenon of imposition of trade remedies on renewable technologies as problematic.[56] They were early commentators to highlight the shift in focus of trade and environment disputes, identifying "the next generation of trade and environment conflicts."[57] The rise of green industrial policy does not face the WTO rules with the problem that too few policy space is present for promoting trade in environmental goods, but rather that there is too much policy space for trade remedies to target green subsidies and renewable energy support schemes.[58]

Although the sector of renewable energy has been of central importance, the discussion expands also more generally to environmentally friendly goods sectors and the extractive elements sectors. In fact, any sector where positive externalities would be created for the local and global environment is affected, [59] including for instance electric and low-emission vehicles and batteries, waste management operations, drought and salt-resistant plant varieties, water-saving technologies, heating, cooling and energy conservation technologies, etc.[60]

2.4.1.2   Reducing the Use of Trade Remedy Duties on Green Goods?

The objective to promote green industries by reflecting their positive externalities is commonly exerted through tariff reductions or subsidies as a trade incentive. Another trade incentive may be to lower the trade remedy burden on green industries by limiting the application of trade remedies on green goods.

The seminal work of the *E15 Initiative* and *Kampel* has been indicative for concrete proposals to lower trade remedies.[61] The renewable energy sector is central in this approach, given the tendency of governments to challenge foreign support schemes and the rise in trade remedy action, as well as the importance of the sector in the achievement of SDG and climate change goals. Promotion of renewable energy through lowering trade remedy duties on renewable energy goods—any environmental good, by extension—will contribute to environmental goals. How trade remedy restrictions imposed on investigating authorities can contribute to the promotion of renewable energy and green goods will be dealt with in Chap. 4.

---

[55] Lester and Watson (2013).

[56] Wu and Salzman (2014).

[57] *Ibid.*

[58] Espa (2019), p. 999.

[59] *Ibid*, p. 981.

[60] Cosbey et al. (2017), p. 70.

[61] Kampel (2017). See also Sect. 4.4 below.

2.4.2 Application of Trade Remedy Duties to Level the Environmental Playing Field

2.4.2.1 The Competitive Advantages of Environmental Cost Externalities

A second role for trade remedies to achieve environmental protection goals is by using them as a tool to ensure environmental cost internalisation for imported goods. Trade remedies could act as level playing field measures which aim to include the carbon content of goods and internalise the environmental cost of production of imported goods entering the domestic market.

The commonly used term 'eco-dumping' or 'environmental dumping' has been used to describe situations where dumping prices are a consequence of the non-internalisation of the environmental impact of producing a good in the price of that good on the global market. Countries not ensuring environmental cost internalisation may save production costs and be placed in an advantageous position on the international market when exporting their products. Although free market-theory presupposes that all social, economic, and environmental costs of production will automatically be internalised in the price of a good,[62] government intervention may be necessary if market forces fail to ensure the internalisation of environmental costs. Producers in importing countries that must adhere to cost internalisation measures therefore advocate for measures that make sure that imported goods adhere to similar standards.

In that relation, 'low environmental standards' have been defined as environmental regulations that do not fully internalise all environmental costs—be it carbon costs or any other environmental costs related to compliance or restrictions on air pollution, water pollution, biodiversity protection, etc.[63] Not only insufficient regulation, but also the weak or lacking enforcement can bring states an unfair competitive advantage with their environmental obligations.[64] Non-compliance in this case means failure to give effect to substantive requirements such as the limitation of carbon emissions, or failure to fulfil environmental requirements such as carrying out an environmental impact assessment, not failure to fulfil institutional obligations (e.g. reporting obligations).[65]

Environmental competition and the regulatory level of environmental protection is particularly impactful on the behaviour of so-called 'energy-intensive, trade-exposed' industries (EITE industries), since they are particularly vulnerable for loss of competitiveness.[66] These sectors represent a relatively small share of the economy but have proportionately big effects on emissions leakage as well as

---

[62] See Potts (2008), pp. 3 ff.

[63] Charnovitz (1993), pp. 31–32.

[64] Sands and Peel (2018), p. 145.

[65] *Ibid.*

[66] Fischer (2015), p. 299.

proportionately big political influence.[67] Therefore, they are often successful in lobbying their governments to impose protective measures.

Trade remedies have been considered as so-called environmental level playing field measures, which can remedy the failure to integrate environmental costs into production costs. Level playing field or competitiveness measures are generally designed to offset any competitive disadvantage a producer in a 'high-standard' nation may suffer versus producers in nations with low, or non-existent environmental standards.[68] For exporters and exporting countries, such measures may create an incentive to ensure internalisation of environmental costs of production processes, bolster technological development and innovation in the industry, reduce environmental impact of production, and ultimately push governments to adopt environmental protection regulation.

Nonetheless, there remains an unclear situation on which cost differences may be labelled unfair (since costs in different countries per definition are different), and even more how to quantify these equalising measures.[69] If trade remedies are imposed to countervail environmental policies, this presumes the qualification of the adoption or maintenance of low environmental standards as a form of 'unfair trade'.[70] Although many environmentalists and politicians consider lax environmental standards 'unfair trade', they may not fulfil the definition of unfair trade in the sense of the WTO trade remedy agreements. Nonetheless, trade remedies may be used in several manners to level the environmental playing field.

2.4.2.2 Using Trade Remedies to Level the Environmental Playing Field?

The objective of levelling the environmental playing field is currently debated in the framework of carbon adjustment measures and ETS schemes. Trade remedies, however, may equally play a role in the reflection of competitive prices for environmental costs.

1) Trade remedies could be used as an instrument to increase the price low priced-goods which have been produced in countries with a proven track record of not internalising environmental costs. This refers to the question whether low environmental standards can be qualified as subsidies, be a ground for imposing safeguard measures or allow the imposition of eco-dumping duties.
2) The calculation of trade remedy duties could also recognise that costs and prices may be distorted due to insufficient environmental regulation in the country of production and include adjustments of these costs and prices. In the framework

---

[67] *Ibid*, p. 299.

[68] Fletcher (1996), p. 361.

[69] Trebilcock and Trachtman (2020), pp. 186 ff. See also Doelle (2004), p. 94 for two climate change concerns in trade law.

[70] That is, with the exception of safeguards measures which respond to a sudden increase of imports which are not considered to be the consequence of an unfair trade practice.

of trade remedy rules, several legal questions arise whether and to what extent environmental costs can be reflected in the calculation of ADDs and CVDs.

3) The trade remedy injury concept could also be regarded as including environmental injury. A trade-remedy like instrument which applies duties to remedy environmental injury could be based on the traditional trade remedies.

Chapters 5–8 will zoom in on these questions for each of the three trade remedies. Chapter 5 considers whether low environmental standards or the failure to internalise environmental costs into the price of goods may be qualified as a countervailable subsidy and addresses government distortions in the calculation of the amount of subsidy. Chapter 6 deals with the rules of the ADA to consider the instrument's usability to address 'eco-dumping'. Much of this question relies on the issue of government distortions and calculation methodologies in jurisprudence and literature. Chapter 7 assesses the role of environmental standards under the SGA. Finally, Chap. 8 expands the injury notion under the three agreements to incorporate environmental injury. Thus, these chapters explore trade remedies as instruments to level the environmental playing field.

2.5 Chapter Summary

Trade remedies traditionally do not take a prominent position in the debate on trade and environment. Much of the discussions and jurisprudence of the last years has been centred around the environmental exceptions of Art. XX GATT. Nevertheless, a recent shift in focus has brought trade remedies to the fore. The rise of green industrial policy has led to the introduction of trade remedies—ADDs, CVDs and even safeguard measures—in the framework of trade policy and the environment in the WTO, most notably through challenges of trade remedy duties which have been used as an instrument of trade policy in the services of ensuring environmental protection. Most notably, the WTO challenges of trade remedy duties which had been used as strategic industrial policy instrument in green industry sectors.

As any WTO instrument, trade remedies are subject to the commitment to sustainable development and environmental protection expressed in the first recital of the Preamble to the WTO Agreement. This chapter identified two roles trade remedies can play as border instruments in the achievement of these sustainability goals:

- First, trade remedies may be used as a tool to contribute to the promotion of green industries with positive spill-overs by restricting their use and thereby lowering the additional burden of heavy use of trade remedies. Trade remedies are frequently applied in various renewable energy sectors, which creates a burden on the industry. By restricting the use of trade remedies, governments may relieve these green goods industries from the trade restriction and advance competitive development of the market and the positive spill-over effects it creates.
- Second, trade remedies may be used as a level playing field instrument to internalise environmental costs of production which have not been reflected in the

price of internationally traded goods. The non-internalisation of environmental costs creates a competitive advantage for goods produced in countries with low environmental standards. The application of trade remedies may equal out this difference and restore the environmental level playing field. However, the debate on incorporation of environmental costs into the price of a good through border measures is thus one that needs to consider the balance between the climate ambition of developed WTO Members and the aim for economic development of developing countries.

To achieve both roles, it is necessary to assess the WTO legal framework which governs the application of trade remedy duties. Green policy goals may only be advanced in as far as the applicable WTO rules on trade remedies leave policy space to the domestic legislator and the investigating authority.

References

Bellmann C, Tipping AV (2015) The role of trade and trade policy in advancing the 2030 development agenda. Rev int pol dév 6(2):1–27

Brewster R, Brunel C, Mayda AM (2016) Trade in environmental goods: a review of the WTO appellate body's ruling in *US – Countervailing Measures (China)*. World Trade Rev 15(2):327–349

Charnovitz S (1993) A taxonomy of environmental trade measures. Georgetown Int Environ Law Rev 6(1):1–46

Cosbey A, Wooders P, Bridle R, Casier L (2017) In with the good, out with the bad: phasing out polluting sectors as green industrial policy. In: Altenburg T, Assmann C (eds) Green industrial policy: concept, policies, country experiences. UNEP/DIE, Geneva/Bonn, pp 69–86

Dawson A (2020) Safeguarding the planet? Renewable energy, solar panel tariffs, and the World Trade Organization's rules on safeguards. Trade Law Dev 11(2):334–371

Dhanania K, Chantramitra W (2014) Addressing the rise of trade remedies against environmental goods. Graduate Institute Geneva Trade and Investment Law Clinic Papers

Doelle M (2004) Climate change and the WTO: opportunities to motivate state action on climate change through the World Trade Organization. Rev Eur Comp Int Environ Law 13(1):85–103

Eliason A (2019) Using the WTO to facilitate the Paris Agreement: a tripartite approach. Vanderbilt J Transnatl Law 52(3):545–575

Espa I (2019) New features of green industrial policy and the limits of WTO rules: what options for the twenty-first century? J World Trade 53(6):979–1000

Espa I, Rolland SE (2015) Subsidies, clean energy, and climate change. E15 Initiative Think Piece

Fischer C (2015) Options for avoiding carbon leakage. In: Barrett S, Carraro C, de Melo J (eds) Towards a workable and effective climate regime. CEPR Press, London, pp 297–311

Fletcher CR (1996) Greening world trade: reconciling GATT and multilateral environmental agreements within the existing world trade regime. J Transnatl Law Policy 5(2):341–372

Frey C (2016) Tackling climate change through the elimination of trade barriers for low-carbon goods: multilateral, plurilateral and regional approaches. In: Mauerhofer V (ed) Legal aspects of sustainable development. Springer, Berlin/Heidelberg, pp 449–468

Gehring MW (2005) The 'Singapore Issues', competition and sustainable development. In: Gehring MW, Cordonier Segger MC (eds) Sustainable development in world trade law. Kluwer Law International, The Hague, pp 355–374

Gustafsson M, Crochet V (2020) At the crossroads of trade and environment. The growing influence of environmental policy on EU trade law. In: Orsini A, Kavvatha E (eds) EU environmental governance. Current and future challenges. Taylor & Francis, London, pp 187–206

Hestermeyer H, Grotto AJ (2008) Preamble WTO Agreement. In: Wolfrum R, Stoll PT, Hestermeyer H (eds) Max Planck commentaries on world trade law, WTO – trade in goods. Brill, Leiden

Kampel K (2017) Options for disciplining the use of trade remedies in clean energy technologies. ICTSD Issue Paper

Kasteng J (2013) Trade remedies on clean energy: a new trend in need of multilateral initiatives. In: E15 Expert Group on Clean Energy Technologies and the Trade System (ed) Clean energy and the trade system: proposals and analysis. ICTSD/WEF, Geneva, pp 60–68

Kaufmann C (2014) Trade and labour standards. In: Wolfrum R (ed) Max Planck Encyclopaedia of Public International Law. Online edition. https://opil.ouplaw.com/home/mpil. Accessed 24 June 2023

Kreier J (2021) The Solar Safeguards Panel Report - Some First Reactions. IELP blog https://ielp.worldtradelaw.net/2021/09/the-solar-safeguards-panel-report-some-first-reactions.html. Accessed 24 June 2023

Kulovesi K (2014) International trade disputes on renewable energy: testing ground for the mutual supportiveness of WTO law and climate change law. Rev Eur Community Int Environ Law 23(2):342–353

Lester S, Watson KW (2013) Free trade in environmental goods: the trade remedy problem. Free Trade Bulletin No. 54

Mavroidis PC (2015) Reaching out for green policies – national environmental policies in the WTO legal order. In: Wouters J, Marx A, Geraets D, Natens B (eds) Global governance through trade. EU policies and approaches. Edward Elgar Publishing, Cheltenham/Northampton, pp 303–328

Mbengue MM (2008) Preamble to the WTO Agreement. In: Wolfrum R, Stoll PT, Hestermeyer H (eds) Max Planck commentaries on world trade law, WTO – trade in goods. Brill, Leiden

PAGE (2017) Green industrial policy and trade: a tool-box. UNEP, Geneva/Bonn

Potts J (2008) The legality of PPMs under the GATT. Challenges and opportunities for sustainable trade policy. IISD, Winnipeg

Quick R (2013) Do we need trade and environment negotiations or has the appellate body done the job? J World Trade 47(5):957–984

Sands P, Peel J (2018) Principles of international environmental law, 4th edn. Cambridge University Press, Cambridge

Trebilcock MJ, Trachtman J (2020) Advanced introduction to international trade law, 2nd edn. Edward Elgar, Cheltenham/Northampton

UNCTAD (2014) Trade remedies: targeting the renewable energy sector. UNCTAD, Geneva

Van den Bossche P, Zdouc W (2017) The law and policy of the World Trade Organization. Text, cases and materials, 4th edn. Cambridge University Press, Cambridge

Vermulst E, Meng M (2017) Dumping and subsidy issues in the renewable energy sector. In: Cottier T, Espa I (eds) International trade in sustainable electricity regulatory challenges in international economic law. Cambridge University Press, Cambridge, pp 336–355

Vikhlyaev A (2004) Environmental goods and services: defining negotiations or negotiating definitions? J World Trade 38(1):93–122

Wu M, Salzman J (2014) The next generation of trade and environment conflicts: the rise of green industrial policy. Northwest Univ Law Rev 108(2):401–474

Chapter 3
WTO Rules for Greening Trade Remedies

3.1 Introduction

This chapter evaluates the WTO legal framework regulating trade remedies to assess whether and to what extent trade remedies can become a tool to exert environmental and sustainability policy goals. Generally, the WTO rules on trade remedies contain highly detailed provisions of technical nature, which do not create a suitable setting for investigating authorities to exert wider import policy objectives.[1] Legislators and/or investigating authorities in WTO Members have therefore only limited opportunity within the applicable international legal framework to promote green values and environmental protection through trade remedy practice.

Trade remedies are regulated on the WTO level in various sources, including the GATT, three specialised trade remedy agreements, accession protocols and RTAs, which each grant different levels of policy discretion available for exerting environmental goals (Sect. 3.2). Only a very limited number of WTO Members have incorporated green considerations in their domestic trade remedy rules (Sect. 3.3). The chapter concludes that certain flexibilities exist and may be a gateway for investigating authorities to put trade remedy practice in service of environmental protection goals (Sect. 3.4).

---

[1] Müller et al. (2009), para. I.04.

3.2   Regulation of Trade Remedies in the WTO

At the WTO level, trade remedies are not only regulated in the GATT but also in three specialised multilateral agreements dedicated to each type of trade remedy: The Anti-Dumping Agreement, Agreement on Subsidies and Countervailing Measures, and Safeguards Agreement.[2] This chapter reviews the history and emergence of trade remedy rules (Sect. 3.2.1), the underlying concepts on which the agreements are built (Sect. 3.2.2), and technical and procedural rules prescribed at the WTO level (Sect. 3.2.3). It reveals that due to the detailed and technical nature of the rules, policy options are limited. In addition, it reviews two further sources of trade remedy regulation relevant for the imposition and application of trade remedies: WTO accession protocols (Sect. 3.2.4) and RTAs (Sect. 3.2.5).

3.2.1   History and Emergence of the WTO Trade Remedy Rules

Trade remedy rules have been part of international trade regulations for more than a century.[3] Emerging originally rather from anti-trust concerns, countries such as Canada (1904), New Zealand (1905), Australia (1906), South Africa (1914), the United States (1916/1921) and Great Britain (1921) were the first countries to adopt anti-dumping rules.[4] Anti-subsidy rules and countervailing duty practice originated in the United States (1890) and Belgium (1892).[5] These domestic laws formed the foundation of the inclusion of an anti-dumping and anti-subsidy provision in the GATT 1947.[6] Art. VI was included in the GATT 1947 dealing with both anti-dumping and anti-subsidy measures in an attempt to multilateralise these disciplines. Accordingly, Art. VI GATT allows WTO Members to react to unfair trade by offsetting the effects of dumping practices or a subsidy bestowed on the production of goods through the imposition of duties.

After developing the Dumping Code and Subsidies Code, the Uruguay Round resulted in the adoption of multilateral agreements dealing with anti-dumping and subsidies practices. The ADA and ASCM have not been amended since their adoption, but have been included in the 2001 Doha Development Agenda.[7] WTO

---

[2] Agreement on Implementation of Article VI of the General Agreement on Tariffs and Trade 1994, LT/UR/A-1A/3, 15 April 1994; Agreement on Subsidies and Countervailing Measures, LT/UR/A-1A/9, 15 April 1994; Agreement on Safeguards, LT/UR/A-1A/8, 15 April 1994.

[3] See Jackson (1997), pp. 175–211, 247–278 and 279–303. *Jacob Viner* traces trade remedy practices back even further. See Viner (1923).

[4] Müller et al. (2009), para. I.02.

[5] Irwin (2016), p. 12.

[6] General Agreement on Tariffs and Trade 1994, LT/UR/A-1A/1, 15 April 1994. See Stewart (2001), pp. 1391–1392.

[7] Doha Development Agenda, para. 28.

Members undertook to maintain the basic concepts and principles of the currently existing rules, while improving the disciplines, particularly for least-developed countries (LDCs).[8] This formulation attempted to balance interests of Members such as the US that opposed to any negotiation that would loosen anti-dumping rules, and other members such as China, Japan and Korea that advocated for reviewing and strengthening those rules.[9] The underlying concepts of dumping and subsidisation will therefore remain unaltered, even in the unlikely case that a legislative change to the trade remedy rules may occur.[10]

By contrast to anti-dumping and anti-subsidy measures, safeguard measures find their origins in 'escape clauses' contained in early trade agreements with the US,[11] and found their way into the GATT 1947 in a separate provision. Art. XIX GATT allowed Members to undo tariff concessions to protect domestic industries from import competition through emergency action on imports of individual products.[12] Although no 'Safeguards Code' was ever developed, the Uruguay Round resulted in a set of multilateral rules on safeguards. The Preamble of the SGA explicitly refers to the overall objectives of the GATT and the disciplines of Art. XIX GATT specifically.[13] Art. XIX GATT and the Safeguards Agreement allow WTO Members to take safeguard action, *i.e.* measures to temporarily restrict imports of a certain product which threatens to cause serious injury to domestic industry. The SGA has not been amended since its adoption and is neither part of ongoing negotiations.

3.2.2 The Foundations Underlying the ADA, ASCM and SGA

The concepts of dumping and subsidisation are targeted at a distortive trade policy, *i.e.* 'unfair trade', whereas safeguards measures react to competition that is in principle 'fair', but nonetheless causes injury to domestic producers.[14] The concepts of

---

[8] *Ibid.*

[9] Kessie (2010), p. 381.

[10] A consolidated text for Members' consideration was circulated on 30 November 2007. See Draft Consolidated Chair Texts of the Antidumping and Subsidies Agreement, TN/RL/W/214, 30 November 2007 and Working Document from the chairman of the Negotiations Group on Rules, TN/RL/W/232, 28 May 2008. The ADA text covered proposals on the initiation of investigations, due process and transparency, injury determinations, dumping margin calculations and reviews and duration of measures, but *not* on the LDR, negligible imports, SDT and *de minimis* thresholds. The ASCM text covered proposals on definition of a benefit, allocation of benefits, export credits, specificity and regulated prices and benefit calculation, but not on dual pricing, non-actionable subsidies and presumption of serious injury. See Kessie (2010), p. 382.

[11] See, for instance, the 1935 US-Belgium trade agreement and later the trade agreements with Sweden, the Netherlands and in 1943 the US-Mexico trade agreement. See Eckes Jr. (1995), pp. 221 ff.

[12] Art. XIX GATT.

[13] SGA, Preamble.

[14] Appellate Body report, *United States – Definitive Safeguard Measures on Imports of Circular Welded Carbon Quality Line Pipe from Korea*, WT/DS202/AB/R, adopted 8 March 2002, para. 80.

dumping (Sect. 3.2.2.1), subsidies (Sect. 3.2.2.2) and safeguards (Sect. 3.2.2.3) are not defined to provide a remedy against the consequences of low environmental standards.

3.2.2.1 The Concept of Dumping

GATT Members discussed various types of dumping, including service dumping, exchange rate dumping, social dumping, and price dumping. Dumping may mean 'social dumping' where export prices are extremely low due to low wage costs in comparison to other countries, or where the level of working conditions is low.[15] Similarly, dumping may mean 'eco-dumping', where price levels are low due to the absence of, or insufficient enforcement of, environmental regulatory standards. Yet, ultimately, only price dumping is subject to the application of anti-dumping measures under the GATT.[16]

The text of the GATT condemned dumping practices "by which products of one country are introduced into the commerce of another country at less than the normal value of the products."[17] Dumping was thus defined as a form of price discrimination and the GATT/WTO rules rooted on a concept spurred by competitiveness considerations and economic factors.[18] Much of the literature on the economic rationale of anti-dumping laws is vested on the seminal work of *Viner*[19] and the focus of early trade remedy practice relied on the existence of predatory intent behind dumping practices.[20]

Accordingly, whether a policy concern linked to social or environmental dumping could be included in the legal framework of dumping is contentious. In principle, the drafters have explicitly excluded such forms of dumping. Anti-dumping provisions in the GATT and ADA are neutral as to the policy considerations or intent of the exporting company that sells its goods at dumping prices in foreign markets.[21] Therefore, any form of dumping resulting in an unfair price differentiation may lead to anti-dumping measures. Only those forms of eco-dumping practices which also result in price discrimination will be captured by the current concept of dumping.

---

[15] Matsushita et al. (2015), p. 375.

[16] Adamantopoulos (2008), Art. VI GATT, para. 4. See UN ECOSOC Council, Preparatory Committee of the International Conference on Trade and Employment, Committee II, Summary Record of Technical Sub-Committee, E/PC/T/C. 11/48, 11 November 1946, available at https://docs.wto.org/gattdocs/q/UN/EPCT/CII-48.PDF (last accessed 21 June 2023).

[17] Art. VI:1 GATT.

[18] See Sect. 3.2.1 above.

[19] Viner (1923).

[20] Nedumpara (2016), pp. 26–27.

[21] Appellate Body report, *United States – Anti-Dumping Act of 1916*, WT/DS136/AB/R, adopted 26 September 2000, para. 107.

3.2.2.2   The Concept of a Subsidy

The failure of a government to set adequate levels of environmental protection may be labelled as a subsidy. Art. 1 ASCM defines a subsidy as a financial contribution by a government or public body which confers a benefit upon the recipient and prescribes an additional requirement of specificity for a subsidy to be considered countervailable by means of anti-subsidy duties. The Uruguay Round GATT negotiators did not accept an implicit subsidy based on low environmental standards in the ASCM.[22] Therefore, although environmental regulation may take away some costs that producers may otherwise incur or takes away a regulatory burden which also comes at a cost, these purely non-financial regulatory action or inaction with subsidising effects have not been treated as a subsidy.[23] For general (environmental) government policies to be included, a broadened definition of a subsidy is required, which would have to include any government intervention (or inaction) in the marketplace as a subsidy.

Subsidies themselves (and subsidisation policy), however, may be driven by factors not relating to the competitive position of exporters, including objectives of environmental protection, climate change, reducing emissions, energy security, development of disadvantaged regions, counteracting unemployment on the labour market, etc.[24] For five years after the conclusion of the Uruguay Round, the ASCM also made certain types of subsidies motivated by non-economic factors immune to challenges and countervailing duties. Subsidies granting assistance to R&D activities, subsidies to disadvantaged regions, and subsidies to promote adaptation of existing facilities to new environmental requirements were deemed non-actionable under Art. 8(2) ASCM. Since these temporary green light subsidies have not been renewed, action against subsidies is currently permitted irrespective the policy objective pursued by the country that grants subsidies.[25]

3.2.2.3   Safeguards

Safeguard measures are imposed as a reaction against a sudden increase in imports to such an extent it causes injury to domestic producers. The inclusion of the safeguard clause in the GATT was driven by non-economic motives. Safeguard clauses had entered in previous trade agreements to enable political concessions at a later stage to protect industries in times of for instance economic or financial difficulties.[26] Underlying that logic are fairness rationales on which the safeguard regimes are vested, particularly in relation to the impact of increasing imports of low-priced

---

[22] Esty (1994), p. 164.

[23] Horlick and Clarke (2017), p. 674.

[24] Müller (2017), pp. 4–6.

[25] Art. 31 ASCM.

[26] Piérola (2014), pp. 95 ff.; Sykes (2003), pp. 288 ff.

goods, the redistributive effects of increased imports, and socially unfair conse-quences thereof.[27] This underlying policy reason of social protection behind impos-ing safeguards already links to the social pillar of sustainable development.[28]

Moreover, political discretion in the imposition of safeguard measures could therefore distinguish safeguards from the strictly administrative determinations under anti-dumping and countervailing duty rules. This was discussed but not adopted when WTO Members attempted to negotiate a Code on Safeguards.[29] Pointing to the danger that governments would abuse the system of safeguards mea-sures motivated by political considerations, the inclusion of strict and detailed pro-cedural and substantive rules was deemed necessary nonetheless, resulting in the Safeguard Agreement.[30]

3.2.3 Policy Discretion in the Rules of the ADA and ASCM

Over the course of an administrative investigation, domestic authorities make sev-eral discretionary decisions and have policy freedom in making administrative deci-sions, which could be put in service of pursuing environmental protection goals. This section highlights the policy space in making the administrative decision to open a trade remedy investigation (Sect. 3.2.3.1), the price calculation methodolo-gies and comparison techniques (Sect. 3.2.3.2), the assessment of injury and causa-tion (Sect. 3.2.3.3), the application of the public interest test (Sect. 3.2.3.4), and finally the decision to initiate administrative or judicial review processes (Sect. 3.2.3.5).

3.2.3.1 Initiation and Conduct of a Trade Remedy Investigation

Investigating authorities maintain policy discretion in deciding whether investiga-tions are opened, which can be guided by environmental policy considerations. Decisions to impose trade remedy duties are different from typical state actions. Trade remedy laws are unilaterally enforced by domestic authorities that act (usu-ally) upon a complaint by industry representatives from the domestic industry or following an *ex officio* decision by the investigating authority itself.[31] As such, investigating authorities can for instance consider the environmental impact of the production process of certain goods from certain countries.

---

[27] Trebilcock and Trachtman (2020), p. 110.

[28] Matsushita et al. (2015), p. 410.

[29] Trebilcock and Trachtman (2020), p. 101.

[30] Bourgeois (2008) Preamble SGA, para. 3.

[31] See Art. 5 ADA and Art. 11 ASCM.

Similarly, the administrative procedure for conducting the investigation, collection of data, surveillance of the industry, etc. are left entirely to the discretion of the investigation authority, leaving considerable policy space for domestic actors to consider environmental impact of the investigated goods. These administrative decisions in the course of the procedure are subject to the procedural discretion for the investigating authorities.

Furthermore, investigating authorities can consider the type of remedy applied. The ADA and ASCM continue with detailed rules on the imposition of remedies (provisional duties, undertakings, definitive duties, a prohibition of retroactivity). Although trade remedies usually take the form of duties, price undertakings can be concluded with individual exporters. Investigating authorities have broad discretion to accept or refuse undertakings, and they may be motivated by reasons of general policy,[32] including environmental policy.

3.2.3.2   Calculation of Trade Remedy Duties

3.2.3.2.1   Under the ADA

In case of dumping, the investigating authority in the country of importation is charged with calculating the dumping margin. This calculation includes a comparison between the price of a product for export to another country (export price) and the price of the like product for domestic consumption in the country of production (normal value).[33] Throughout the administrative procedure, investigating authorities take several decisions, which all may take account of environmental costs of the production process.

For instance, when investigating authorities deem it impossible to rely on *actual* export prices and domestic prices to establish the normal value,[34] the Appellate Body confirmed there may be any number of reasons to consider sales outside the ordinary course of trade.[35] Whether the absence of environmental regulation in the country of production constitutes a particular market situation, or renders the sales outside the ordinary course of trade is therefore a decision the investigating authority can consider such policy goals.[36]

Furthermore, when authorities construct the normal value of goods, in principle, production costs shall be calculated on the basis of records kept by the exporter or

---

[32] Art. 8.3 ADA and Art. 18.3 ASCM. See also Panel report, *United States – Continued Dumping and Subsidy Offset Act of 2000*, WT/DS217/R, adopted 27 January 2003, para. 7.80–7.81.

[33] Stewart and Mueller (2008), Art. 2 ADA, para. 18.

[34] Art. 2.2 ADA foresees that when there are no sales in the ordinary course of trade (OCT), when a particular market situation (PMS) affects price comparability, or when a low volume of sale (less than 5%) affects price comparability, domestic prices may be disregarded.

[35] Appellate Body report, *United States – Anti-Dumping Measures on Certain Hot-Rolled Steel Products from Japan*, WT/DS184/AB/R, adopted 23 August 2001, para. 147.

[36] See, in detail, Sect. 6.3 below.

producer, pursuant to Art. 2.2.1.1 ADA. There is a certain degree of discretion in the assessment whether these costs are to be used, on account of the wording "normally".[37] Bringing about other costs into the normal value through this mechanism would mean constructing the normal value not at the level of the *normal* value but "at the level of trade *equivalent* to the level of trade of the constructed export price."[38]

Investigating authorities then must add of a reasonable amount of selling, general and administrative (SG&A) costs and profit to the normal value.[39] Where actual data from the exporter of producer under investigation is not available, the investigating authorities make a determination based on a number of alternative methodologies.[40] This level of SG&A costs may be influenced by the costs for environmental compliance, for instance. If the authority relies on its own methodology, it must include an explanation of its decision that is reasoned and adequate.[41]

Alternatively, investigating authorities may also resort to comparable prices of the like product when exported to an appropriate third country, provided that this price is representative.[42] The ADA does not prescribe criteria for the selection of an appropriate third country, so environmental criteria could be applied to determine the level of 'appropriateness' and 'representativeness' of third countries.

Finally, an obligation rests on investigating authorities to carry out a fair comparison between export prices and normal value. Art. VI:1 GATT notes that due allowance shall be given to "other differences affecting price comparability", which could include environmental costs differences.[43] In addition, Art. 2.4 ADA prescribes that "due allowance" shall be made for certain circumstances.[44] This leaves freedom as to how this is exerted in practice, where a Panel could only examine whether the investigating authority has acted in an unbiased and even-handed manner.[45] In that regard, it should be noted that an accounting principles analysis of dumping margin investigations indicates that there is a great of range of accounting discretions available for investigating authorities to be used to reconstruct normal value, export price and in turn computing dumping margin.[46]

---

[37] See Panel report, *Australia – Anti-Dumping Measures on A4 Copy Paper*, WT/DS529/R, adopted 4 December 2019, para. 7.110.

[38] Choi and Lee (2017), pp. 30–31 (emphasis added).

[39] De Baere et al. (2021), para. 229 ff.

[40] Art. 2.2.2. See also Panel report, *European Communities – Anti-Dumping Duties on Imports of Cotton-type Bed Linen from India*, WT/DS141/R, adopted 12 March 2001, para. 6.62.

[41] Panel report, *China – Anti-Dumping and Countervailing Duty Measures on Broiler Products from the United States, Recourse to Art. 21.5 of the DSU by the United States*, WT/DS427/RW, adopted 28 February 2018, para. 7.52. See also *ibid.* para. 7.62.

[42] Art. 2.2 ADA or Art. 2.7 ADA.

[43] Sands and Peel (2018), p. 899.

[44] De Baere et al. (2021), para. 298 ff.

[45] Panel report, *European Communities – Anti-Dumping Duties on Malleable Cast Iron Tube or Pipe Fittings from Brazil*, WT/DS219/R, adopted 18 August 2003, para. 7.178.

[46] Cheaseth and Samreth (2009).

3.2.3.2.2 Under the ASCM

In anti-subsidy investigations, domestic authorities are charged with determining whether a financial contribution by a government or public body which confers a benefit can be qualified as a countervailable subsidy.[47] The focus of the authorities lies on an assessment of the constituent elements of a subsidy and the question whether low environmental standards can be qualified as a subsidy.

Besides that, the investigating authorities also determine the level of subsidisation, which is—similarly to the anti-dumping investigation—subject to a broad discretion for the investigating authority. The chapeau of Art. 14 ASCM leaves it up to investigating authorities to define "any method" for the determination of the amount of subsidy in terms of benefit conferred. WTO Members must thus foresee national legislation or implementing regulations that determine the method used by investigating authorities.[48] This wide discretion is only subject to guidelines for four types of subsidies. In fact, Panels have effectively endorsed national practices.[49]

Generally, the amount of benefit in CVD investigations is calculated in terms of commercial benchmarks.[50] Investigating authorities must therefore determine comparable private transactions on the market,[51] which could include environmental costs and distorted prices of certain energy or raw material inputs. In exceptional cases, investigating authorities may also decide to depart from market prices as a benchmark.[52] In such cases, environmental costs could be considered when determining an alternative benchmark by the investigating authority.

3.2.3.2.3 Under the SGA

Domestic trade remedy authorities also deal with investigations to impose safeguards measures. Although not as frequently imposed as ADDs and CVDs, safeguard measures also allow the authorities to exert a certain level of discretion. Especially when investigating unforeseen developments, investigating authorities have the possibility to include environmental aspects in their assessment of what

---

[47] Art. 1 and 2 ASCM.

[48] Panel report, *European Communities – Countervailing Measures on Dynamic Random Access Memory Chips from Korea*, WT/DS299/R, circulated 3 August 2005, para. 7.213; Panel report, *Mexico – Definitive Countervailing Measures on Olive Oil from the European Communities*, WT/DS341, adopted 21 October 2008, fn 63. See also Durling (2008), Art. 14 SCMA, para. 19.

[49] Durling (2008), Art. 14 SCMA, para. 22. See, for instance, Panel report, *United States – Countervailing Measures on Softwood Lumber from Canada*, WT/DS533/R, circulated 23 August 2020, para. 7.562.

[50] Appellate Body report, *European Communities – Imposition of Countervailing Duties on Certain Hot-Rolled Lead and Bismuth Carbon Steel Products Originating in the United Kingdom*, WT/DS138/AB/R, adopted 7 June 2000, para. 57–74.

[51] Durling (2008), Art. 14 SCMA, para. 9.

[52] See Sect. 5.4.1.2 below.

caused the surge of imports. The SGA prescribes that the moment in time to judge the unforeseeable nature of the developments is the time of the last tariff negotiation that was concluded, *i.e.* the conclusion of the Uruguay Round negotiation.[53]

Furthermore, the SGA leaves the discretion to the investigating authorities to choose the form of safeguard measures. Measures may take the form of temporary tariff increases or quantitative restrictions.[54] The SGA leaves investigating authorities with discretion to determine the form and level of a safeguard measure. Importantly, Members imposing them (generally) must pay compensation to the Members whose trade is affected. Such requirement does not exist for ADDs/CVDs.[55]

3.2.3.3 Examination of Injury and Causation

The assessment of injury and causation also leaves investigating authorities with certain policy freedom which can be oriented towards environmental injury. Investigating authorities' determination of injury rests on an examination of all relevant economic factors and indices having an influence. The indicative list in Art. 3.4 ADA and Art. 15.4 ASCM is not exhaustive, so any environmental harm resulting in economic losses for the domestic industry could be considered by the investigating authorities. The assessment of these relevant economic factors under Art. 3.4 ADA amounts to a certain degree to a discretionary assessment by the investigating authority.[56] Similarly, Art. 4.2 of the SGA sets out that investigating authorities must consider whether increased imports have caused or are threatening to cause serious injury to a domestic industry.[57]

The application of the Lesser-Duty Rule (LDR) is another step in the investigation where domestic authorities have the option to consider environmental aspects.[58] The LDR is an optional provision, which is only "desirable" under the WTO rules.[59] It gives investigating authorities the option to impose a lower duty if such duty level would suffice to alleviate the injury from the domestic market. As illustrated by

---

[53] Panel report, *Argentina – Definitive Safeguard Measure on Imports of Preserved Peaches*, WT/DS238/R, adopted 15 April 2003, para. 7.35; Panel Report, *Dominican Republic – Safeguard Measures on Imports of Polypropylene Bags and Tubular Fabric*, WT/DS417/R, adopted 22 February 2012, para. 128–129.

[54] In case a WTO Member applies provisional safeguard measures, they should take the form of refundable tariff increases. See Art. 6 SGA.

[55] Wu (2012), p. 69.

[56] See, for instance, Panel report, *Morocco – Anti-Dumping Measures on Certain Hot-Rolled Steel from Turkey*, WT/DS513/R, adopted 8 January 2020, para. 7.261.

[57] Nedumpara (2016), p. 62. For a comparison between injury factors in trade remedy agreement under the WTO, see *ibid*, p. 75, Table 1, and the interplay between these factors, see *ibid*, p. 77.

[58] In detail, see Sect. 4.4.2.6.

[59] Art. 7.4 and 9.1 ADA. This is also true for undertakings, Art. 8.1 ADA; see also Art. 17.5, 19.2 and 18.1(a) ASCM. See also Appellate Body report, *European Communities – Definitive Anti-Dumping Measures on Certain Iron or Steel Fasteners from China*, WT/DS397/AB/R, adopted 28 July 2011, para. 336.

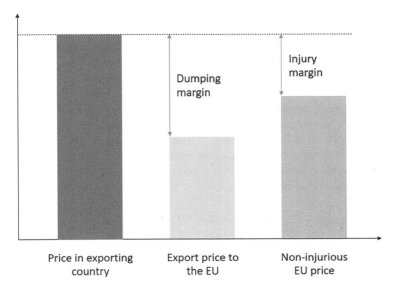

Fig. 3.1 The Lesser-Duty Rule. Source: Author's own creation

Fig. 3.1, investigating authorities have the possibility to impose a duty at the level of the injury margin instead of the dumping margin. The ADA does not prescribe a method for calculating the injury margin.[60] This leaves the investigating authority with a broad discretion as regards the calculation method. Options to 'green' the LDR include a mandatory application of the rule for environmental goods or the inclusion of environmental costs in the determination of the injury on the domestic level.

3.2.3.4   Public Interest Test

The application of the public interest test leaves investigating authorities with the possibility to include considerations of various groups of the broader public, other stakeholders in the investigations. Although the public interest test has an economic character and general policy considerations normally do not play a role in the public interest test,[61] such considerations may include environmental aspects in certain cases.

The public interest test may result in a decision not to impose duties driven by environmental considerations despite the fulfilment of all substantive requirements. The current Uruguay Round texts of the ADA and ASCM neither provide for an

---

[60] Panel report, *European Union – Anti-Dumping Measures on Certain Footwear from China*, WT/DS405/R, adopted 22 February 2012, para. 7.927.

[61] Müller et al. (2009), para. 21.53.

explicit public interest test, nor prohibit a public interest consideration.[62] The agreements merely include a permissive, rather than mandatory choice of the Members.[63] By contrast, the SGA includes an obligatory public interest test in Art. 3.1 SGA. In fact, interested parties play a central role in safeguards investigations in that they are the primary source of information to the competent authorities.[64]

Only some WTO Members have adopted a public interest test in their domestic legal framework. Whereas the EU systematically applies the Union interest test, other countries like Australia and Canada occasionally, and other countries like the US do not apply a public interest test.[65] The EU interest test is a public interest clause and provides that measures cannot be applied if it is established that they are contrary to the overall economic interest of the EU, but has nonetheless taken into account environmental considerations in as far as they were brought up by interested parties.[66]

3.2.3.5 Administrative and Judicial Review of Trade Remedy Measures

Administrative review procedures grant investigating authorities again discretionary freedom to decide whether to prolong the imposition of duties, as well as similar freedom in the calculation or re-calculation of the amount of duty. Such administrative review process could again consider the environmentally friendly nature of the goods in question. The EU, for instance, allows the Commission to initiate interim reviews where the Union industry faces increased costs resulting from higher social and environmental standards or changed circumstances in exporting countries relating to social and environmental standards.[67] This provision is not transposed in the operative part of the BADR, neither has it led to interim review procedures in practice.[68]

In addition, WTO Members may also challenge trade remedies at the WTO level. All three agreements foresee that the Dispute Settlement Understanding (DSU) is applicable to disputes arising under the specialised trade remedy agreements. The ADA contains a special dispute resolution rule of Art. 17.6 ADA, which limits the review of WTO Panels. When the Panel assesses the facts of the matters, it shall determine whether (1) the national authorities have established the facts properly, (2) whether the national authorities have evaluated them in an unbiased way, and (3)

---

[62] The legal basis for imposition of a public interest test is the formulation in Art. 9.1 ADA that is "desirable that the imposition be permissive in the territory of all Members." Several WTO Members have implemented this provision by means of a public interest test.

[63] See Appellate Body report, *United States – Anti-Dumping Act of 1916*, WT/DS136/AB/R, adopted 26 September 2000, para. 113 and 116.

[64] Appellate Body report, *United States – Definitive Safeguard Measures on Imports of Wheat Gluten from the European Communities*, WT/DS166/AB/R, adopted 19 January 2001, para. 54.

[65] *Ibid*, para. 21.02.

[66] See Sect. 3.3.2 below.

[67] Recital 12 tot the amended BADR.

[68] Gustafsson and Crochet (2020), p. 200.

in an objective way. Even if Panels may disagree with the decision of an investigating authority, they shall not overturn their decision if these two requirements are met. This safeguards the discretion of the investigating authorities in conducting their investigations free from judicial review.

3.2.4 Trade Remedy Rules in WTO Accession Protocols

WTO accession protocols are another source of trade remedy rules besides the GATT and the specialised multilateral agreements. Notably, these WTO-plus obligations may include additional discretionary powers for investigating authorities in relation to imports from specific acceded countries, which are important to consider when assessing the possibility to include environmental considerations in trade remedy practice.

Obligations relating to trade remedies include *inter alia* transitional safeguard provisions and commitments on price comparability in determining subsidies and dumping have been included in WTO accession protocols. Accession protocols must be situated in the context of worries expressed by WTO Members on state-distorted prices and government policies affecting prices in certain countries which had retained a significant degree of control over the economy.[69] This resulted in an "entry fee" through additional commitments upon accession. The imposition of very stringent accession commitments was a part of the transition into a market economy through reduction of the impact of the state on the economy.[70]

The most prominent example is China's Accession Protocol (CAP) to the WTO, which details out important rules for the conduct of trade remedy investigations against imports from China.[71] China was one of the original signatories of the GATT 1947 but remained inactive since 1949 and finally retreated in 1950. In 1986, China applied to resume its status as a Contracting Party again.[72] After 15 years of negotiations between China and the WTO Members, China accepted the protocol of accession in November 2001 and has been a Member since December 2001.

The CAP contains several rules relevant for the application of trade remedies against Chinese imports.[73] First, Sect. 15 CAP contains special price comparability rules for the determination of subsidies and dumping. Absent specific rules on treatment of imports from NMEs in the ADA, incumbent WTO Members and China

---

[69] Examples of NMEs that acceded the WTO include Georgia (2000), China (2001), Armenia (2003), Cambodia (2004), Vietnam (2007), Tajikistan (2013) and Kazakhstan (2015).

[70] See Geraets (2018), pp. 207 ff.

[71] Accession of the People's Republic of China, Decision of 10 November 2001, WT/L/432, Section 15 and Report of the Working Party on the Accession of China, WT/CC/CHN/49, 1 October 2001.

[72] Communication from the People's Republic of China, China's Status as a Contracting Partner, GATT doc. L/6017, 14 July 1986.

[73] For an overview, see Geraets (2018), pp. 240 ff; Qin (2004); Yamaoka (2013); Halverson (2004).

included in the CAP that a strict comparison between domestic Chinese price and the export price may not always be appropriate and that investigating authorities can rely on external benchmarks when domestic Chinese prices are deemed not reliable. Similar obligations are contained in the working party reports on the accessions of Vietnam and Tajikistan.[74] In relation to China, Sect. 15(d) CAP foresees that the provisions shall expire 15 years after the date of accession and even prior to the expiry of that 15-year period, should China establish that market economy conditions prevail in a particular industry or sector. By contrast, Vietnam's provisions contain an exact expiry date of 31 December 2018 (12 years after accession). In case of Tajikistan, again a 15-year time period after accession was included.

Second, the CAP contains special rules relating to Chinese subsidies. Pursuant to Sect. 10.2 CAP, China accepted it shall notify subsidies within the meaning of Art. 1 ASCM following the requirements of Art. 25 ASCM. It also accepted that all subsidies *to* Chinese SOEs will automatically be viewed as specific for the purposes of applying Art. 1.2 and 2 ASCM. This presumption of specificity applies particularly when SOEs are the predominant recipients of subsidies or when SOEs receive proportionally large amounts of subsidies, according to Sect. 10.2 CAP. Moreover, Set. 10.3 CAP foresees the elimination of all subsidy programmes including prohibited subsidies contingent on export performance or the use of domestic over imported goods.

Third, Sect. 16 CAP includes a Transitional Product-Specific Safeguard Mechanism (TPSSM), which aims at preventing injury to domestic industries in WTO Members because of a sudden and unexpected increase in imports. This is a unique feature of China's accession to the WTO, linked to the concern that China's accession to the WTO would increase cheap imports across the globe.[75] One WTO dispute, *US – Tyres*, was initiated during the application of the mechanism, but the Appellate Body did not find that the US acted inconsistent with Sect. 16 CAP.[76] The TPSSM was terminated in 2013.[77]

Finally, the CAP contains general commitments including the topics of transparency (Sect. 2c CAP), state trading (Sect. 6 CAP), price controls (Sect. 9 CAP) and agricultural subsidies (Sect 12 CAP). These commitments are not directly relevant in the field of trade remedies, but shed light on the general rationale of the CAP.

---

[74] Accession of the People's Republic of China, Decision of 10 November 2001, WT/L/432, section 15 and Report of the Working Party on the Accession of China, WT/CC/CHN/49, 1 October 2001; Report of the Working Party on the Accession of Viet Nam, WT/ACC/VNM/48, 27 October 2006, para. 255; Report of the Working Party on the Accession of Tajikistan, WT/ACC/TJK/30, 6 November 2012, para. 164.

[75] See Lingliang (2008), p. 98; Anderson and Lau (2002), pp. 405 ff.

[76] Appellate Body report, *United States – Measures Affecting Imports of Certain Passenger Vehicle and Light Truck Tyres from China*, WT/DS399/AB/R, adopted 5 October 2011.

[77] See Sect. 16.9 CAP.

3.2.5   Trade Remedy Rules in RTAs

Regional Trade Agreements (RTAs) in the WTO are reciprocal trade agreements between two or more trade partners, aiming at facilitating trade between the parties. WTO Members have the possibility to include trade remedy provisions which may be driven by common environmental goals. Trade remedy provisions in RTAs may be categorised into largely three groups:

- *WTO provisions*: Most trade remedy rules in RTAs are limited to a reference that trade partners will respect and abide by the WTO rights and obligations concerning trade remedies.[78] Such confirmation of the WTO disciplines is legally not necessary, because the rules will continue to apply between RTA partners also absent express reference in RTAs. The relative unimportance of trade remedy rules in RTA negotiations can be traced back to the fact that they are a safety-valve. By the implementation of the Uruguay Round negotiations under the GATT, industrial tariffs had already been significantly reduced, to approximately 4%. Most developing countries had 'replaced' these tariffs by resorting increasingly to anti-dumping duties as a protectionist 'back-door' industrial policy tool. As such, trade remedies act as a safety valve for countries to re-introduce certain tariffs.[79] In addition, the fact that the majority of RTAs is negotiated between trade partners that have never imposed trade remedies between one another is relevant.[80]
- *WTO-plus provisions*: Some RTAs contain innovations to the ADA and ASCM, that are usually more restrictive than the default WTO rules. Similarly to accession commitments, trade partners may agree on more stringent trade remedy disciplines to facilitate bilateral trade flows. For example, they set a higher *de minimis* level for the initiation of procedures, shorter duration for imposed trade remedies duties,[81] or best endeavour clauses not to impose trade remedy duties.[82] These commitments limit the application of trade remedies. By contrast, product-specific transitional safeguards measures, which are also frequently included in RTAs, increase the use of trade remedies among WTO Members.[83]
- *Elimination of trade remedies*: A small share of RTAs include provisions eliminating the possibility to impose anti-dumping and/or anti-subsidy and/or safeguards measures. The abolition of anti-dumping measures is associated with deep levels of integration: the deeper the market integration, the more likely

---

[78] Around 90% of RTAs merely confirm the WTO disciplines. See Kommerskollegium (2013), p. 4.

[79] Horlick and Shea (1995), pp. 6–7.

[80] Kommerskollegium (2013), p. 4.

[81] See, for instance, Singapore-New Zealand, Art. 9; Singapore-Jordan, Art. 2.8; Taiwan-Panama, Art. 7.02(1)–(2); Taiwan-Nicaragua, Art. 7.5.

[82] See, for instance, EFTA-South Korea, Art. 2.10(1).

[83] Voon (2010), p. 639.

trade remedies are abolished.[84] Particularly, harmonised competition policy or competition rules appear to be an important, yet not necessary, precondition for the abolition of anti-dumping in RTAs.[85] This occurs largely between closely connected trade partners: customs unions (EU), single countries (China-Hong Kong, China-Taiwan), deeply integrated economies (EEA, EFTA, Australia-New Zealand) or associations of countries with strong liberalisation agendas (Australia, Canada, Chile, New Zealand, Singapore).[86] For all three forms of contingent protection measures to be abolished, it appears a particularly high level of integration is necessary, which may expand beyond competition policy integration. Only one RTA, the EU treaty, has abolished all three forms of trade remedies among its members. Generally, the elimination of anti-dumping rules (and anti-subsidy rules) has been balanced out by retaining the option of keeping safeguard measures.

As such, RTA negotiations grant willing trade partners a possibility to modify the conditions for imposition of trade remedies. This presents an opportunity and a forum to agree on greening trade remedies in bilateral relations. This would fit into the general provisions (e.g. in the Preamble) or specific commitments, providing the context in RTAs for other environmental provisions, such as the commitment to liberalise environmental goods and services.[87]

3.3 Domestic Legislation on Trade Remedies in Selected WTO Members

3.3.1 Overview

WTO Members show no strong record of implementing green considerations in their domestic legal framework for trade remedies. According to the WTO's environmental database, between 2009 and 2019, out of some 14,000 environment-related measures notified by WTO Members, five notifications (or <0.1%) related to

---

[84] See Prusa (2011), pp. 181 ff.; Teh et al. (2009), pp. 166–248; Voon (2010); Marceau (1994), pp. 312 ff.; Farha (2012); Hoekman (1999).

[85] *Ibid.*

[86] EU Treaty of Rome, Art. 91(1). This rule has later been applied in all successive EU enlargements in 1973, 1981, 1986, 1995, 2004, 2007 and 2013 when the EU expanded from 6 to 28 Member States; EEA Agreement, Art. 26 and Protocol 13; EFTA, Art. 36; EU-EFTA; EU-Andorra; EU-San Marino; Australia-New Zealand (ANZCERTA), Art. 4(1) and (2); EFTA-Singapore, Art. 16(1) and (2); EFTA-Chile, Art. 18(1) and (2); Canada-Chile, Art. M-01 and M-04; China-Hong Kong, Art. 7; China-Taiwan, Art. 7. See *Voon* (2010), p. 647.

[87] See, for instance, CETA, Art. 24.9(1) ("effort to facilitate and promote trade and investment in environmental goods and services"); New Zealand-Taiwan, Art. 3.2(2) ("eliminate all tariffs on environmental goods"); USMCA, Art. 24.24 ("the Parties shall strive to facilitate and promote trade and investment in environmental goods and services").

domestic rules on anti-dumping investigations, 209 (or 1.5%) to anti-subsidy investigations, and 13 (or 0.1%) to safeguard measures.[88]

In relation to anti-dumping, most notifications come from the EU legislation, which was modernised in 2018.[89] The EU takes into consideration the relevant multilateral environmental conventions as well as the increased costs resulting from higher social and environmental standards in anti-dumping investigations. Furthermore, under Brazilian law, applying companies in anti-dumping investigations, as well as in sunset reviews, must provide the investigating authority with information on various performance indicators of the domestic industry and the company in question. Investigating authorities may consider investments carried out by domestic companies during the investigation period which were required to adhere to environmental regulation in the determination of the injury and the calculation of the injury margin.[90]

Countervailing measures notified to the WTO have dealt with environmental aspects, including air pollution reduction, energy conservation, biodiversity, alternative and renewable energy, energy conservation and efficiency, water management and conservation, climate change mitigation and adaptation, sustainable and environmentally friendly production, etc. The EU's legislation features prominently for its inclusion of environmental measures, namely the consideration of environmental standards in CVD investigations.[91] Other jurisdictions have included an Art. 8 ASCM-type of exception to the challenge of subsidies in national legislation (including Liberia[92] and Montenegro[93]). The bulk of notifications, however, pertains countervailing measures against products receiving environment-related subsidies from other jurisdictions, mostly in energy and manufacturing sectors.

Regarding safeguards, all notifications relate to environmental considerations in the application, design, or modification of the measure. Examples include the progressive reduction in safeguard duty rates to respect national commitments to the Paris Agreements (India[94]), adjustment plans by the domestic industry in a

---

[88] See WTO Environmental Database, https://edb.wto.org/ (last accessed 21 June 2023).

[89] See Sect. 3.3.2 below.

[90] See Committee on Anti-Dumping Practice, Committee on Subsidies and Countervailing Measures, and Committee on Safeguards, Notification of Laws and Regulations under Articles 18.5, 32.6 and 12.6 of the Agreements, Brazil, G/ADP/N/1/BRA/3/Suppl.2 and G/ADP/N/1/BRA/3/Suppl.5, 18 September 2014 and 31 January 2019.

[91] See Sect. 3.3.2 below.

[92] Regulation C/Reg.05/06/13 Relating to the Imposition of Countervailing Duties, Art. 5(6), available at https://www.wto.org/english/thewto_e/acc_e/lbr_e/wtacclbr15_leg_49.pdf (last accessed 21 June 2023).

[93] Decree for the Implementation of the Law on Foreign Trade, Art. 16.

[94] See Committee on Safeguards, Notification Under Article 12.1(b) of the Agreement on Safeguards on Finding a Serious Injury or Threat Thereof Caused by Increased Imports, Notification of a Proposal to Impose a Measure, Notification Pursuant to Article 9, Footnote 2, of the Agreement on Safeguards, India, Solar Cells Whether or not assembled in modules or panels, G/SG/N/8/IND/31/SUPPL.1, 2 August 2018.

safeguard investigation to comply with environmental requirements (Egypt[95]), environmental considerations relating to sustainable forest management and environmentally friendly production facilities and test machines (Indonesia[96]), and the non-application of safeguards measures linked to environmental national interest considerations (Ukraine[97]).

Furthermore, the link between trade remedies and the environment has been made in the Trade Poly Report Mechanism (TPRM). Entries regarding ADDs, CVDs and safeguard measures rank lowest in the list, with 10, 9 and 1 mention(s), respectively.[98] These entries pertain cases of trade remedy investigations on environmentally friendly goods.[99] Despite the relevance of monitoring trade remedy action on environmentally friendly goods, the WTO is not consistently monitoring the phenomenon in the TPRMs.

3.3.2   Case-Study: EU Trade Defence Instruments Regulations

"To be free, trade must be fair."[100] With this quote, the European Commission opened its first annual report on the use of Trade Defence Instruments (TDI) in 2019 after the reform of the anti-dumping and anti-subsidy rules that addressed environmental considerations. The EU maintains a policy discourse that open trade policy can only be built on sustainable trade, including in the field of trade remedies.[101] The

---

[95] See Committee on Safeguards, Notification under Article 12.1(b) of the Agreement on Safeguards on Finding a Serious Injury or Threat Thereof Caused by Increased Imports, Notification under Article 12.1(c) of the Agreement on Safeguards on Taking a Decision to Apply a Safeguard Measure, Notification Pursuant to Article 9, Footnote 2, of the Agreement on Safeguards, Egypt, Automotive Batteries, G/SG/N/8/EGY/8; G/SG/N/10/EGY/8; G/SG/N/11/EGY/10, 26 October 2015.

[96] See Committee on Safeguards, Notification Under Article 12.1(b) of the Agreement on Safeguard on Finding a Serious Injury or Threat Thereof Caused by Increased Imports, Notification of a Proposal to Extend a Measure, Indonesia, I and H Sections of Other Alloy Steel, G/SG/N/8/IDN/4/SUPPL.3; G/SG/N/10/IDN/4/SUPPL.3, 13 May 2022.

[97] See Committee on Safeguards, Notifications Under Article 12.1(b) to the Committee on Safeguards on Finding a Serious Injury or Threat Thereof Caused by Increased Imports, Notification Under Article 12.1(a) of the Agreement on Safeguards on Initiation of an Investigation and the Reasons for it, Ukraine, Casing and pump-compressor seamless steel pipes, G/SG/N/14/UKR/1; G/SG/N/8/UKR/1/SUPPL.1, 31 March 2015.

[98] See WTO Environmental Database, https://edb.wto.org/ (last accessed 21 June 2023).

[99] See, for instance, Trade Policy Review Body, Trade Policy Review, Report by the Secretariat, Canada, WT/TPR/S/389/Rev.1, 23 August 2019, S-Table-A3.1 and Trade Policy Review Body, Trade Policy Review, Report by the Secretariat, Peru, WT/TPR/S/393/Rev.2, 13 February 2020, para. 2.20, 2.61, 2.135 and S-Table-II.2.

[100] European Commission, 37th Annual Report from the Commission to the Council and the European Parliament on the EU's Anti-Dumping, Anti-Subsidy and Safeguard activities and the Use of trade defence instruments by Third Countries targeting the EU in 2018, 27 March 2019, COM(2019) 158 final, p. 3.

[101] *Ibid*, p. 7.

EU has been a front-runner when it included environmental objectives into its modernised legal framework of trade remedies.

As a result, green governance is now exerted through the recently reformed Basic Anti-Dumping and Basic Anti-Subsidy Regulations (BADR, BASR).[102] In December 2017 and May 2018, the European Parliament and the Council modernised the EU's trade defence rules in two successive legislative amendments.[103] It was particularly the European Parliament that pushed its stance that tougher duties should be imposed against environmental or social dumping.[104] The Parliament demanded that imported goods from countries that do not have sufficient levels of environmental protection be charged with stiffer duties. As a result, for the first time, social and environmental considerations have been included in the legal framework.[105]

Green elements in the updated legal framework include:

- **Existence of significant distortions**—The new rules introduce a "significant distortions" exception to using domestic prices in the comparison of the export price and the normal value by the Commission. Art. 2(6a)(b) BADR includes only consideration of the impact of government involvement or SOE presence in the market in determining whether significant distortions exist. Although the definition of significant distortions does not include compliance with social and environmental standards, Recital 4 to the Modernisation Package does link the concept of significant distortions to sustainability, by providing that "relevant

---

[102] Regulation (EU) 2016/1036 of the European Parliament and of the Council of 8 June 2016 on protection against dumped imports from countries not members of the European Union, OJ 2016 L 176/21, codified version available at https://eur-lex.europa.eu/legal-content/EN/TXT/PDF/?uri=C ELEX:02016R1036-20180608&from=EN (last accessed 21 June 2023); Regulation (EU) 2016/1037 of 8 June 2016 of the European Parliament and of the Council on protection against subsidised imports from countries not members of the European Union, OJ 2016 L 176/55 codified version available at https://eur-lex.europa.eu/legal-content/EN/TXT/PDF/?uri=CELEX:0201 6R1037-20180608&from=EN (last accessed 21 June 2023).

[103] Regulation (EU) 2016/1036 of the European Parliament and of the Council of 8 June 2016 on protection against dumped imports from countries not members of the European Union, OJ 2016 L 176/21, codified version available at https://eur-lex.europa.eu/legal-content/EN/TXT/?uri=CELE X:02016R1036-20180608 (last accessed 21 June 2023); Regulation (EU) 2016/1037 of 8 June 2016 of the European Parliament and of the Council on protection against subsidised imports from countries not members of the European Union, OJ 2016 L 176/55 codified version available at https://eur-lex.europa.eu/legal-content/EN/TXT/?qid=1528439971388&uri=CELE X:02016R1037-20180608 (last accessed 21 June 2023).

[104] See European Parliament, MEPs call for tougher measures against unfair imports from third countries, European Parliament Press Room, 5 February 2014, available at https://www.europarl. europa.eu/news/en/press-room/20140203IPR34509/MEPs-call-for-tougher-measures-against-unfair-imports-from-third-countries (last accessed 21 June 2023); European Parliament, Tougher Defence Tools Against Unfair Imports, MEPs Strike a deal with Ministers, 6 December 2017, available at https://www.europarl.europa.eu/news/de/press-room/20171205IPR89528/tougher-defence-tools-against-unfair-imports-meps-strike-deal-with-ministers (last accessed 21 June 2023).

[105] See European Commission, EU modernises its trade defence instruments, European Commission Press Corner, 23 January 2018, available at https://ec.europa.eu/commission/presscorner/detail/en/ MEMO_18_396 (last accessed 21 June 2023).

international standards, including core conventions of the [ILO] and relevant [MEAs]" shall be taken into account. This does not amount to an obligation for the Commission, as evidenced by the absence of reliance on this aspect in practice.[106] Moreover, the country reports of China and Russia the Commission produced for the assessment of significant distortions under the new methodology do not systematically refer to social and environmental conventions.

- **Social and environmental standards in selection of 3rd country**—Once the Commission decided to disregard domestic prices in the anti-dumping investigation, it will construct the normal value on the basis of undistorted prices or benchmarks. To that extent, Art. 2(6a) BADR foresees that corresponding costs of production and sale in an appropriate country will be used, and that "preference shall be given, where appropriate, to countries with an adequate level of social and environmental protection." The Basic Regulation includes a list of ILO Conventions, as well as MEAs in Annex 1a. However, in practice, this criterion plays only a limited role, as the Commission highlighted that social and environmental standards will only be considered as a secondary criterion when more than one appropriate third country exists. Similarly, the selection of representative countries in investigations on goods imported from non-WTO Members will consider environmental standards as a secondary selection criterion.[107]

- **Cost of production in injury margin calculation includes costs resulting from MEAs and protocols**—In most cases, the Commission applies duties on the injury margin level, which corresponds to the level of duty needed to eliminate the injury incurred to the EU industry. Given that imports may have already impacted the sales prices of EU producers, the Commission normally constructs the domestic sales prices for the purpose of comparison. Art. 7(2d) BADR now foresees that future costs to comply with multilateral environmental agreements of ILO Conventions to which the EU is a party must be added to the target price. Importantly, not only actual costs but also future costs resulting from these conventions are to be calculated. This is the most significant change to the dumping rules, as it will jack up the determination of the target price, therefore the injury margin in the calculation, and ultimately the imposed ADD.[108] However, this rule may potentially overlap with state aid for the implementation of EU environmental legislation.[109]

- **LDR linked to raw material distortions**—Until recently, the EU counted as one of the most consistent users of the LDR.[110] The LDR is a beneficial measure a WTO Member can voluntarily apply to impose lower ADDs and CVDs. The Commission does not apply the LDR anymore in case it finds raw material dis-

---

[106] Gustafsson and Crochet (2020), pp. 196–197.

[107] See new Art. 2(7) BADR.

[108] Gustafsson and Crochet (2020), pp. 198–199.

[109] Trapp (2021), p. 198.

[110] See Müller et al. (2009), para. 14.02 ff; Van Bael & Bellis (2019), pp. 295–297.

tortions exist (Art. 7(2a) BADR). The LDR will only be applied if three conditions are met: raw material distortions exist regarding the product concerned, the raw material accounts for at least 17% of the cost of production of the product, and it is in the Union's interest to not resort to the LDR.[111] This is an indirect environmental measure, as it will lead to higher duties for environmentally unfriendly raw materials distortions. The distortions noted include dual pricing schemes, export taxes, export surtaxes, export quota, export prohibitions, fiscal taxes on exports, licensing requirements, minimum export prices, VAT tax refund reductions or withdrawals, restriction on customs clearance point for exporters, qualified exporter lists, domestic market obligations, captive mining—all of which lead to prices of raw materials lower than the international price. This list is based and linked to the OECD Inventory on export restriction on industrial raw materials. The Commission gets powers under Art. 290 TFEU to make a list based on the OECD Inventory or any other OECD list which replaces the current list (Recital 25). In anti-subsidy cases, the LDR will simply no longer apply at all, so CVDs will always be applied at the (higher) subsidy margin.[112] It must be noted that, in both cases, an additional Union interest test could work to the benefit of the EU's climate policy and sustainable development on a global level—if the position of environmental stakeholders and environmental considerations in the Union interest test is improved.[113]

- **Social and environmental considerations in the acceptance of undertakings**—Pursuant Art. 8(3) BADR, undertakings offered by exporters from countries may be refused with reference to the principles and obligations set out in MEAs to which the EU is a party and ILO Conventions. Undertakings could in the past already be refused because of reasons of general policy, but now this is further concretised to MEA violations. In practice, the Commission is very reluctant to accept undertakings, so the amended provision will likely only have limited effects.

- **Environmental reporting obligations**—The Commission's reporting obligations in the annual report are extended to detailing how social and environmental standards have been considered and taken into account in the investigations in accordance with Art. 23(1) BADR. In addition thereto, the reporting obligation regarding the non-application of the LDR and the acceptance of undertakings would include notions on the environmental standards too. The reports also include considerations regarding ILO conventions and MEAs.[114]

- **Interim reviews and environmental considerations**—The Commission would be entitled to initiate interim reviews, *ex officio*, in case the costs of the EU indus-

---

[111] See new Art. 7(2a), 7(2b) and 9(4) BADR.

[112] See new Art. 12(1) and 15(1) BASR.

[113] See Sect. 4.4.2.8 below.

[114] Recital 4 of Regulation (EU) 2017/2321 of the European Parliament and of the Council of 12 December 2017 amending Regulation (EU) 2016/1036 on protection against dumped imports from countries not members of the European Union and Regulation (EU) 2016/1037 on protection against subsidised imports from countries not members of the European Union.

try increase as a result of higher social and environmental standards, or circumstances in the exporting countries change related to social and environmental standards. This is foreseen Recital 12 but is not reproduced in the operative part of the amended Basic Regulation. The scope of these reviews will depend on the precise nature of the change, but if a country for instance withdraws from a MEA, the interim review could result in the withdrawal of the undertakings in force.

Most of these measures can be labelled as rather policy provisions, not yet a real stamp of the new sustainability commitment in the EU. Commentators have questioned the real impact of these inclusions in practice and called out the EU for mostly including signpost provisions with little to no measurable effect in practice.[115] Only the inclusion of costs resulting from MEAs and protocols into the injury margin calculation has the potential to affect the level of ADDs or CVDs. Yet the new provisions exemplify a policy in the EU to pursue a value-based approach in developing its instruments of common commercial policy.

3.4 Chapter Summary

The WTO ruleset on trade remedies contains highly technical calculation rules and detailed procedural provisions. They are generally deemed unfit to exert non-economic policy goals such as environmental protection and climate change mitigation.

Trade remedies are historically vested on economic considerations. The underlying concepts and definitions of the notion of dumping and subsidisation under the WTO Agreements does not include eco-dumping or regulatory failure subsidies. Art. VI GATT is not intended to address environmental or social dumping, nor is the subsidy concept designed to include regulatory failures. Nonetheless, the legal framework on trade remedies leaves policy discretion for domestic legislators and national investigating authorities, which can be put into service of achieving green goals. Investigating authorities make several discretionary administrative decisions which may include a policy consideration in favour of environmental goods. The WTO rules contain complex calculation methods for dumping and injury margins. The calculation methodologies used by investigating authorities include discretionary freedoms to influence the dumping margin, amount of subsidy, as well as the injury margin. Therefore, whether a policy concern linked to social or environmental dumping could be included in the legal framework of dumping remains contentious.

The EU has taken the forefront by explicitly linking goals of social and environmental protection to the trade remedy action. Whether this is a true token of green governance, or rather a hidden form of green protectionism is debated. In any case, the EU example outlines various options for linking green objectives to trade

---

[115] See, for instance, Gustafsson and Crochet (2020), p. 200.

remedy investigations, including in the newly developed significant distortions methodology, the application of the LDR, the choice of appropriate third countries and reporting obligations. With these legislative changes, the EU has been a first-mover to explore the possibilities to pursue green governance objectives in the field of trade defence instruments. Whether other WTO Members will follow suit is questionable and must be awaited.

References

Adamantopoulos K (2008) Art. VI GATT. In: Wolfrum R, Stoll PT, Hestermeyer H (eds) Max Planck Commentaries on World Trade Law, WTO – trade in goods. Brill, Leiden

Anderson S, Lau C (2002) Hedging hopes with fears in China's Accession to the World Trade Organization: the transitional special product-safeguard for Chinese exports. J World Intellect Prop 5(3):405–476

Bourgeois K (2008) Preamble SGA. In: Wolfrum R, Stoll PT, Hestermeyer H (eds) Max Planck Commentaries on World Trade Law, WTO – trade in goods. Brill, Leiden

Cheaseth S, Samreth S (2009) Dumping determination discretions analysis: through lenses of relevant accounting principles. https://papers.ssrn.com/sol3/papers.cfm?abstract_id=1482992. Accessed 24 June 2023

Choi H, Lee SH (2017) Using modified anti-dumping mechanisms for sustainable development: the case of the Chinese Iron and Steel Industry. ASAN Report

De Baere P, du Parc C, Van Damme I (2021) The WTO anti-dumping agreement. A detailed commentary. Cambridge University Press, Cambridge

Durling JP (2008) Art. 14 SCMA. In: Wolfrum R, Stoll PT, Hestermeyer H (eds) Max Planck Commentaries on World Trade Law, WTO – trade in goods. Brill, Leiden

Eckes AE Jr (1995) Opening America's market: U.S. foreign trade policy since 1776. University of North Carolina Press, Chapel Hill

Esty DC (1994) Greening the GATT. Trade, environment, and the future. Institute for International Economics, Washington

Farha R (2012) A right unexercised is a right lost?: Abolishing antidumping in regional trade agreements. Georgetown J Int Law 44(1):211–248

Geraets D (2018) Accession to the World Trade Organization. A legal analysis. Edward Elgar Publishing, Cheltenham/Northampton

Gustafsson M, Crochet V (2020) At the crossroads of trade and environment. The growing influence of environmental policy on EU trade law. In: Orsini A, Kavvatha E (eds) EU environmental governance. Current and future challenges. Taylor & Francis, London, pp 187–206

Halverson K (2004) China's WTO Accession: economic, legal, and political implications. Boston College Int & Comp L Rev:319–370

Hoekman (1999) Free trade and deep integration: antidumping and antitrust in regional agreements, World Bank paper

Horlick G, Clarke PA (2017) Rethinking subsidy disciplines for the future: policy options for reform. J Int Econ Law 20(3):673–703

Horlick GN, Shea EC (1995) The World Trade Organization Anti-Dumping Agreement. J World Trade 29(1):5–31

Irwin D (2016) Historical notes on subsidies and the trading system. In: Rubini L, Hawkins J (eds) What shapes the law? Reflections on the history, law, politics and economics of international and European subsidy disciplines. European University Institute, Italy, pp 11–13

Jackson JH (1997) The world trading system. Law and policy of international economic relations, 2nd edn. The MIT Press, Cambridge/London

Kessie E (2010) The Doha Development Agenda at a crossroads: what are the remaining obstacles to the conclusion of the round? In: Herrmann C, Terhechte JP (eds) European Yearbook of International Economic Law 2010. Springer, Berlin/Heidelberg, pp 361–390

Kommerskollegium (2013) Eliminating anti-dumping measures in regional trade agreements, the European Union example. National Board of Trade, Sweden

Lingliang Z (2008) The legal effectiveness and appropriateness of transitional product-specific safeguard mechanism against China. In: Goa H, Lewis D (eds) China's participation in the WTO. Cameron May, London

Marceau G (1994) Anti-dumping and anti-trust issues in free-trade areas. Clarendon Press, Oxford

Matsushita M, Schoenbaum T, Mavroidis P, Hahn M (2015) The World Trade Organization, law, practice, and policy, 3rd edn. Oxford University Press, Oxford

Müller W (2017) WTO agreement on subsidies and countervailing measures: a commentary. Cambridge University Press, Cambridge

Müller W, Khan N, Scharf T (2009) EC and WTO anti-dumping law. A handbook, 2nd edn. Oxford University Press, Oxford

Nedumpara JJ (2016) Injury and causation in trade remedy law. A study of WTO law and country practices. Springer, Singapore

Piérola F (2014) The challenge of safeguards in the WTO. Cambridge University Press, Cambridge

Prusa TJ (2011) Trade remedy provisions. In: Chauffour JP, Maur JC (eds) Preferential trade agreement policies for development. A handbook. World Bank, Washington, pp 179–196

Qin JY (2004) WTO Regulation of Subsidies to State-Owned Enterprises (SOEs) – a critical appraisal of the China Accession Protocol. J Int Econ Law 7(4):863–919

Sands P, Peel J (2018) Principles of international environmental law, 4th edn. Cambridge University Press, Cambridge

Stewart TP (2001) Antidumping. In: Stewart TP, Dwyer AS (eds) Handbook on WTO Trade Remedy Disputes: the first six years (1995-2000). Brill/Nijhoff, Leiden/Boston

Stewart TP, Mueller DP (2008) Art. 1-2 ADA. In: Wolfrum R, Stoll PT, Hestermeyer H (eds) Max Planck Commentaries on World Trade Law, WTO – trade in goods. Brill, Leiden

Sykes AO (2003) The safeguards mess: a critique of WTO jurisprudence. J World Trade 2(3):261–295

Teh R, Prusa TJ, Budetta M (2009) Trade remedy provisions in regional trade agreements. In: Estevadeordal A, Suominen K, Teh R (eds) Regional rules in the global trading system. Cambridge University Press, Cambridge, pp 166–248

Trapp P (2021) "Global Green Governance" oder "Veiled Protectionism"? Die Berücksichtigung sozial- und umweltpolitischer Belange in den reformierten Grundverordnungen der EU zur Verhängung von Anti-Dumping- und Ausgleichsmaßnahmen. Nachhaltigkeitsrecht 1(2):195–204

Trebilcock MJ, Trachtman J (2020) Advanced introduction to international trade law, 2nd edn. Edward Elgar, Cheltenham/Northampton

Van Bael & Bellis (2019) EU anti-dumping and other trade defence instruments, 6th edn. Wolters Kluwer, Alphen aan den Rijn

Viner JA (1923) Dumping: a problem in international trade. The University of Chicago Press, Chicago

Voon T (2010) Eliminating trade remedies from the WTO: lessons from regional trade agreements. Int Comp Law Q 59(3):625–667

Wu M (2012) Antidumping in Asia's emerging giants. Harv Int Law J 53(1):1–84

Yamaoka T (2013) Analysis of China's Accession Commitments in the WTO: new taxonomy of more and less stringent commitments, and the struggle for mitigation by China. J World Trade 47(1):105–157

Chapter 4
The Use of Trade Remedies on Green Goods

4.1 Introduction

In 2002, the WTO included a stance on sustainable development in its working agenda under the Doha Development Agenda (DDA), by committing to reduce all trade barriers on environmental goods and services (EGS):

> 31. With a view to enhancing the mutual supportiveness of trade and environment, we agree to negotiations, without prejudging their outcome, on:
>
>   (iii) the reduction or, as appropriate, elimination of tariff and non-tariff barriers to environmental goods and services.[1]

Reducing trade barriers on EGS would generate "win-win" outcomes whereby developed countries win in terms of market access, and developing countries win in terms of access to EGS. However, this DDA commitment has not been converted into practice yet. So far, the work on the so-called 'environmental package'[2] of the DDA focuses on negotiations on the relationship between multilateral environmental agreements (MEAs) and WTO disciplines and information exchange between MEA secretariats,[3] and the role of the Committee on Trade and Environment (CTE) in fostering debates within the working sphere of trade and environment to identify developmental and environmental aspects of rules negotiations.[4] The reduction of non-tariff barriers (NTBs) on environmental goods and services was discussed between 2011–2016 but has been dormant since. Recently, initiatives on trade and

---

[1] Doha Development Agenda, para. 31 (emphasis added).

[2] Kennedy (2009), p. 532.

[3] Doha Development Agenda, para. 31(i) and 31(ii).

[4] Doha Development Agenda, para. 51.

© The Author(s), under exclusive license to Springer Nature Switzerland AG 2023   49
P. Van Vaerenbergh, *Greening Trade Remedies*, EYIEL Monographs - Studies in European and International Economic Law 31,
https://doi.org/10.1007/978-3-031-38172-0_4

sustainability bring the liberalisation of environmental goods back to the forefront of multilateral discussion, both within as well as outside the WTO auspices.[5]

Trade remedies are an important example of non-tariff barriers, which have a significant impact on certain EGS sectors. This chapter considers how to materialise the commitment in para. 31(iii) DDA to lower or reduce tariffs and non-tariff barriers on environmental goods on account of trade remedies. It opens by considering the value of resorting to tariff reductions to achieve environmental protection (Sect. 4.2). Then, three steps must be taken to discipline the use of trade remedies on green goods: First, WTO Members must agree on the definition of environmental goods and services to set out the range of environmentally friendly goods that may be exempted from trade remedies (Sect. 4.3). Second, an agreement between WTO Members to remove trade barriers on environmental goods shall deal with both complete eliminations of as well as other limitations on the use of trade remedies on green goods (Sect. 4.4). Finally, multilateral, bilateral, plurilateral, or sectoral agreements shall implement the limitations on trade remedies (Sect. 4.5). This chapter concludes with a summary of the most feasible measures investigating authorities may implement to show a non-economic policy preference for green purposes in trade remedy investigations (Sect. 4.6).

4.2   The Case for Liberalising the Environmental Goods Market

It is a commendable effort to liberalise tariffs on trade in environmental goods, but governments may see these efforts nullified through the imposition of other, so-called non-tariff barriers (NTBs). As a prime example of NTBs, trade remedy measures are an important border measure applied to imports from goods.[6] The massive imposition of trade remedies is an example of a significant burden in the sector of environmental goods, which renders efforts to liberalise the EGS sector through lowering tariff barriers meaningless, or at least reduces the effectivity of the efforts.[7]

---

[5] In November 2020, 53 WTO Members launched the Trade and Environmental Sustainability Structured Discussions (TESSD); negotiations on an Agreement on Climate Change. See WTO News, First meeting held to advance work on trade and environmental sustainability, 5 March 2021, available at https://www.wto.org/english/news_e/news21_e/tessd_08mar21_e.htm (last accessed 21 June 2023). Moreover, New Zealand, Costa Rica, Fiji, Iceland, Norway and Switzerland have launched negotiations on an Agreement on Climate Change, Trade and Sustainability (ACCTS), which aims to lower tariff barriers on environmental goods and services by means of a binding ceiling on the potential tariff. See https://www.mfat.govt.nz/en/trade/free-trade-agreements/trade-and-climate/agreement-on-climate-change-trade-and-sustainability-accts-negotiations/ (last accessed 21 June 2023).

[6] UNCTAD's classification of NTBs includes "Contingent trade-protective measures" as a category of non-technical measures. See UNCTAD (2014), pp. 18 ff. Similarly, the OECD defined core NTBs in 1997 including anti-dumping and countervailing actions. See Deardorff and Stern (1997).

[7] See Sect. 2.4.1.1 above.

Trade remedies thus may result in the *de facto* re-instatement of tariff barriers that impede the development and innovation in the EGS sector.[8]

Against that background, with the aim of addressing the trade barrier created by the imposition of trade remedy duties, proposals have been formulated for governments to reduce this trade obstacle—particularly in the sector of environmentally friendly goods. Preferably, the pursuit of a green policy agenda in relation to trade remedies exists in a complete abolition of trade remedy duties on environmental goods.[9] Alternatively, by reducing the amount of trade remedies in the EGS sector, governments may also use trade remedy policy as a tool to promote the green industries with positive spill-overs.

As such, in this approach, environmental protection is not achieved through putting a price on carbon emissions or environmental regulation, but rather through lowering (or not increasing) the price of environmentally friendly goods, thereby fostering market forces and growth of the EGS sectors. Due to low percentage of tariffs on environmental goods, removing trade remedy burden on environmental goods might even have a bigger impact on environmental goods than further tariff reductions.[10] This proposal aims to achieve freer trade in environmental goods and thus promote environment and renewable energy and remove trade barriers to let the market forces strengthen the environmental goods market. This also contributes to the competitive position of environmental goods on the market. On the other hand, companies may interpret this temporary relief from trade remedies as an incentive to engage in additional dumping practices.

4.3 Defining Environmental Goods

Differentiating between 'good' green and 'bad' industrial goods requires a definition on the level of tariff lines that allows to distinguish goods on their environmental impact (Sect. 4.3.1). Various approaches to the negotiations have been suggested, but this section focusses on the so-called 'list approach', where a positive list of environmentally friendly goods and services is attempted to be agreed on.[11] Such list may be based on a combination of criteria such as end-uses, properties, nature and quality, consumer tastes and habits, tariff classification and product-related PPMs to make it WTO-agreeable.[12] However, negotiations on environmental goods have proven a difficult task (Sect. 4.3.2) and raise various WTO compatibility questions (Sect. 4.3.3).

---

[8] The Peterson Institute for International Economics quantified in 2014 that trade remedies on environmental goods reduced trade in such goods by approximately $14 billion annually. See UNCTAD (2014), pp. 12–13.

[9] Meléndez-Ortiz (2016), p. 11; Horlick (2013), p. 69.

[10] Brewster et al. (2016), p. 328.

[11] See Zhang (2013), pp. 677 ff.

[12] Vikhlyaev (2004), p. 103.

4.3.1   Tariff Lines for Environmental Goods

The GATT and WTO rely on the World Customs Organisation (WCO) and its predecessors in defining tariff classifications in trade negotiations and application of tariff schedules in the WTO.[13] The Harmonized Commodity Description and Coding System (HS Convention) of tariff nomenclature is the international standardised system of names and numbers to classify traded products.[14] The WCO developed the system and maintained it since 1988.[15] It has since been widely used by practically all countries in the world for various purposes.

The HS Convention knows 21 sections organised by economic activity or component material, which have 99 chapters (first two digits), then developed into 1244 headings (next two digits) and 5224 subheadings (last two digits). This totals the 6-digit nomenclature which is internationally agreed upon. Legal notes at every section and chapter, which clarify the proper classification of goods, are available for the assistance of the Members.[16] Figure 4.1 shows an example of the hierarchical structure of the HS:

The WCO Members have based their national tariff schedules on this classification. This is one example of the use of the HS codes, *i.e.* trade negotiations at the WTO schedules of tariff concessions.[17]

Fig. 4.1 Example of the hierarchical structure of the Harmonized System. Source: Author's own creation

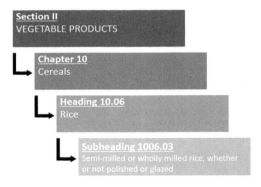

---

[13] Appellate Body report, *European Communities – Customs Classification of Frozen Boneless Chicken Cuts*, WT/DS269/AB/R, adopted 12 September 2005, para. 198.

[14] For the status as a source of public international law in the WTO jurisprudence, see Matsushita et al. (2015), p. 226.

[15] HS 2022, the 7th edition of the HS, shall enter into force on 1 January 2022. Addressing environmental and social issues of global concern was one of the major features of the HS 2022 amendments. See WCO Newsroom, The new 2022 Edition of the Harmonized System has been accepted, 8 January 2020, available at http://www.wcoomd.org/en/media/newsroom/2020/january/the-new-2022-edition-of-the-harmonized-system-has-been-accepted.aspx (last accessed 21 June 2023).

[16] In the EU, for instance, the ECJ has confirmed these play an important role in the EU for ensuring uniform application of the tariffs. See ECJ, *Daiber v. Hauptzollamt Reutlingen*, Case 200/84, judgment of 10 October 1985, ECLI:EU:C:1985:403, para. 14.

[17] They are also used for custom tariff administration, collection of international trade statistics, rules of origin, collection of international taxes, transport tariffs and statistics, monitoring of controlled goods etc.

At the HS 6-digit level, tariff lines are expressed in a regulation-neutral manner. After the Tokyo Round of negotiations, many countries of the Organisation for Economic Cooperation and Development (OECD), including the US and the EU, started negotiating concessions beyond the 6-digit level, at the 8-, 10- or 12-digit level too. At these lower levels, countries may already differentiate classes of goods based on their environmental impact. This is legally allowed under the HS Convention:

> Nothing in this Article shall prevent a Contracting Party from establishing, in its Customs tariff or statistical nomenclatures, subdivisions classifying goods beyond the level of the Harmonized System, provided that any such subdivision is added and coded at a <u>level beyond that of the six-digit numerical code</u> set out in the Annex to this Convention.[18]

Such subdivisions and subheadings beyond the 6-digit level are called 'ex-outs'.[19] GATT Panels have recognised that such classifications may need to differentiate between products that are otherwise like products and might therefore violate the MFN principle.[20] Nonetheless, at the WTO, the bound tariffs are applied until the 6-digit level based on the HS qualification. Hence, it is possible that a Member adds 8 and 8+ levels to distinguish between products made using renewable energy or the same products using fossil fuels. The WCO may even facilitate policy choices based on categorisations of goods for a certain purpose. One example is a classification of environmental goods, which may form an important basis to regulate trade and negotiate trade deals that carry out values of environmental protection.

4.3.2   Environmental Goods: Impossible to Define or Impossible to Negotiate?

4.3.2.1   Environmental Goods Negotiations: An Overview

Environmental tariff lines beyond the 6-digit level can be formulated unilaterally in national schemes, in a bilateral/plurilateral context or through multilateral negotiations. Several plurilateral initiatives have attempted negotiations of environmental goods on and beyond the 6-digit level between smaller groups of like-minded WTO Members. The work of the plurilateral initiatives is centred around overcoming the definitional problems on the multilateral level.

---

[18] Art. 3(3) HS Convention (emphasis added).

[19] Mavroidis and Neven (2019), p. 377.

[20] See GATT Panel report, *Spain – Tariff Treatment of Unroasted Coffee*, L/5135, BISD 28S/102, adopted 11 June 1981, para. 4.4. The Panel found all unroasted, non-decaffeinated coffee beans like products. Differently, see GATT Panel report, *Canada/Japan – Tariff on Imports of Spruce, Pine, Fir (SPF) Dimension Lumber*, L/6470, BISD 36S/167, adopted 19 July 1989, para. 5.8. The Panel found that both varieties of lumber were not like products.

At the international level, the OECD published an indicative list of environmental goods and services in 1992,[21] based on their exercise to map out the environmental industry—for analytical, rather than tariff negotiation purposes.[22] The OECD list is therefore broad, because it had no specific policy purpose. One category of goods is the environmentally preferable products (EPPs), which typically includes products which cause significantly less environmental harm at some stage of their life cycle (production, processing, consumption, or disposal).[23] Examples include products superior to petroleum-based products (e.g. biofuels), environmentally friendly produced goods (e.g. organic coffee, tea, or cocoa, chemical-free cotton, timber from sustainable forests…) and goods contributing to preserving the environment (e.g. biopesticides).[24]

Leading example of plurilateral EGS negotiations is the so-called 'Early Voluntary Sector Liberalization Initiative' of the Asia Pacific Economic Cooperation (APEC).[25] Initiated in 1997 by the Quad countries, the APEC grew to an initiative among 21 countries. The APEC published a list of 54 environmental goods for preferential tariffs in 2012, based on the OECD definitional work.[26] The outcome is based on individual nominations by the participating countries, rather than on a common understanding of the industry of environmental goods. The list aimed to achieve rapid liberalisation of products that customs authorities could readily distinguish. The list includes goods relating to clean energy technologies such as solar panel and wind turbines. It has been concluded and, although not formally adopted yet, already applied on a voluntary basis and on an MFN basis.[27] This distinguishes the APEC plurilateral agreement from an RTA approach. Remarkably, the APEC has used this project for consumption purposes solely, and maybe not for environmental reasons, evidenced by the fact that the environmental commitments only apply to the trading and not the production aspects of the various HS-lines.[28]

Within the WTO, negotiations on reducing trade barriers on environmental goods and services have been stalled after a decade of negotiations in the Doha Round. Both in the Committee on Trade and the Environment (CTE) and the Committee on

---

[21] OECD, The OECD Environment Industry: Situation, Prospects and Government Policy, 1992; OECD, The Global Environment Goods and Services Industry, 1996.

[22] Zhang (2013), p. 677.

[23] Vikhlyaev (2004), p. 96.

[24] Ibid, p. 96.

[25] The APEC includes 21 so-called Member Economies: Australia, Brunei, Canada, Chile, China, Hong Kong, Indonesia, Japan, Malaysia, Mexico, New Zealand, Papua New Guinea, Peru, Philippines, Russia, Singapore, South Korea, Chinese Taipei, Thailand, United States and Vietnam. See https://www.apec.org/About-Us/About-APEC/Member-Economies (last accessed 21 June 2023).

[26] APEC List of Environmental Goods, Annex C to the 2012 Leaders' Declaration, November 2012, available at https://www.apec.org/Meeting-Papers/Leaders-Declarations/2012/2012_aelm/2012_aelm_annexC.aspx (last accessed 21 June 2023). For a comparison between the OECD and the APEC Lists, see Steenblik (2005).

[27] Mavroidis and Neven (2019), p. 377.

[28] Ibid, p. 378.

Rules Negotiations (CNR), negotiations are ongoing. The WTO Committee on Trade and Environment in Special Session (CTE-SS) foresaw in 2011 that the four issues of focus will be (i) scope of liberalisation, (ii) exact coverage of goods and services, (iii) modalities of treatment and (iv) development elements.[29] The US supported these negotiations in 2013 and pushed forward trade negotiations on environmental goods and services.[30] The WTO tried facilitating the process by removing NTBs and environmental services from the agenda, but a tariff-only negotiation proved equally unfruitful. Although the Committee published a list of 408 tariff lines on goods relating to air pollution control, renewable energy, waste management and water treatment, environmental technologies, carbon capture and storage and others, further multilateral negotiations appeared impossible.[31] Submissions of WTO Members established mercantilist behaviour by the WTO Members, systematically avoiding goods where comparative advantages or high tariffs were noted.[32] The majority of submissions to the WTO regard renewable energy, energy efficiency, heat and energy management and carbon capture and storage.[33]

Against that background, Environmental Goods Agreement (EGA) negotiations were launched in July 2014 by 46 WTO Members under leadership of the EU and the US.[34] The aim was to promote trade with respect to environmentally friendly products, including goods related to renewable energy production (wind turbines and solar panels and energy saving products), waste management, noise, and air pollution, etc. However, negotiations are frozen since December 2016, when US-EU relations deteriorated in the verge of the negotiations on the Transatlantic Trade and Investment Partnership (TTIP). The EGA initiative built further on the APEC list of 54 environmental goods. Like the WTO negotiations, difficult hurdles had to be overcome on individual products. Even the proposed inclusion of uncontroversial goods which may be considered environmental goods absent any discussion on technological characteristics have led to opposition by certain WTO Members. For instance, when China proposed to include bicycles and bicycle parts, the EU opposed.[35] This might be traced back to the decades-long imposition of anti-dumping duties by the EU on bicycles from China.[36] This illustrates the difficulty of

---

[29] Committee on Trade and Environment Special Session, Report by the Chairman, TN/TE/20, para. 11.

[30] See Executive Office of the President, The President's Climate Action Plan, June 2013, pp. 19–20.

[31] Frey (2016), p. 459.

[32] de Melo and Solleder (2020), p. 335.

[33] Sugathan (2013).

[34] The EGA includes 46 Members (many of which are also part of the APEC initiative: Australia, Canada, China, Costa Rica, European Union, Hong Kong, Iceland, Israel, Japan, South Korea, New Zealand, Norway, Singapore, Switzerland, Liechtenstein, Chinese Taipei, Turkey, and the United States. See World Trade Organization, Map of EGA participants, available at https://www.wto.org/english/tratop_e/envir_e/ega_map_e.htm (last accessed 21 June 2023).

[35] de Melo and Solleder (2020), p. 336.

[36] The European Commission has imposed and maintained anti-dumping investigations on bicycles from China since 1996 until (at least) 2024. See, most recently, Commission Implementing

agreeing on a list of environmental goods, because the challenge is to overcome political differences and making sure negotiations stay clean from political influences.[37] Moreover, broadening the scope beyond tariffs will increase developing countries' interest in joining the EGA project.[38] Whilst the EGA is being negotiated as a plurilateral agreement, there is hope that it will later evolve into a multilateral agreement adopted by all WTO Members. Recently, the elimination of NTBs on EGS has been placed on the trade and environment Agenda at the WTO again, for instance by the work of the Structured Discussions on Trade and Environmental Sustainability (TESSD).

There are also other multilateral and bilateral initiatives concluded on the definition of EGS, for instance by the World Bank. One example of a mini-plurilateral negotiation on reducing tariffs on environmental goods on an MFN-basis advancing the EGA is the Agreement on Climate Change, Trade and Sustainability (ACCTS) between Costa Rica, Fiji, Iceland, New Zealand, and Norway, which also aims to remove fossil fuel subsidies and voluntary eco-labelling programmes.[39]

Finally, it could also be an initiative of the WCO itself to publish a list of environmental goods,[40] or even unilateral initiatives from certain countries. The EU, for instance, has already pursued a 'green' list beyond the 6-digit level. The advantage is that this can be easily implemented, especially upon initiative of the WCO—as opposed to including ex-outs beyond the 6-digit level that indicate for instance production externalities or end-uses.

4.3.2.2 Shortcomings of Environmental Goods Negotiations

Such plurilateral initiatives defining environmental goods are commendable for pushing forward multilaterally committed targets within the WTO. One aspect of the EGA merits highlighting: the MFN treatment of the EGA goods is planned to be extended to all WTO members and not just those participating in the agreement.[41] This amounts to a *de facto* multilateralisation of the zero-tariffs on green goods.

Regulation (EU) 2019/1379 of 28 August 2019 imposing a definitive anti-dumping duty on imports of bicycles originating in the People's Republic of China, OJ 2019 L 225/1.

[37] Eliason (2019), p. 568.

[38] Wu (2014), pp. 173–174.

[39] See Steenblik and Droege (2019).

[40] Amidst the COVID-19 pandemic, the WCO published a list of goods that expressed policy considerations, (the "HS classification reference for Covid-19 medical supplies") to facilitate management of cross-border movement of medical goods, apply contingent tariff and non-tariff measures, survey and combat movement falsified supplies, and address shortages. See WCO, HS classification reference for Covid-19 medical supplies, 2nd edition, as updated 9 April 2020.

[41] Report from the 14th round of negotiations for an Environmental Goods Agreement (EGA), available at https://trade.ec.europa.eu/doclib/docs/2016/july/tradoc_154784.pdf (last accessed 21 June 2023).

Necessary requirement is that a critical mass is achieved, which means 85–90% of trade in the relevant products is covered and no other WTO Members object.

However, the current initiatives suffer from several shortcoming. First, the average tariff of environmental goods in for instance the APEC-list is relatively low (2.6%). Many goods with high tariffs are excluded, therefore missing the goal of contributing to the achievement of sustainable development goals.[42] In fact, negotiations are limited only to focus on tariffs and nothing beyond that, which has been criticised. Second, developing countries are largely absent from the negotiations. For instance, China and Costa Rica are the only developing countries currently involved in the EGA negotiations. Reportedly, whereas China is only looking for market access through its participation, Costa Rica is seeking to put its economy on a green industrialisation track.[43] Third, negotiations of environmental goods are mostly carried out at the HS 6-digit level, where tariff lines do not yet necessarily distinguish by end-use (dual use problem), neither how products are produced (process and production method problem, PPM problem), nor do they necessarily show their impact on the environment. In that sense, national tariff lines going beyond the 6-digit level would be better fit for identifying goods.[44] In any case, negotiations should make use of the updated HS list on account of for instance LED-bulbs or hybrid and all-electric cars which have just been added.[45] Fourth, the list approach must include flexibilities that allow the list to change and develop over time. A mechanism to add elements, remove elements, and revise the position of elements must be included in the list-system.[46]

Most importantly, for the negotiations carried out under the auspices of the WTO, discussions under para. 31(iii) have excluded environmental services and NTBs. Especially NTBs are very important especially in the renewable energy sector and include contingent protection measures, local-content requirements, growing anti-dumping duties. The environmental services aspect of para. 31 has been separated from the EGA into the negotiations on the Trade in Services Agreement (TiSA) in the GATS committee since 2013 among 23 WTO Members where negotiations are conducted in a similar fashion.[47] However, since trade remedies only relate to trade in goods, TiSA negotiations are not of particular importance.

---

[42] Wouters et al. (2020), pp. 16–17.

[43] de Melo and Solleder (2020), p. 338.

[44] See Sect. 4.3.1 above.

[45] de Melo and Solleder (2020), p. 341.

[46] Cosbey (2014).

[47] There have been attempts to define the concept of "environmental services" in the literature. See for instance Gelosso Grosso (2007); Vikhlyaev (2004), pp. 108 ff.

4.3.3   WTO Compatibility of Environmental Tariff Lines

Even though schedules of commitments are negotiated, their validity can still be challenged after the end of negotiations.[48] Singling out certain renewable energy products in separate tariff lines beyond the 6-digit level for reasons relating to policy preferences can thus raise WTO-compatibility questions. This section focuses on the question whether environmentally friendly produced goods and environmentally unfriendly produced goods "like products" (Sect. 4.3.3.1). Furthermore, the environmental justification debate equally may arise (Sect. 4.3.3.2).

4.3.3.1   Are Products with Different Carbon Content 'Like' Products?

In the remit of environmental protection and climate change, the question arises whether two products are 'like products' if they are produced using renewable energy and fossil fuels respectively. Climate change policies that target a reduction of GHG emissions, however, generally focus on the production process and not the product *per se*—the very definition of PPMs. The result is that climate change measures may be particularly vulnerable on this account for the non-discrimination principles under the GATT. In some scenarios, it might be fair to conclude that carbon-intensive and climate-friendly products are not like.[49] This would influence whether WTO Members could treat environmental goods differently with regard to customs duties.

PPM jurisprudence mainly developed under Art. III GATT,[50] but may *mutatis mutandis* be applied to Art. I GATT.[51] Only product-related PPMs (which affect the physical characteristics of the product which they produce) are permissible under WTO law, but not not-product related PPMs (which leave no physical traces in the product). In the seminal *Tuna/Dolphin* case, the GATT Panel did not apply Art. III

---

[48] See GATT Panel report, *United States – Restrictions on the Importation of Sugar and Sugar-Containing Products Applied Under the 1955 Waiver and Under the Headnote to the Schedule of Tariff Concessions*, BISD 36S/331, adopted 7 November 1990, para. 5.2; Appellate Body report, *European Communities – Regime for the Importation, Sale and Distribution of Bananas*, WT/DS27/AB/R, adopted 25 September 1997, para. 153–158. See Hoekman and Mavroidis (2017), pp. 392 ff.

[49] Doelle (2004), p. 95.

[50] The seminal *Tuna/Dolphin* cases seemed to close the door on considering PPMs in likeness determination under Art. I or III GATT. In *Salmon and Herring*, PPMs were considered relevant under Art. XX GATT, but Panels did not consider PPMs for the scope of application of Art. I GATT. In *Shrimp/Turtle*, the Appellate Body found a violation of Art. XI GATT, thereby effectively escaping the PPM question under Art. I and III GATT. Hence, the question whether PPMs are a basis for distinguishing between products remains open, in absence of a definitive ruling in that direction. Ultimately, The WTO chose to tackle the differentiation under Art. XX GATT where PPM differences are specifically allowed. See also Sect. 4.3.3.2 below.

[51] The meaning of the term 'like product' under both provisions is identical. See Potts (2008), pp. 11–12.

GATT but suggested that dolphin-friendly tuna would be "like" conventionally har-
vested tuna.[52] Thus stemmed the conventional belief that PPM-based different treatment would violate per se the national treatment obligations of the GATT.

At present, the concept of environmental likeness is still debated at large in WTO
jurisprudence and scholarship. The question of likeness must be assessed on a case-
by-case basis, taking into account both the factual background, as well as the provision of the GATT in question.[53] The Appellate Body focusses on four criteria when
analysing likeness: (i) the physical properties, nature and quality of the products, (ii)
the extent to which the products may serve the same or similar end uses in a given
market, (iii) the extent to which consumers perceive and treat the products as alternative means of satisfying a want or demand, and (iv) tariff classification of the
products.[54]

Two criteria—properties, nature and quality, and end-uses—will normally not
change on the basis of non-product related PPMs. [55] The other two—consumer preference and the criterion of tariff classification—may become relevant to distinguish
carbon-intensive from carbon-neutral goods. First, a stronger consumer preference
aspect in the likeness debate can affect the PPM debate effectively. The growing
market of eco-labelled products and fair-trade awareness of consumers stands that
point. The consumer tastes and habits criterion applied in *EC –Asbestos* might constitute a ground to make an analogous argument.[56] The Appellate Body concluded
that otherwise like products may be unlike due to health risks associated with the
product.[57] At present, maybe the consumer has enough climate change and environmental protection interest (*i.e.* the ability to link climate change to PPMs and negative health impacts), to conclude that products with different levels of emissions are
not like. However, the consumer criterion has rarely been applied as primary basis
for determining likeness of products—criteria relating to functionality of products
seem more important. Nonetheless, since *EC – Asbestos*, the Appellate Body underlined the need to consider all relevant criteria for likeness on their own individual
merit, thereby suggesting that a single criterion may be sufficient for conclusions,

---

[52] GATT Panel report, *United States – Restrictions on Imports of Tuna*, 3 September 1991,
unadopted, BISD 39S/155, para. 5.15.

[53] Potts (2008), pp. 14–15.

[54] See Appellate Body report, *European Communities – Measures Affecting Asbestos and Products
Containing Asbestos*, WT/DS135/AB/R, adopted 5 April 2001, para. 91; Appellate Body/Panel
report, *Japan – Alcoholic Beverages II*, WT/DS8/AB/R, WT/DS10/AB/R, WT/DS11/AB/R,
adopted 1 November 1996, para. 28–37 and 67–75. Nothing prevents addition of additional sustainable development-oriented criteria for like product interpretations. Potts (2008), p. 14: Based
on evolutionary approach and WTO principle of sustainable development, there may be compel-
ling arguments to do so.

[55] Potts (2008), p. 14.

[56] Doelle (2004), p. 95.

[57] Appellate Body report, *European Communities – Measures Affecting Asbestos and Asbestos-
Containing Products*, WT/DS135/AB/R, adopted 5 April 2001.

and vice versa that one single criterion is necessarily more important.[58] This may boost the value of the consumers tastes and habits as a criterion again.

Second, the importance of PPM tariff lines must be underlined. The tariff classification criterion for likeness investigations has been explicitly defined at the 6-digit level in *Japan – Alcoholic Beverages II*[59] and *Japan – SPF Dimension Lumber*[60] and may therefore be useless for policy considerations at the 8-digit level. Consequently, very few HS 6-digit level codes reflect differences of production. Products within the same 6-digit category but differences reflecting environmental harm on the 8-digit level would necessarily be categorised as like products for the MFN obligation under Art. I:1 GATT and therefore differentiation in applicable tariffs found WTO-inconsistent.[61]

In the literature on PPMs, authors put forth various solutions for acceptable PPMs under the current WTO state of play. *Mavroidis/Neven* have proposed to accept policy likeness under Art. I:1 GATT, by importing some sort of necessity or consistency test from Art. XX GATT to assess whether the policy dimension is authentic.[62] However, in the field of services, the predominant understanding of the term 'like service' does not include policy likeness.[63] *Potts* suggests using PPM trade measures on these products which have a clear market, e.g. the ones from eco-labelling schemes. Finally, overwhelming international research can help the case.[64]

In conclusion, it is unlikely that environmentally friendly and environmentally-unfriendly goods would be classified as like products. Treating them differently in terms of customs or NTBs at the border is therefore not a possibility. Consequently, currently, because most Members argue against it, PPM products (goods with eco-labels, goods with environmentally friendly procedures, and organic products) are excluded from negotiations on defining environmentally friendly goods.[65]

---

[58] *Ibid*, para. 109 ff.

[59] Appellate Body report, *Japan – Alcoholic Beverages II*, WT/DS8/AB/R, WT/DS10/AB/R, WT/DS11/AB/R, adopted 1 November 1996, para. 25.

[60] GATT Panel report, *Canada/Japan — Tariff on Imports of Spruce, Pine, Fir (SPF) Dimension Lumber*, L/6470, adopted 19 July 1989, para. 5.11–5.12.

[61] Mavroidis and Neven (2019), p. 386.

[62] *Ibid*.

[63] Appellate Body report, *Argentina – Measures Relating to Trade in Goods and Services*, WT/DS453/AB/R, adopted 9 May 2016.

[64] Potts (2008).

[65] Zhang (2013), p. 682.

4.3.3.2   Could Justifications Under Art. XX GATT Be Applied?

Violations of the MFN obligation can be justified in a specific case through recourse to the general exceptions to the GATT. In such case, the defending Member carries the burden of proof to furnish reasons why measures may be justified for environmental reasons.[66]

There is no definitive Panel/Appellate Body finding on whether these exceptions know a jurisdictional limitation. In other words, it is not decided whether justifications the defending Member relies upon may relate to environmental concerns *outside* the territory of the invoking Member. Early Panel reports including *Tuna/Dolphin I*, *Tuna/Dolphin II* and *US – Shrimp* suggested a rather restrictive approach.[67] The Appellate Body in *US – Shrimp*, however, took a different stance, opining that "[i]t is not necessary to assume that requiring from exporting countries compliance with, or adoption of certain policies [...] renders a measure *a priori* incapable of justification of Article XX."[68] Criteria are not formulated, but some domestic effects would already suffice. Although not explicitly addressing the possible implied jurisdictional limitations under Art. XX GATT, the Appellate Body resorted to the 'sufficient nexus' test between the protected non-trade value (in that case migratory and endangered marine populations involved) and the defending Member (in that case the US) for the purposes of Art. XX(g) GATT.[69] The jurisprudence then turned towards a test of the existence of sufficient 'legitimate interest' in the case law on *US – Tuna II (Mexico)*, assessing the legitimacy of the policy goal pursued by the measures at issue rather than the existence of a sufficient jurisdictional nexus.[70]

Under Art. XX(b) GATT, the two-step test involves establishing (1) whether the policy objective pursued by the measure is to protect human, animal or plant life or health, and (2) whether this measure is necessary to fulfil that policy objective. A broad range of environmental objectives has been accepted under this exception.

---

[66] See for instance, Panel report, *China – Measures related to the Exportation of Rare Earths, Tungsten, and Molybdenum*, WT/DS431/R, WT/DS432/R, WT/DS433/R, adopted 29 August 2014, para. 7.261; Appellate Body report, *China – Measures related to the Exportation of Rare Earths, Tungsten, and Molybdenum*, WT/DS431/AB/R, WT/DS432/AB/R, WT/DS433/AB/R, adopted 29 August 2014, para. 5.94. Van den Bossche and Zdouc (2017), pp. 543–582.

[67] GATT Panel report, *United States – Restrictions on Imports of Tuna*, DS21/R, 3 September 1991, unadopted, para. 5.531–5.532; GATT Panel report, *United States – Restrictions on Imports of Tuna*, DS29/R, 16 June 1994, unadopted, para. 5.20; the Panel in *US – Shrimp* did not address the issue of extraterritorial jurisdiction.

[68] Appellate Body report, *United States – Import Prohibition of Certain Shrimp and Shrimp Products*, WT/DS58/AB/R, adopted 6 November 1998, para. 121.

[69] Appellate Body report, *United States – Import Prohibition of Certain Shrimp and Shrimp Products*, WT/DS58/AB/R, adopted 6 November 1998, para. 133.

[70] Panel report, *United States – Measures Concerning the Importation, Marketing and Sale of Tuna and Tuna Products*, WT/DS381/R, adopted 13 June 2002, para. 7.444; Appellate Body report, *United States – Measures Concerning the Importation, Marketing and Sale of Tuna and Tuna Products*, WT/DS381/AB/R, adopted 13 June 2012, para. 338; Panel report, *United States – Measures Concerning the Importation, Marketing and Sale of Tuna and Tuna Products, Recourse to Article 21.5 by Mexico*, WT/DS381/RW, adopted 3 December 2015, para. 7.524–7.525.

According to the Appellate Body in *EC – Seals*, the necessity test consists of a weighting and balancing test including (1) the importance of the objective, (2) the contribution of the measure to the objective, and (3) the trade-restrictiveness of the measure.[71] First, the recognition of climate change and biodiversity is recognised as a common concern under various MEAs (e.g. UNFCCC, CBD) and could therefore satisfy this criterion.[72] Second, the measure must contribute to the realisation of the objective pursued, which has been interpreted as "a genuine relationship of ends and means between the objective pursued and the measure at issue".[73] This does not include a pre-determined threshold of contribution or a standard of 'materiality' in analysing necessity according to the Appellate Body.[74] Third, the level of trade restrictiveness includes an assessment that the benefits of the measure outweigh the costs of the measure in terms of trade-restrictiveness. If this two-step test under Art. XX(b) GATT is concluded positively, the Panel must finally consider alternative measures suggested by the complainant.

Under Art. XX(g) GATT, trade-restrictive measures violating the GATT may be justified after conducting three-step test: (1) measures envisage the conservation of exhaustible natural resources, (2) are relating to such goals, and (3) are made effective in conjunction with restrictions on domestic production or consumption. In short, these are the aim, nexus, and safeguard requirements. First, measures must concern exhaustible natural resources. As soon as a resource is capable of depleting and extinction, it qualifies as an exhaustible natural resource.[75] Both living and non-living resources may be considered as 'exhaustible natural resources'.[76] Traditionally, the focus of the cases investigated under Art. XX(g) GATT were living resources, including migratory sea turtles, salmon and herring, tuna, and dolphins.[77] In

---

[71] Appellate Body report, *European Communities – Measures Prohibiting the Importation and Marketing of Seal Products*, WT/DS400/AB/R and WT/DS401/AB/R, adopted 16 June 2014, para. 5.214.

[72] Limenta (2020), p. 335.

[73] Appellate Body report, *Brazil – Measures Affecting Imports of Retreaded Tyres*, WT/DS332/AB/R, adopted 17 December 2007, para. 210; Appellate Body report, *European Communities – Measures Prohibiting the Importation and Marketing of Seal Products*, WT/DS400/AB/R and WT/DS401/AB/R, adopted 16 June 2014, para. 5.200 ff.

[74] Appellate Body report, *European Communities – Measures Prohibiting the Importation and Marketing of Seal Products*, WT/DS400/AB/R and WT/DS401/AB/R, adopted 16 June 2014, para. 5.209, overturning Appellate Body report, *Brazil – Measures Affecting Imports of Retreaded Tyres*, WT/DS332/AB/R, adopted 17 December 2007, para. 121.

[75] Appellate Body report, *United States – Import Prohibition of Certain Shrimp and Shrimp Products*, WT/DS58/AB/R, adopted 6 November 1998, para. 128.

[76] *Ibid*, para. 141.

[77] See Appellate Body report, *European Communities – Measures Prohibiting the Importation and Marketing of Seal Products*, WT/DS400/AB/R and WT/DS401/AB/R, adopted 16 June 2014; GATT Panel report, *Canada – Measures Affecting Exports of Unprocessed Salmon and Herring*, L/6268-35S/98, adopted 22 March 1988; GATT Panel report, *United States – Prohibition of Imports of Tuna and Tuna Products from Canada*, L/5198-29S/91, adopted 22 February 1982; GATT Panel report, *United States – Restrictions on Imports of Tuna*, DS21/R, 3 September 1991, unadopted.

US – Gasoline, the Appellate Body broadened Art. XX(g) GATT to include measures against air pollution.[78] Natural resources under Art. XX(g) GATT have not
been interpreted yet to include the atmosphere and global climate, but given the
threat to human health, forests, agriculture and biodiversity more generally, such
qualification should be possible—if necessary, climate change could at least be
interpreted as a clean air issue.[79] Second, the measures sought to be justified must be
'relating to' the conservation of exhaustible natural resources. This relating to-test
must be interpreted as less stringent than the necessity test under paragraph (b) as
interpreted to be "a close and genuine relationship of ends and means"[80]—as long
as the respondent can demonstrate a real and close relationship, the test would be
fulfilled. It must be "primarily aimed at" conservation of natural resources.[81] Third,
the measures must be 'made effective in conjunction with' domestic measures. This
is a safeguard against potential abuse of the exception by WTO Members. In *US –
Gasoline*, the Appellate Body specified that this was a requirement of 'even-
handedness' in the imposition of restrictions on imported and domestic products,
but does not amount to a requirement of identical treatment of domestic and
imported products.[82] The burden imposed in conserving the environment must be
distributed between trade partners and domestic producers.[83] Rather, measures on
domestic and imported products should be applied jointly, or measures on imported
products should work together with restrictions on domestic production or consumption to conserve an exhaustible natural resource.[84]

In addition, the chapeau of Art. XX GATT includes an additional test relating to
the way in which a WTO Member applies measures.[85] It includes again two distinguishable elements: arbitrary or unjustifiable discrimination, and disguised restriction on international trade. In that sense, it aims to find out whether invoking the

---

[78] Appellate Body report, *United States – Standards for Reformulated and Conventional Gasoline*, WT/DS2/AB/R, adopted 20 May 1996, p. 16.

[79] See Condon (2009), p. 912; Douma (2016), p. 301.

[80] Appellate Body report, *United States – Import Prohibition of Certain Shrimp and Shrimp Products*, WT/DS58/AB/R, adopted 6 November 1998, para. 135–136; Appellate Body report, *China – Measures related to the Exportation of Various Raw Materials*, WT/DS394/AB/R, WT/DS395/AB/R, WT/DS398/AB/R, adopted 22 February 2012, para. 355; Appellate Body report, *China – Measures related to the Exportation of Rare Earths, Tungsten, and Molybdenum*, WT/DS431/AB/R, WT/DS432/AB/R, WT/DS433/AB/R, adopted 29 August 2014, para. 5.90.

[81] Appellate Body report, *United States – Standards for Reformulated and Conventional Gasoline*, WT/DS2/AB/R, adopted 20 May 1996, p. 18.

[82] Appellate Body report, *United States – Standards for Reformulated and Conventional Gasoline*, WT/DS2/AB/R, adopted 20 May 1996, pp. 20–21; Appellate Body report, *United States – Import Prohibition of Certain Shrimp and Shrimp Products*, WT/DS58/AB/R, adopted 6 November 1998, para. 144.

[83] Liu and Maughan (2012), p. 998.

[84] Appellate Body report, *China – Measures Related to the Exportation of Various Raw Materials*, WT/DS394/AB/R, WT/DS395/AB/R, WT/DS398/AB/R, adopted 22 February 2012, para. 360.

[85] Panel report, *Brazil – Measures Affecting Imports of Retreaded Tyres*, WT/DS332/R, adopted 17 December 2007, para. 7.107.

exceptions would not constitute an abuse or misuse of Art. XX GATT and to find out whether there is a balance between the right of a Member to invoke an exception under Art. XX and the substantive rights of the other Members under the GATT.[86] The first aims to check if other countries in similar conditions are treated differently (arbitrary)[87] or without consideration of the propriety of the measure in the conditions prevailing in the country (unjustifiable).[88] The second aspect reveals whether WTO Members are not simply masking their trade-restrictive measures with environmental protection policy goals.[89] This includes a good faith obligation for WTO Members to make serious efforts to negotiate multilateral solutions to a problem before resorting to trade-restrictive measures.[90] Internationally agreed standards embodied in a treaty with monitoring system may be recommendable—as well as PPMs that related to the product/firm rather than the country.[91] For climate change, States opting for relatively trade-restricting measures which have collateral or environmental benefits must make clear that there are multiple objectives, which all have to be taking into the examination of Art. XX GATT. Most successful would be measures with clear environmental objectives and that have as much flexibility as possible on how to meet those objectives.[92]

4.4 Restrictions on the Use of Trade Remedies on Environmental Goods

The definitional work of environmental goods—despite its political sensitiveness—is the necessary groundwork for the elimination of trade remedies on those goods. This section reviews proposals and possibilities that have been advanced for the reduction or disciplining of trade remedies on environmental goods. Several such

---

[86] Appellate Body report, *United States – Import Prohibition of Certain Shrimp and Shrimp Products*, WT/DS58/AB/R, adopted 6 November 1998, para. 156.

[87] Appellate Body report, *Brazil – Measures Affecting Imports of Retreaded Tyres*, WT/DS332/R, adopted 17 December 2007, para. 229–230.

[88] Appellate Body report, *United States – Measures Concerning the Importation, Marketing and Sale of Tuna and Tuna Products*, WT/DS381/AB/R, adopted 13 June 2012, para. 7.316; Panel report, *European Communities – Conditions for the Granting of Tariff Preferences to Developing Countries*, WT/DS246/R, adopted 1 December 2003, para. 7.228–7.229, 7.232 and 7.234.

[89] Appellate Body report, *United States – Standards for Reformulated and Conventional Gasoline*, WT/DS2/AB/R, adopted 20 May 1996, p. 25.

[90] See Appellate Body report, *United States – Import Prohibition of Certain Shrimp and Shrimp Products*, recourse to Article 21.5 by Malaysia, WT/DS58/AB/RW, adopted 21 November 2001, para. 115–134.

[91] Potts (2008), p. 26.

[92] Doelle (2004), p. 99.

proposals were consolidated in the E15 Initiative from ICTSD and the World Economic Forum[93] and the seminal work of *Wu/Salzman*[94] and *Kampel*.[95]

This section advances that a total abolition of trade remedies on environmental goods would be the strongest action (Sect. 4.4.1). Yet short of a total abolition, several options to impose certain restrictions on the use of trade remedies on environmental goods exist (Sect. 4.4.2).

4.4.1   Abolishing the Imposition of Trade Remedies on Environmental Goods

Preventing the imposition of trade remedies altogether is the preferred strategy to advance a green policy agenda using the instrument of trade remedies. The imposition of ADDs and CVDs is a widespread and frequent phenomenon in the sector of for instance renewable energy goods. The restrictive effects resulting from the application of trade remedy duties in the clean energy sector have been widely documented.[96] Moreover, imposing trade remedy duties raises the price of environmental goods on the market of the importing country, which affects their competitive position as opposed to goods that do not qualify as environmentally friendly goods. Against that background, the elimination of the trade remedy burden on environmental goods would have a significant impact on the promotion of green industrial sectors and promote the development of clean energy.

Eliminating trade remedies on green goods would prevent significant 'chilling effects' caused by the investigative procedure for trade remedy measures. Research has shown that not only the actual imposition of duties impacts the domestic industry of the like product, but already the initiation of an investigation has similar effects on trade flows—that is, even if the investigation concludes no trade remedy duties will be imposed.[97] The probability of the future imposition and the uncertainty about the amount and height thereof has proved to produce a chilling effect on imports, even the mere threat thereof can suffice to produce effects by the exporting companies in for instance accepting undertakings.[98] Moreover, trade remedy investigations also create a spill-over effect, discouraging foreign producers to export other products to the country where the investigation is pending.[99]

---

[93] See, generally, E15 Expert Group on Clean Energy Technologies and the Trade System (2013).

[94] Wu and Salzman (2014).

[95] Kampel (2017).

[96] See Sect. 2.4.1.1 above.

[97] Niels (2000), pp. 470–471.

[98] *Ibid.*

[99] Bloningen and Prusa (2001), pp. 27 ff.; Lima-Campos and Vito (2004); Bloningen and Prusa (2016), p. 142.

Additionally, a WTO challenge of an imposed anti-dumping duty before a Panel and/or the Appellate Body and/or retaliation proceedings also create trade-disruptive effects. Not only does initiating cases take a lot of time, the initiation of a judicial challenge itself also creates immediate trade-disruptive effects. *Horlick* reports on negative impact on exports, even if cases are won at the Panel stage, and that such strategy of challenging trade remedies at the WTO level is an enormous return on investment for the complaining industry—greater than improving service.[100]

In sum, it is recommended to eliminate the imposition of trade remedies on green goods to prevent the significant distortive effects on the free flow of environmental goods. Not only do trade remedies affect the competitive position of green goods on the market by making the products more expensive, the initiation of an investigation or the challenge of an imposed measure also causes the market to react.

4.4.2   Disciplining Trade Remedies on Environmental Goods

Short of preventing the imposition of trade remedy duties entirely, efforts to reduce the impact of trade remedies on imports of green goods may also alleviate the additional pressure created by trade remedies on the sectors producing green goods. This section lists various options to curb, limit or discipline the use of trade remedies imposed on green goods. These proposals exploit so-called 'procedural weaknesses' in the trade remedy agreements in favour of environmental protection and the promotion of green goods and may be more politically feasible than a total elimination.

4.4.2.1   Limiting the Duration of Trade Remedies

The duration of the trade remedy duties on environmental goods can be limited by introducing (shorter) time limits.[101] In case of environmental goods, by apply trade remedies for a shorter time frame, investigating authorities can help protect those goods but limit the distortive effects in time.[102]

According to the ADA and ASCM, duties shall remain in force only as long as and to the extent necessary to counteract dumping or subsidisation but are in any case to be terminated after five years.[103] Investigating authorities may therefore opt to impose duties for a timeframe of less than five years, and still fulfil the "general

---

[100] Horlick (2013), pp. 69–70.

[101] Meléndez-Ortiz (2016), p. 11; Wu and Salzman (2014), p. 471; Kampel (2017), p. 20. See for instance, Singapore-Jordan FTA, Art. 2.8(f).

[102] UNCTAD (2014), p. 15.

[103] Art. 11.3 ADA; Art. 21.3 ASCM.

necessity requirement" included in these provisions.[104] Moreover, domestic authorities may also try to halt the practice to consistently apply for prolongations of trade remedy measures beyond the initial five years, by considering strictly applications for administrative review on measures imposed on green goods.[105]

By contrast, the SGA contains more restrictive rules on the duration of safeguard measures. Art. 7 SGA foresees that the period of application of the initial safeguard measure shall not exceed four years and the total period of application shall not exceed eight years. These time limits include the period of investigation by the national authorities. Furthermore, safeguard measures may only be applied again on imports of the same product after a time period equal to the application of the measure (with a minimum of two years) has lapsed. In addition, the SGA also prescribes an obligation to progressively liberalise the safeguard measures in regular intervals after the first year of application. Such additional restrictions on the timeframe and prolongation of measures may have a major influence in the field of renewable energy, particularly because the renewable energy sector develops according to Moore's Law and learning curve effects heavily.[106]

Thus, limitations on the duration of trade remedy measures can be formulated regarding termination provisions or limitations regarding review to reconsider long-lasting duties and overcome automatic prolongation. Putting a halt on the initial duration or calling for prudence in review procedures may alleviate some of the burden of trade remedy measures on environmental goods. Moreover, the SGA provisions may serve as an inspiration on how to shorten the duration.

4.4.2.2 Limiting the Scope of Trade Remedies

Limiting the scope of trade remedy action is another option to discipline trade remedy action on green goods.[107] Such limitations may be numerical or linked to specific values of imports.[108] In the former case, the total number of trade remedies that are applied simultaneously against environmental goods are limited. In the latter case, limitations are defined on the total amount of import value of environmental goods on which trade remedy duties may be imposed.

Such limitations would have to be negotiated by WTO Members in respect to specific environmental goods at specific numbers or values. Governments could work with a system of 'credits' representing trade remedy measures on environmental goods. If, for instance, investigating authorities have only three credits for trade remedy measures on environmental goods, this will make the governments reluctant

---

[104] See Panel report, *United States – Anti-Dumping Duty on Dynamic Random Access Memory Semiconductors (DRAMS) of One Megabit or Above from Korea*, WT/DS99/R, adopted 19 March 1999, para. 6.41.

[105] See Art. 11.2, 11.3 and 9.5 ADA; Art. 21.2, 21.2 ASCM.

[106] See Sect. 2.4.1.1 above.

[107] Meléndez-Ortiz (2016), p. 11; UNCTAD (2014), p. 15; Kampel (2017), p. 19.

[108] Kampel (2017), p. 19.

and think twice about potential trade-offs between various options of trade remedy action, and make them consider ending long-lasting duties to focus on new threats.[109] Trade-offs between different green goods shall then be made by governments, ultimately benefitting the entire sector. This works on the sector that gets a certain on-average relief from trade remedies.

4.4.2.3   Raising the *De Minimis* Level and/or Capping the Upper Level of Trade Remedy Duties

Limitations can also be instated in the level of the trade remedy duty imposed on green goods. This may include capping the upper level of duties allowed trade remedy duties or raising the bottom level before duties may be imposed.

Numerical upper bounds would prevent detrimental effects on green goods sectors, which could be a pertinent halt on very high duties of for instance 250% imposed by investigating authorities in certain countries.[110] *Horlick* proposes to cap the level of ADDs at such level that they do not raise the price of renewable energy to a level where it could not compete anymore with fossil fuel energy.[111] Discussions on the upper bound of trade remedy duty levels also relate to the discussion on a mandatory LDR for environmental goods.[112]

Regarding the bottom level, it has been put forth to raise the *de minimis* level of duties and raise the negligible amounts for environmental goods.[113] WTO rules require a margin of at least 2% expressed as a percentage of the export price in case of dumping, and 1% *ad valorem* in case of subsidisation.[114] For instance, the *de minimis* level for environmental goods could be raised to 5%.[115] These proposals aim to raise the threshold for an investigation to be initiated. Whether these kinds of measures would have a meaningful impact is disputed, but it could amount to a gesture of political goodwill.[116]

4.4.2.4   Defining the Like Product and Domestic Industry

The definition of the product under consideration and like product are the first two elements in the injury investigation, where environmental considerations may affect the targeted product of the investigation. Investigating authorities have a broad

---

[109] Wu and Salzman (2014), pp. 470–471; Kampel (2017), pp. 19–20.

[110] Wu and Salzman (2014), pp. 471–472.

[111] Horlick (2013), p. 70.

[112] See Sect. 4.4.2.4 below.

[113] Kampel (2017), p. 19.

[114] Art. 5.9 ADA; Art. 11.9 ASCM.

[115] See for instance Singapore-Jordan FTA, Art. 2.8(a).

[116] See Horlick (2013), p. 70.

discretionary power to determine the scope of the like product.[117] Accordingly, practice among investigating authorities in different countries varies greatly.[118] Closely related is the definition of the domestic industry, which refers to all domestic producers of the like product or those of them accounting for a major proportion of the total domestic production,[119] according to Art. 4 ADA and 16 ASCM.

Since the definition of the like product and the domestic industry affect the remainder of the anti-dumping or anti-subsidy investigation, it may be relevant to consider environmental protection goals already at that stage. *Meléndez-Ortiz*, for instance, argues to consider the entire value chain of the product so that ADDs or CVDs are not imposed for multiple parts of the assembly across global value chains.[120] Focusing particularly on clean energy technology products, he points out that reducing barriers to market access is crucial for optimising supply chains, but that governments often wish to retain a degree of policy space to pursue various goals related to sustainable development.[121]

Against that background, it has been suggested to repurpose the like product determination to a market-based test to limit the discretion of the investigating authorities and to increase legal certainty. A market-based test would mean that products in direct competition with each other are considered.[122] *Bronckers/McNelis*, for instance, take the market-based approach for like products from the GATT and transpose it to the ADA, and have considered like products in relation to environmental protection.[123] In this manner, the consideration of market-based elements in defining the targeted product in trade remedy investigations may have positive environmental effects.

4.4.2.5   Redefining Material Injury

The finding of "material injury" represents the second essential legal step in the investigation for the imposition of ADDs or CVDs. Also the assessment of injury offers investigating authorities an option to include environmental considerations in the procedure. Factors to be considered when determining injury include all relevant economic factors and indices having a bearing on the state of the industry.[124] Given

---

[117] Andersen (2009), pp. 72 ff.

[118] See Adamantopoulos and De Notaris (2000), pp. 36–38.

[119] It is often held that "a major proportion" instead of the major proportion would mean that the domestic industry must not represent more than 50% of the domestic producers. See *Vermulst* (2005), p. 67; see, for instance, Panel report, *European Communities – Measures Affecting Importation of Certain Poultry Products*, WT/DS69/R, adopted 23 July 1998, para. 7.341.

[120] Meléndez-Ortiz (2016), p. 10.

[121] *Ibid.*

[122] See, in detail, Choi (2002).

[123] Bronckers and McNelis (2000), pp. 345–385.

[124] Other factors include actual and potential decline in output, sales, market share, profits, productivity, return on investments, or utilization of capacity; factors affecting domestic prices; actual and

that the list is possible factors to consider is not exhaustive, domestic authorities can in principle take into account any environmental impact which results in harm to the domestic industry.[125] Against that background, and to spur environmental protection in the assessment of material injury, *Howse* proposes an interpretive understanding that positive environmental and other impacts in the importing country of the policies and practices being responded to by trade remedies be netted out when injury is determined.[126]

Related to the definition of injury is the discussion whether the injury notion should orient more to competitive harm rather than economic harm. This would involve, *inter alia*, revision of the definition of abuse of dominant position and of dumping so that the rules specifically target anti-competitive behaviour (rather than simple price discrimination).[127] A definition of material injury under the ADA and ASCM more closely to the competition or anti-trust rules to only remedy truly anti-competitive behaviour would, for example, require higher thresholds on dominant position and price undercutting for initiating anti-dumping investigations than in the current rules.[128] This could also be beneficial for environmental goods.

4.4.2.6   Applying a Mandatory Lesser-Duty Rule

The introduction of a mandatory Lesser-Duty Rule (LDR) on environmental goods would result in lower duties which may still alleviate the injury to the domestic industry but ensure less restrictions on the green goods sectors.[129] Under the LDR, investigating authorities apply a lower duty at the injury margin level instead of countervailing at the full level of dumping or subsidisation. Accordingly, the application of the LDR for environmental products could lead to lower duties, thereby fostering the EGS sector. This is beneficial for goods in the renewable energy sector as it does not inflate prices of renewable energy goods more than necessary to remedy the injury suffered by the domestic industry.

WTO Members could also consider conditioning the application of the LDR on environmental compliance with MEA standards. Thereby, the LDR would be abolished in cases where trade partners did not have sufficient levels of environment standards, so that trade partners would have an incentive to raise their environmental standard to shelter their domestic industry from higher trade remedy duties, but this would not lead to additional protection or beneficial effects for the domestic industry.

---

potential negative effects on cash flow, inventories, employment, wages, growth, ability to raise capital or investments and, in the case of agriculture, whether there has been an increased burden on government support programmes. See Art. 3.4 ADA; Art. 15.4 ASCM.

[125] See also Sect. 8.2.1 below.

[126] Howse (2013), p. 51.

[127] Meléndez-Ortiz (2016), p. 11.

[128] Kasteng (2013), p. 66.

[129] UNCTAD (2014), p. 15.

As the application of the LDR is voluntary, WTO Members have the choice to include the LDR in their domestic legal framework or not. Some major players, such as the US, do not apply the LDR, whereas others, such as the EU, do. Nonetheless, breaking a long-standing tradition of consistently applying the LDR, the EU has changed its approach in its recent legislative amendment. The European Commission included a removal of the LDR in case of raw material distortions and subsidies in the proposal of 2013.[130] During its first reading in 2014, the European Parliament proposed to remove the LDR in cases involving countries with insufficient social or environmental standards or where complainants were SMEs.[131] Unable to agree on this proposal and with certain countries pressured by their steel industries, the matter was left open. In 2016, the final agreement on a new LDR meant that the LDR would be removed in cases of structural raw material distortions where such raw materials account for more than 17% of the cost of production of the investigated product, and always in case of subsidisation.[132] This revised LDR was adopted in 2018.[133]

4.4.2.7   Tightening Causation and Non-Attribution Rules

A more robust causation and non-attribution analysis with respect to ADDs, CVDs and safeguard measures could also be an option to discourage trade remedy imposition on environmental goods. The causation requirement is the third step in the investigation process, where domestic authorities establish a causal link between the dumped or subsidised imports and the injury to the domestic industry on the basis of all relevant evidence before the authorities.[134] In many cases, the findings tend to be based on correlation rather than causality.[135] Accordingly, to prevent the imposition of trade remedies on green goods, new or clarified rules and definitions involving proof of causality would make the investigation more objective, transparent and predictable.[136] A higher standard of proof required to show that trade remedies are a legitimate response to specific, harmful trade practices—for instance robust statistical tools to determine causality and non-attribution—has been discussed.[137]

---

[130] European Commission, Proposal for a Regulation, COM(2013) 192 final, 10 April 2013.

[131] Vermulst and Sud (2018), pp. 73–75.

[132] Art. 7(2a), subpara. 5 BADR.

[133] For a detailed discussion of the new rules in the EU, see Sect. 4.5.4 below.

[134] Art. 3.5 ADA; Art. 15.5 ASCM.

[135] Kasteng (2013), p. 66.

[136] Kampel (2017), p. 20.

[137] Barthelemy and Peat (2015), pp. 462 ff.; Kasteng (2013), p. 66.

4.4.2.8 Applying a Mandatory Public Interest Test

Climate policy and environmental protection objectives could be considered when applying the public interest test, particularly when it comes to trade remedy duties to environmental goods.[138] The public interest test is not mandatory under the WTO agreements,[139] but merely recommended for WTO Members to impose. A mandatory environmental public interest test would entail an obligation for investigating authorities to consider the environmental consequences of the imposition of trade remedies through their chilling effect and raise in prices of environmental goods. Traditionally, this includes the interest of producers, but not as much the interests of exporters and the consumers. The ASCM specifically highlights the position of the domestic interested parties (*i.e.* consumers and industrial users) whose interests might be adversely affected by the imposition of the countervailing duty.[140] Environmental stakeholders (such as importers, user industry and consumers) or internal debate with the relevant ministries (in case of the EU, the relevant DG, namely DG Environment) might be included as interested parties to a larger degree than today in the public interest test.[141] Many proponents of the idea have linked a mandatory interest test to environmental goods, but it could just as much be a general obligation for investigating authorities to consider all aspects including environmental impacts instead of focusing on the economic impacts of the domestic injury.

The public interest test could thus allow investigating authorities to not apply the duties for reasons of public policy considerations. *Kampel* opines an environmental public interest test appears good in theory but is usually inconsequential to the outcome of the investigation in practice.[142] Therefore, it would be better that if the investigating authority finds that it is not in the interest of the public to apply duties, it can decide *ex ante* to terminate the anti-dumping investigation involving environmental goods, rather than deciding not to apply any additional duty at the end of the procedure. Also *Meléndez-Ortiz* and *Horlick* have proposed a mandatory study of the effects of imposing trade remedies before the opening of the investigation, thereby showing the willingness of the Member that by publishing this study indicates there were really no alternatives.[143] However, in that regard, it should be reminded that any step before the formal initiation of an investigation or imposition of a duty already has certain chilling effects on the market.[144]

---

[138] Kampel (2017), p. 19; UNCTAD (2014), p. 16.

[139] See Sect. 3.2.3.1 above.

[140] Art. 19.2 ASCM.

[141] Meléndez-Ortiz (2016), p. 11; Kasteng (2013), pp. 65–66; UNCTAD (2014).

[142] Kampel (2017), p. 26.

[143] Meléndez-Ortiz (2016); Horlick (2013), pp. 69–73.

[144] See Sect. 4.4.1 above.

4.4.2.9 Conditional Acceptance of Undertakings

A mechanism of conditional acceptance of price undertakings depending on the fulfilment of environmental conditions can also be envisaged as a measure affecting the use of trade remedies on green goods.[145] Investigating authorities have broad discretion to accept or refuse undertakings, and they may be motivated by reasons of general policy.[146] In case of anti-dumping proceedings, the acceptance of price undertakings by some of the most important companies concerned may move the investigating authority to terminate or suspend proceedings, or to lower the all others rate significantly. However, no obligation exists for exporters to accept price undertakings and refusals to accept undertakings shall in no way prejudice the consideration of the case by the investigating authority.[147] In case of CVDs, the acceptance by the government suffices.[148] *Kampel*, however, points out that these proposals will not necessarily result in fewer procedures against environmental goods, but rather lead to greater complexity of the investigations.[149]

The EU allows refusing the acceptance of undertakings for "reasons of general policy which comprise in particular the principles and obligations set out in multilateral environmental agreements and protocols thereunder, to which the Union is a party, and of ILO Conventions listed in Annex Ia to this Regulation."[150] The Commission is known to have rejected undertakings for reasons of general policy in past practice.[151] A first reference to environmental considerations in a rejection of an undertaking offer is still to be awaited. The Commission, however, maintains a very reluctant stance to accept undertakings, so the amended provision will likely only have limited effects.

4.4.2.10 Ensuring Procedural Neutrality

The current ADA and ASCM rules as applied by the national investigation authorities suffer from procedural weaknesses and an inherent bias in investigations towards a protectionist outcome for the domestic industry.[152] The domestic investigative process carries a bias towards the interests of import-competing groups, who are the petitioners of the contingent protection with their government and the

---

[145] Kampel (2017), p. 19.

[146] Art. 8.3 ADA and Art. 18.3 ASCM. See also Panel report, *United States – Continued Dumping and Subsidy Offset Act of 2000*, WT/DS217/R, adopted 27 January 2003, para. 7.80–7.81.

[147] Art. 8.5 ADA. See also Art. 18.5 ASCM.

[148] See also Panel report, *European Communities – Definitive Anti-Dumping Measures on Certain Iron or Steel Fasteners from China*, WT/DS397/R, adopted 28 July 2011, fn. 279.

[149] Kampel (2017).

[150] Art. 8(3) BADR.

[151] Van Bael & Bellis (2019), pp. 278–279.

[152] Kasteng (2013), pp. 60–68; Espa and Marín Durán (2018), pp. 137–138; Meléndez-Ortiz (2016), pp. 10–11.

obvious beneficiaries of protective measures. More detailed rules on the multilateral level should shift the job of the investigating authorities away from the view that they must protect the domestic injury, in the direction of more objective, transparent and predictable procedures.[153]

Due process rights in the ADA could be extended effectively to all interested groups under the public interest test, including environmental interest groups and consumer organisations.[154] More, or at least more balanced, procedural rights for industrial users and consumers in trade remedy investigations, as opposed to the powerful position of the complaining domestic industry, will improve the position of the latter in order to promote climate change, and environmental protection.[155] On the other hand, stricter rules on procedural weaknesses may result in a greater effort of the investigating authorities to ultimately successfully complete investigations rather than a lower incidence of trade remedies in the renewable energy sectors.[156]

Similar concerns have been raised in relation to other aspects of trade remedy investigations, such as the product definition, the selection of a sample of companies, the identification of indicators on injury, and verification of causality between dumping or subsidisation and injury, which may have to be reconsidered to alleviate the bias towards a certain outcome the rules hold.[157] The finding of material injury will be made by not-so-neutral institutions (investigating authorities rather than the DSB) that often tend to hang closer to industrial interests than promotion of global environmental gains.[158] Injury determination practices are sometimes not transparent, so that new rules to clarify procedures and standards of proof of injury may be considered. Proposals include making anti-dumping and anti-subsidy investigations more objective, transparent, and predictable when it comes to the definition of injury.[159]

4.5   Options for Implementation

Implementing options to discipline the use of trade remedies on green goods include possibilities on the multi-, pluri- and bilateral level. Within each potential level, possibilities to preclude the initiation of trade remedy investigations and mitigating the effect of trade remedies on green goods will be addressed, respectively.

---

[153] *Ibid.*

[154] For instance, to influence the application of the public interest test. See Sect. 4.4.2.8 above.

[155] Espa and Marín Durán (2018), pp. 137–138.

[156] Kampel (2017), p. 26.

[157] Kasteng (2013), p. 66; Meléndez-Ortiz (2016), p. 11.

[158] Espa and Marín Durán (2018), p. 641.

[159] *Ibid.*

4.5.1   Amendments to the ADA, ASCM and SGA

On the multilateral level, the option to agree on a general or temporary 'peace clause' for environmental goods may be considered.[160] Such clauses limit recourse to ADD or CVD measures among WTO Members by temporarily calling for non-use of trade remedies. In this context, a peace clause would envisage a self-imposed restraint on the use of unilateral trade remedies when an investigation is targeting environmental goods.

Another option is the introduction of an environmental LDR. Discussions in the Anti-Dumping Committee noted that WTO Members are sharply divided on the matter of mandatorily applying the rule. Not all WTO Members apply the LDR.[161] The EU was one of the prime examples of users of the LDR. In 2018, in almost half of the cases, the anti-dumping measures for individual exporting companies are set at the level of the injury margin instead of the higher dumping margin.[162] Most recently, the EU cut back on the application of the LDR by conditioning its application for ADDs and completely stepping away from it for CVDs.[163]

However, whether a consensus to amend the multilateral agreements—be it for the inclusion of a peace clause, or any other of the measures discussed above—could be reached is doubtful. WTO Members have made various proposals for improving transparency and due process in the trade remedy agreements, no agreements are found to amend the basic agreements. Moreover, the very limited legislative progress at the WTO made during the first 25 years since the last round of negotiations is illustrative of the fact that multilateral negotiations are likely.[164]

In effect, a peace clause would replicate the category of non-actionable environmental subsidies. Therefore, a revival of Art. 8.2(c) ASCM could be an alternative option in the field of anti-subsidy measures. According to the expired provision, green subsidies were exempted from being challenged by CVD duties when

---

[160] See Wu and Salzman (2014), p. 468; Lester and Watson (2013); Meléndez-Ortiz (2016), p. 11; UNCTAD (2014); Kampel (2017).

[161] See WTO Negotiating Group on Rules, New Draft Consolidated Chair Texts of the AD And SCM Agreements, TN/RL/W/236, 19 December 2008, para. 18–19.

[162] European Commission, Commission Staff Working Document accompanying the Report from the Commission to the European Parliament on the EU's Anti-Dumping, Anti-Subsidy and Safeguard activities and the Use of trade defence instruments by Third Countries targeting the EU in 2018, 27 March 2019, COM(2019) 158 final, p. 5.

[163] See Sect. 4.4.2.4 below.

[164] Nairobi Decision to eliminate agricultural export subsidies (2015), TRIPS amendment (2017), Trade Facilitation Agreement (2017), ongoing Fisheries Subsidies negotiations (ongoing). Moreover, two plurilateral agreements were agreed upon: Expansion of Information Technology Agreement (2015), Revision of the Government Procurement Agreement (2014).

fulfilling certain conditions.[165] This category existed for five years after the entry into force of the WTO Agreement,[166] but was not prolonged because Members could not come to an agreement.[167] Unlike non-actionable development-oriented subsidies,[168] the environmental subsidies are not explicitly part of the DDA and therefore not part of the current possible negotiations on the ASCM. Nonetheless, scholars have formulated several proposals on the category of non-actionable environmental subsidies.[169] One potential advantage would be that a mere revival of an existing provision would be easier for the WTO Membership to agree on than formulating a novel provision.

A mere revival of the old provision may be ineffective due to the too narrow scope of the environmental subsidy exception. Art. 8.2(c) ASCM applies only to subsidies for the assistance to promote adaptation of existing facilities to new environmental requirements which puts greater constraints and financial burdens on firms. In addition, the provision sets out five criteria to be fulfilled to qualify as a non-countervailable subsidy. This sets a high burden. This is illustrated by the fact that during the period which the article was in force, not a single subsidy was notified to the WTO under the exception.[170] This was due to burdensome procedures, fear of legal challenges, lack of incentive in absence of a legal obligation to notify and a high threshold to meet the prescribed criteria.[171] Case law on the provision does not exist either.[172]

Rather, the introduction of a revamped concept of non-actionable environmental subsidies with a specific mention of environmental protection, climate change mitigation or carbon emission mitigation goals would be more effective. If such a category of non-actionable green subsidies is formulated, then procedural safeguards including surveillance, notification and arbitration provisions should be included to

---

[165] Art. 8.2(c) ASCM: "assistance to promote adaptation of existing facilities to new environmental requirements imposed by law and/or regulations which result in greater constraints and financial burden on firms" were non-actionable, provided the particular requirements are fulfilled.

[166] Art. 31 ASCM.

[167] Committee on Subsidies and Countervailing Measures, Minutes of the Regular Meeting Held on 1–2 November 1999, G/SCM/M/24, 26 April 2000, para. 47.

[168] Doha Development Agenda, para. 10.2.

[169] See for instance Kasteng (2013), pp. 60–68; Cosbey and Rubini (2013), pp. 39–46; Kennedy (2009); Horlick (2013), pp. 69–73; Kampel (2017); Farah and Cima (2015), p. 536; Matsushita et al. (2015), p. 736.

[170] Committee on Subsidies and Countervailing Measures, Notification provisions under the Agreement on Subsidies and Countervailing Measures, Background note by the Secretariat, G/SCM/546/Rev.11, 1 May 2020, para. 18.

[171] Shadikhodjaev (2015), p. 494.

[172] However, the Panel in *US – Large Civil Aircraft* addressed Art. 8(2)(a) ASCM. It disregarded the EU's argument that the notion of R&D subsidies in Art. 8 ASCM necessarily implies that governmental purchases of R&D services are covered by the ASCM. See Panel report, *United States – Measures Affecting Trade in Large Civil Aircraft – Second Complaint*, WT/DS353/RW, adopted 23 March 2012, para. 7.958.

ensure acceptance by the WTO Members.[173] While acknowledging the potential value of (similarly drafted) exceptions in Art. 8.2(c) ASCM, some have opined that this may not suffice.[174] Instead, those scholars argue that newly introduced exceptions modelled after or inspired by the general exceptions of Art. XX GATT would be preferrable.[175]

Another alternative to introducing a peace clause in the ASCM is to formulate a defence under Art. XX GATT to protect green subsidies from being challenged be applicable to the ASCM. Since the ASCM builds upon a provision in the GATT, so it is argued, the applicability of Art. XX GATT could be inferred. Nonetheless, WTO jurisprudence seems to require an explicit textual reference to the GATT for the general exceptions to be applicable in other agreements.[176] Footnote 56 to Article 32.1 ASCM provides that no specific action against a subsidy may be taken unless it is "not intended to preclude action under other relevant provisions of GATT 1994".[177] This would open the possibility to argue that the exceptions of Art. XX GATT relating to the environment could be applied when challenging subsidies, *i.e.* through CVDs or undertakings.[178] The Appellate Body interpreted this provision in the sense that "an action that is not 'specific' within the meaning of Art. 18.1 ADA and of Art. 32.1 ASCM, but is nevertheless related to dumping or subsidisation, is not prohibited by Art. 18.1 ADA or Art. 32.1 ASCM."[179]

Further options to safeguard renewable energy subsidies can include, for instance, an interpretative note to Art. XX GATT that explicitly allows the flexibilities to be used for ASCM subsidies.[180] Also a waiver for clean energy policies may be considered for subsidy schemes that respect the national treatment and MFN obligations, or an interpretative understanding of the ASCM regarding local content rules (LCRs), which are currently ASCM-inconsistent, to convert them into WTO-consistent measures.[181] Finally, a country may prepare to challenge the imposition of CVDs imposed on goods benefitting from their green subsidies, for instance by pointing out that green support programs necessarily fail the definition of a countervailable subsidy, due to non-specificity and absence of a benefit. Following that

---

[173] See Art. 8.3, 8.4 and 8.5 ASCM.

[174] Cosbey and Mavroidis (2017), pp. 3–43; Rubini (2012).

[175] *Ibid.*

[176] See Appellate Body report, *China – Measures Affecting Trading Rights and Distribution Services for Certain Publications and Audiovisual Entertainment Products*, WT/DS363/AB/R, adopted 19 January 2010, para. 230 and 233. Absent a textual reference to the GATT, general exceptions do not apply. See Appellate Body report, *China – Measures related to the Exportation of Various Raw Materials*, WT/DS394/AB/R, WT/DS395/AB/R, WT/DS398/AB/R, adopted 22 February 2012, para. 307.

[177] See also footnote 24 to Article 18.1 ADA.

[178] Shadikhodjaev (2015), pp. 499–500.

[179] Appellate Body report, *United States – Continued Dumping and Subsidy Offset Act of 2000*, WT/DS217/AB/R, adopted 27 January 2003, para. 262.

[180] Meléndez-Ortiz (2016), p. 10.

[181] *Ibid*, pp. 10–11.

avenue, for instance, *Lee* has analysed how products that benefited green subsidies in Korea that have faced CVD investigations in the US.[182] These are all residual options to safeguard policy space in the anti-subsidy rules.

4.5.2   Environmental Goods Agreement

The EGA negotiations are the most prominent legislative initiative for a sectoral agreement on environmental goods.[183] Such a sectoral agreement for environmental goods may be more likely to include barriers on the use of trade remedies than explicit provisions in the ADA, ASCM or SGA. Although EGA-negotiations currently exclude trade remedies and are on hold, it is worth exploring the value of such sectoral agreement for green goods. A peace clause on the use of trade remedies may be considered in the framework of (future) negotiations. It has been raised that sectoral agreements would not be fit to include a peace clause, because it would leave participating WTO Members (1) without any remedy against unfair dumping or subsidies practice amongst each other, and (2) vulnerable to third parties, since participating members are bound to the MFN requirement *vis-à-vis* third countries.[184] A peace clause limited in time (temporal peace clause) may take away such concerns.

At the WTO level, a sectoral agreement may be implemented either on the multilateral or plurilateral level.[185] Whether sectoral negotiations on EGS including trade remedy restrictions would be legally, politically, and practically feasible to move forward on the multilateral level remains to be seen. Plurilateral agreements can be a suitable manner for climate change like-minded countries to agree on an 'optimal' regulatory standard, which gives outsiders an incentive to raise their standard of production processes sufficiently to get market access by joining the club.[186] Plurilateral agreements start off with a narrow group of signatories among the WTO Membership but have the objective to be multilateralised.

Should the EGA be concluded as a plurilateral agreement, potential WTO-inconsistencies may have to be prevented. Plurilateral agreements already exist in the WTO legal framework and are hence considered feasible as long as they do not impose obligations on non-participants,[187] but the entire WTO Membership must approve.[188] The current practice of agreeing amongst like-minded countries and

---

[182] Lee (2016), pp. 209 ff.

[183] See Sect. 4.3.2.1 above.

[184] Kampel (2017), p. 36.

[185] Ultimately, also a stand-alone agreement outside the framework of the WTO can be considered. ICTSD has launched such potential project in 2011. See Brewer (2012).

[186] Mavroidis and de Melo (2015), p. 234.

[187] Art. II:3 WTO Agreement.

[188] Art. X:9 WTO Agreement.

then applying on an MFN-basis would work too, thereby complying with Art. II.3 but without needing Art. X:9 of the WTO Agreement (it creates rights, free-riding rights, but not obligations).[189] Reaching a 'critical mass' is a necessary prerequisite for plurilateral agreements to be multilateralised,[190] because then there is no free-riding and it adds up to make a plurilateral agreement where multilateral is not possible: the critical mass is just to make sure there is no backlash possible.[191] An interesting aspect is that the key traders in clean energy products, like solar panels and wind turbines, are often also the major greenhouse gas-emitting countries. Thus, the "critical mass", if it were to be defined as such, for both climate mitigation as well as trade in clean energy products comprises a handful of countries and often the same ones—China, the US, and the EU being fundamentally important in both spheres.[192]

4.5.3   Regional Trade Agreements

RTAs foresee the mutual reduction or elimination of tariffs among developing country members on products imported from one another. RTAs are an exception to MFN treatment under WTO law—although for trade remedies no MFN issues arise since they pertain exporter-specific actions.[193] As tariffs are already low across the board and applied on a non-discriminatory basis because of the multilateral WTO rules, the biggest benefit of RTAs is rather liberalisation on account of NTBs.[194] Against that background, RTAs have the potential to curb trade remedies on environmental goods.

RTAs may abolish the use of trade remedies between trade partners altogether.[195] There is, however, a considerable political hurdle to prohibit the use of trade remedies in the framework of RTA negotiations. In fact, the EU customs union is one of the only RTAs in which all three forms of TDIs have been abolished successfully.[196] There are other examples of RTAs that have curbed the use of one or more types of trade remedies,[197] but generally there is no tendency noted in RTA practice to abolish the possibility to resort to trade remedies. Whether a peace clause on trade remedies on a specific sub-set of goods, *in casu* environmental goods, would be legally

---

[189] Mavroidis and Neven (2019), p. 382.

[190] Frey (2016), p. 460.

[191] In the Trade Facilitation Agreement, the critical mass was set at 90%. For the APEC, Parties did not even wait until the critical mass was reached.

[192] Sugathan (2013), p. 3.

[193] Art. XXIV GATT.

[194] Van den Bossche and Zdouc (2017), pp. 677–678.

[195] Voon (2010).

[196] Art. 28(1) TFEU. See Teh et al. (2009), pp. 166–248.

[197] See, for instance, EFTA-Chile Art. 18.1 and 18.2 (anti-dumping), EFTA-Ukraine, Art. 2.14 (anti-dumping).

allowed, depends on an interpretation of Art. XXIV of the GATT. An RTA with sectoral limitations, *i.e.* a sectoral agreement focussed on environmental goods and services, may not be in accordance with the requirement under Art. XXIV:8 GATT that RTAs eliminate trade barriers on "substantially all the trade" (SAT). Inserting tariff provisions and by extension NTB disciplines in RTAs may therefore violate this provision.[198] Although for others, the SAT requirement does not pose any problems.[199] WTO jurisprudence confirmed WTO Members have never reached agreement on the extent of SAT—it is less than all trade, and more than some trade.[200]

Short of a peace clause eliminating the use of trade remedies amongst RTA partners, countries may also include other measures to restrict the use of trade remedies in their trade partners. The width of possible commitments and provisions is broader and leans more in the direction of current practice on trade remedies chapters in RTAs:

- First, the stricter enforcement of, or specific application of, existing trade remedy rules on green goods may be agreed upon by trade partners. This includes the proposals on limiting duration,[201] amount or upper level of the duties, raising the de minimis level,[202] adapting the product definition, and several procedural issues such as compulsory consultations before the initiation of investigations.
- Second, also amendments to the LDR to make it mandatory for environmental goods could be included in the RTAs. By extension, it can also be considered to agree on specific conditions for the application of the LDR.[203] Lower duties through mandatory application of the LDR is useful for green goods and green industries. In addition, more detailed rules on the use of the LDR, e.g. stipulation on the determination of the non-injurious price, can be considered. Such tendency cannot be noted in practice. Even the EU, which is known to include a wide variety of environmental provisions in the new generation of FTAs,[204] remains cautious and does not go much further than the confirmation of the WTO disciplines of the ADA and ASCM and adds a traditional set of LDR/public interest commitment, transparency obligations, bilateral safeguards clauses and exclusion from dispute settlement to the chapters on trade remedies.[205] None of the EU's FTAs or FTA proposals go beyond the WTO language and make the LDR mandatory, although the WTO provisions explicitly allow to do so. The recent changes to the LDR do reveal the EU's motivation to keep discretion to

---

[198] Mavroidis and Neven (2019), p. 382.

[199] Zhang (2013), p. 692.

[200] Appellate Body report, *Turkey – Restrictions on Imports of Textile and Clothing Products*, WT/DS34/AB/R, adopted 19 November 1999, para. 48.

[201] See, for instance, Singapore-Jordan FTA, Art. 2.8.

[202] *Ibid.*

[203] Kampel (2017), p. 61.

[204] Current sustainability inclusions in new EU trade policy are outlined in the TREND database, available at https://klimalog.die-gdi.de/trend/ (last accessed 21 June 2023).

[205] See Van Vaerenbergh (2018), pp. 227–228.

raise trade remedies in certain other sectors.[206] In fact, the new LDR does consider distortions.[207]

- Third, a mandatory environmental interest test in the public interest test may be considered. *Espa/Marin Duran* have proposed to strengthen the environmental aspects of RTAs through a mandatory public interest test which takes environmental considerations into account.[208] Since WTO rules allow for a such test to be included, it is a relatively easy and WTO-conform way to strengthen green considerations in bilateral arrangements on trade remedies. Most notably, the EU focuses on provisions relating to the public interest test.[209] The EU practice varies: some FTAs have an obligatory public interest test ("shall take into account"),[210] whereas others are more vague ("shall endeavour to consider").[211] Other FTAs choose a middle ground in the form of obligatory public interest considerations without specifying which interests,[212] or obligatory considerations without providing consequences.[213] Further watering down the power of these provisions is the fact that the trade remedy chapters of EU FTAs are not subject to dispute settlement and mediation mechanisms.[214] As best practices, the EU may (1) push for an obligatory nature, (2) outline the interested parties to be considered, (3) apply sanctions/institutional features, or (4) even design a separate clause specially for environmental considerations.[215]

The effectiveness of environmentally-specific trade remedy commitments in RTAs are undermined by the fact that many RTAs exclude dispute resolution on the topic.[216] It is therefore also relevant to consider institutional possibilities within the RTA framework to ensure at least mutual discussion or administrative procedures. Some bilateral safeguards surrounding the imposition of trade remedies may be considered. For instance, compulsory consultations can be organised bilaterally in a trade remedies committee under an RTA (and by extension a general forum to discuss issues on the legal framework in the respective jurisdictions, for instance on the LDR, duration of application of duties, practices, and policy considerations). Trade

---

[206] Espa and Marín Durán (2018), p. 147.

[207] See Sect. 3.3.2 above.

[208] Espa and Marín Durán (2018), pp. 140 ff.

[209] *Ibid*, pp. 140 ff.

[210] EU-Ukraine AA, Art. 48 or EU-Singapore FTA, Art. 3.4, or similarly EU-Vietnam FTA, Art. 3.3.

[211] EU-Korea FTA, Art. 3.10.

[212] CETA, Art. 3.3(1), EU-Central America AA, Art. 94 EU-Japan FTA, Art. 5.13.

[213] EU-Japan FTA, Art. 5.13, EU-COPE FTA, Art. 39.

[214] But see EU-Ukraine AA which does have consultations (Art. 50*bis*) and institutional dialogue on trade remedies (Art. 51). The AA/DCFTA between EU-Moldova and EU-Georgia largely follow the provisions of the EU-Ukraine FTA on the topic of trade remedies, albeit with minor differences. See Van der Loo (2016), pp. 243–245. Also outside the EU, similar provisions exist. See for instance US-Korea FTA, Art. 10.8 and Canada-Korea FTA, Art. 7.8, both providing for a forum for Parties to exchange information on trade remedies.

[215] Espa and Marín Durán (2018), p. 146.

[216] See, generally, Bucholtz (1995).

partners may enter into an agreement to engage in consultations on the topic of trade remedies. This obligation may range from a preliminary discussion of the foreseen initiation of an investigation a few days ahead of the initiation to a mandatory publication of an objective study of the costs and benefits of the measures of the envisaged trade remedy duties.[217] Consultation requirements have frequently been included in FTAs.[218]

Furthermore, making use of an RTA framework to discipline trade remedies on green goods, trade remedy provisions may be subject to general procedural options included. For instance, the necessity of maintaining the option to impose trade remedies between trade partners may be subject to periodical review. Making use of such review clauses, considering recent developments in sustainable development or climate change, parties can decide to curb or to eliminate trade remedies on green goods after all.[219] Review clauses for trade remedy action between trade partners are already included in FTAs in practice.[220] Furthermore, transparency obligations may include reports on trade remedies. Finally, trade remedies may be embedded in the broader strategy towards environmental and sustainability provisions in RTAs. This would provide relevant context for specific action on trade remedies on green goods.

4.5.4 Unilateral Policy Choices: Who Sets the Right Example?

WTO Members may also opt to unilaterally include some of the mitigation or prevention options in the domestic legal framework or by introducing policy changes in the practice of the competent authority. This may include self-commitment to the LDR and the public interest test, additional administrative steps of self-reflection before initiating trade remedy investigations on green goods, and policy considerations to not target renewable energy goods, loosen review procedures, or restrict the duration of duties in the green goods sector in general. Whether governments may voluntarily give up contingent protection tools in favour of highly competitive markets of renewable energy goods is uncertain. A unilateral decision to stop the imposition of trade remedies on green goods is therefore unlikely for domestic legislators or authorities to be pursued, as it effectively excludes the possibility for contingent protection in EGS sectors.

WTO Members show no record of implementing green considerations in their domestic legal framework for trade remedies.[221] Besides the EU, no significant other environment-related amendments to domestic legislation have been notified to the WTO database and included in the WTO's environmental database. The EU's

---

[217] Meléndez-Ortiz (2016), p. 11.

[218] See, for instance, US-Korea FTA, Art. 10.7.3(a) and 10.8, Canada-Korea FTA, Art. 7.7.2 and 7.8.

[219] Kampel (2017), p. 58.

[220] See, for instance, EFTA-South Korea FTA, Art. 2.10(2) and Art. 2.11(10).

[221] See Sect. 3.3.1 above.

legislative changes are not focused on green goods as a distinct category, but rather include the consideration of obligations in MEAs into the legal framework. Besides this recent development, which has been reviewed above,[222] discussions surrounding an environmental public interest test have also spurred in the EU—albeit without leading to a legislative amendment.

The EU adopts a public interest test when conducting anti-dumping and anti-subsidy investigations. The EU has developed the test throughout several years of practice.[223] The Commission maps out the various interests of all relevant parties, whereby interested parties must particularly note how the duties need to eliminate trade distortive effects and how they restore effective competition.[224] The Commission includes various parties into the analysis: the complaining industry, trade unions, other producers of the like product, individual traders/importers, representative users, suppliers of inputs, representative consumer organisations—but not exporting producers of the product concerned since they are located outside the EU.[225] The Commission must balance out all positive and negative economic effects of each involved party.[226] The Commission does not have to adopt any of the suggested views, but only has the obligation to examine all information submitted, and thus is not in any risk of finding itself obliged to follow every suggestion.

General policy considerations (for environmental protection) cannot play a role in the Union interest test. The 2006 Green Paper on TDI highlighted the economic character of the Union interest test.[227] The Commission confirmed this in *Polyester staple fibre*, where it held that "[t]he Community interest analysis in anti-dumping proceedings focuses on the economic impact of measures on the economic operators concerned and is not directly related to environmental concerns."[228] A 2013 communication from the Commission to the Council and the Parliament on the modernisation of TDI confirmed that position.[229]

---

[222] See Sect. 3.3.2 above.

[223] This test exists in the EU since the very beginning in 1962 and was confirmed in the later versions of the Basic Regulations. See Melin (2016), p. 90; Wellhausen (2001), pp. 1032 f and 1046 f.

[224] Art. 21(1) BADR.

[225] DG Trade Working Document, Draft Commission guidelines on the Union interest test, not adopted, para. 5–6.

[226] *Ibid*, para. 21.03. See ECJ, *T.KUP SAS v Belgium*, case C-349/16, judgment of 15 June 2017, ECLI:EU:C:2017:469, para. 44; General Court, *VTZ OAO and Others v Council*, T-432/12, Order of 17 May 2017, ECLI:EU:T:2017:397, para. 143.

[227] European Commission, Commission Clarification Paper on the Community Interest Test in Anti-dumping and Anti-subsidy Proceedings, TRADE.B.1/AS D(2005) D/568, 13 January 2006.

[228] Council Regulation (EC) No 893/2008 of 10 September 2008 maintaining the anti-dumping duties on imports of polyester staple fibres originating in Belarus, the People's Republic of China, Saudi Arabia and Korea following a partial interim review pursuant to Article 11(3) of Regulation (EC) No 384/96, OJ 2008 L 247/1, rec. 80.

[229] European Commission, Communication from the Commission to the Council and the European Parliament on Modernisation of Trade Defence Instruments adapting trade defence instruments to the current needs of the European economy, COM(2013) 191 final, 10 April 2013.

The Commission only addresses environmental considerations when parties bring it up, *i.e.* when the environmental considerations coincide with the aims of the parties.[230] Doing so would at first sight contradict the technical nature of the investigation.[231] Nonetheless, the Union interest has been interpreted in existing practice surrounding the interests of the Union industry as "safeguarding employment", "protecting the environment" and reasons relating to raw materials.[232] In *PSF*, the Commission considered that the imposition of duties would guarantee the viability of the PSF industry in the recycling of PET bottles, thereby contributing to the achievement of environmental objectives and waste management in the EU.[233] In *Solar Panels*, regarding renewable energy sources, the Commission considered environmental arguments brought up by the interested parties, but finally dismissed the plea as not having impact on the achievement of the Agenda 2020 goals.[234] In *Flat-Rolled Steel*, the Commission considered that anti-dumping duties were necessary to enable the Union industry to continue investment and development of the steel products to meet the requirements of the EcoDesign Regulation, which contributes to climate change objectives and energy efficiency of products.[235] Such arguments are only considered exceptionally, as exemplified in the *Lamps* case, where the Commission did not accept the argument against the imposition of anti-dumping duties on energy-saving lamps for the purpose of energy saving policies.[236]

The Commission tried to reintroduce non-economic considerations in the latest round of legislative adjustments, but the Council took issue with that.[237] Since 2018, special consideration must be given to raw material distortions according to Art. 7(2b) BADR. That provision now foresees a second Union interest test regarding the application of the LDR: the LDR shall not apply when raw materials distortions

---

[230] Melin (2016), p. 110; Sinnaeve (2007), p. 162.

[231] Melin (2016), p. 109.

[232] Van Bael & Bellis (2019), pp. 281–282.

[233] Council Regulation (EC) No 428/2005 of 10 March 2005 imposing a definitive anti-dumping duty on imports of polyester staple fibres originating in the People's Republic of China and Saudi Arabia, amending Regulation (EC) No 2852/2000 imposing a definitive anti-dumping duty on imports of polyester staple fibres originating in the Republic of Korea and terminating the anti-dumping proceeding in respect of such imports originating in Taiwan, OJ 2005 L 71/1, rec. 278–281.

[234] Commission Delegated Regulation (EU) No 152/2013 of 19 December 2012 supplementing Regulation (EU) No 648/2012 of the European Parliament and of the Council with regard to regulatory technical standards on capital requirements for central counterparties, OJ 2013 L 152/37, rec. 257–258.

[235] Commission Implementing Regulation (EU) 2015/1953 of 29 October 2015 imposing a definitive anti-dumping duty on imports of certain grain-oriented flat-rolled products of silicon-electrical steel originating in the People's Republic of China, Japan, the Republic of Korea, the Russian Federation and the United States of America, OJ 2015 L 284/109, rec. 144.

[236] Council Regulation (EC) No 1470/2001 of 16 July 2001 imposing a definitive anti-dumping duty and collecting definitively the provisional duty imposed on imports of integrated electronic compact fluorescent lamps (CFL-i) originating in the People's Republic of China, OJ 2001 L 195/8, rec. 36–46.

[237] Hoffmeister (2015), p. 375.

exist. Importantly, this provision should lead to a high level of cooperation because in absence of cooperation, the Commission may conclude that the LDR will apply—in the past this did not happen because the Commission did not give enough weight to the Union interest test.[238] In that connection, some have even argued that the non-economic considerations are not genuinely taken into account, but merely mentioned.[239]

As a reaction in the literature, many voices raised that broadening the scope of the public interest test to for instance development policy, labour or environmental policy is a possibility.[240] A standalone public interest test for environmental reasons would have to meet the high threshold of Art. 21(1) BADR that the Commission decides against the imposition of any duty based on these environmental considerations. The practice of the Commission shows that the Union interest test is rarely used to refuse or modify anti-dumping duties.[241] In the past, it was suggested that the test could also have the effect of a downward adjustment of the duty (to the injury or dumping margin, whichever is lower—upwards is at odds with the LDR)[242] or exemptions for certain products.[243] Quantifying or modulating based on public interest was difficult and not wished for.[244] Scarce examples of successful applications of the Union interest test include change of form of duty[245] and the duration of the duty.[246]

Not only in the EU are examples to be found where the interest of certain interested parties align with environmental interests. In a safeguards measure on certain types of cars with hybrid propulsion applied by the Ukrainian investigating authority, it was found that Ukraine's national interests required non-application of special

---

[238] Van Bael & Bellis (2019), p. 277.

[239] Kotsiubska (2011), p. 28.

[240] See, e.g. Sinnaeve (2007), pp. 176–177; Kommerskollegium (2013).

[241] Van Bael & Bellis (2019), pp. 278–279. For an exemplary list of cases, see Müller et al. (2009), para. 21.62.

[242] Sinnaeve (2007), p. 177.

[243] European Commission, Communication from the Commission to the Council and the European Parliament on Modernisation of Trade Defence Instruments adapting trade defence instruments to the current needs of the European economy, COM(2013) 191 final, 10 April 2013, pp. 9–12.

[244] Sinnaeve (2007), p. 177.

[245] See, for instance, Commission Implementing Regulation (EU) 2015/1953 of 29 October 2015 imposing a definitive anti-dumping duty on imports of certain grain-oriented flat-rolled products of silicon-electrical steel originating in the People's Republic of China, Japan, the Republic of Korea, the Russian Federation and the United States of America, OJ 2015 L 284/109, rec. 110–112, 147–149 and 169.

[246] See, for instance, Commission Implementing Regulation (EU) 2017/367 of 1 March 2017 imposing a definitive anti-dumping duty on imports of crystalline silicon photovoltaic modules and key components (i.e. cells) originating in or consigned from the People's Republic of China following an expiry review pursuant to Article 11(2) of Regulation (EU) 2016/1036 of the European Parliament and of the Council and terminating the partial interim review investigation pursuant to Article 11(3) of Regulation (EU) 2016/1036, OJ 2017 L 56/131, rec. 334–335.

measures concerning import into Ukraine of certain types of cars with hybrid propulsion, which led to the non-application of a safeguards measure.[247]

Also the recently adopted UK trade remedies legislation provides for the option to account for climate change considerations as part of the trade remedy investigation.[248] The recently established investigating authority, the Trade Remedies Authority (TRA), can consider any submissions as part of the economic interest consideration by any interested party to the investigation. Similarly, the Secretary of State required to give due consideration to such submissions as part of the public interest test.

4.6 Chapter Summary

The observation that the renewable energy sector became a prime target for the imposition of sometimes very heavy trade remedy duties has led to the consideration that some restrictions on the use of such trade remedies would be an appropriate policy standpoint for WTO Members. Against this background, the goal of this chapter was to formulate policy options that would prevent that the imposition of trade remedies on environmental goods stand in the way of development of the renewable energy sector to become a worthy competitor of fossil fuel energy. This breaks down into three main questions: What kind of 'environmental goods' merit preferential trade remedy treatment? What are the procedural restrictions in trade remedy investigations possible in practice? And how can these restrictions be implemented in practice?

The first question on the definition of environmental goods has led to years of political and economic discussions without a definitive outcome—although some initiatives like the APEC list have been considered a successful step. Finding an agreement would mean a novel approach where tariff qualification is the basis for exerting policy instruments for climate mitigation, environmental protection, and sustainability. Short of outcomes on the WTO level, this is a first important hurdle to be overcome before systemic trade remedy policy changes may be implemented.

Regarding the second question, the ideal solution would be for trade remedies not to be imposed at all. However, exploiting so-called 'procedural weaknesses' in the trade remedy agreements in favour of environmental protection is more feasible. This chapter has reviewed a list of possibilities ranging from reducing the amounts, durations, level, or scope of trade remedies. UNCTAD suggests focussing on a

---

[247] Committee on Safeguards, Notification under Article 12.1(b) of the Agreement on Safeguards on Finding a Serious Injury or Threat Thereof Caused by Increased Imports, Notification under Article 12.1(c) of the Agreement on Safeguards on Taking a Decision to Apply a Safeguard Measure, Notification Pursuant to Article 9, Footnote 2, of the Agreement on Safeguards, Ukraine, Motor cars, Supplement, G/SG/N/8/UKR/3/Suppl.2, G/SG/N/10/UKR/3/Suppl.3, G/SG/N/11/UKR/1/Suppl.2, 27 February 2015.

[248] Merlo (2021).

mandatory LDR and shorter time limits for imposition of trade remedies for environmental goods.[249] Also a due consideration of environmental stakeholders, not only in the application of an environmental public interest test, but throughout the investigation procedure should also lead to policy decisions by investigating authorities in favour of environmental protection.

As to the implementation, multilateral, plurilateral and sectoral initiatives (most notably the EGA initiative) seem politically unfeasible as negotiations have proven unable to move forward. Some of the options for disciplining trade remedy action can become self-imposed behavioural reforms implemented by WTO Members unilaterally within their existing domestic legal framework. The core idea is to urge investigating authorities to rethink, ameliorate or mitigate the impact of trade remedy measures on green goods. The EU legal framework provides for a relevant case study. Discussions on a broader, environmental interest test in the EU have not led to changes in legislation or practice. As discussed above, more recently, the EU has taken a forefront position by including some environmental considerations in its legal framework. One remaining question is whether it will be able to move countries to commit to similar or additional trade remedies provisions in their FTAs.

References

Adamantopoulos K, De Notaris D (2000) The future of the WTO and the reform of the anti-dumping agreement: a legal perspective. Fordham Int Law J 24(1/2):30–61

Andersen H (2009) EU dumping determinations and WTO law. Kluwer Law International, Alphen aan den Rijn

Barthelemy C, Peat D (2015) Trade remedies in the renewable energy sector: normal value and double remedies. J World Invest Trade 16(3):436–466

Bloningen BA, Prusa TJ (2001) Antidumping. NBER Working Paper No. 8398

Bloningen BA, Prusa TJ (2016) Dumping and antidumping duties. In: Bagwell K, Staiger RW (eds) Handbook of commercial policy, volume 1, Part B. North-Holland/Elsevier, Amsterdam/Oxford, pp 107–159

Brewer T (2012) International technology diffusion in a Sustainable Energy Trade Agreement (SETA). E15 Initiative

Brewster R, Brunel C, Mayda AM (2016) Trade in environmental goods: a review of the WTO Appellate Body's Ruling in *US – Countervailing Measures (China)*. World Trade Rev 15(2):327–349

Bronckers M, McNelis N (2000) Rethinking the "like product" definition in GATT 1994: anti-dumping and environmental protection. In: Cottier T, Mavroidis PC (eds) Regulatory barriers and the principle of non-discrimination in world trade law. University of Michigan Press, Michigan, pp 345–385

Bucholtz B (1995) Sawing off the third branch: precluding judicial review of anti-dumping and countervailing duty assessments under free trade agreements. Maryland J Int Law Trade 19(2):175–224

Choi WM (2002) 'Like Products' in International Trade Law, Toward a Consistent GATT/WTO Jurisprudence. Oxford University Press, Oxford

---

[249] UNCTAD (2014), p. 16.

Condon BJ (2009) Climate change and unresolved issues in WTO law. J Int Econ Law 12(4):895–926

Cosbey A (2014) The Green Goods Agreement: neither green nor good? IISD Commentary

Cosbey A, Mavroidis PC (2017) A turquoise mess: green subsidies, blue industrial policy and renewable energy: the case for redrafting the subsidies agreement of the WTO. EUI Working Papers RSCAS 2014/17

Cosbey A, Rubini L (2013) Does it FIT? An assessment of the effectiveness of renewable energy measures and of the implications of the Canada – renewable energy/FIT disputes. In: E15 Expert Group on Clean Energy Technologies and the Trade System (ed) Clean energy and the trade system: proposals and analysis. ICTSD/WEF, Geneva, pp 39–46

Deardorff AV, Stern RM (1997) Measurement of non-tariff barriers. OECD Economics Department Working Papers No. 179

de Melo J, Solleder JM (2020) The EGA Negotiations: Why They Are Important, Why They Are Stalled, and Challenges Ahead. J World Trade 54(3):333–348

Doelle M (2004) Climate change and the WTO: opportunities to motivate state action on climate change through the World Trade Organization. Rev Eur Comp Int Environ Law 13(1):85–103

Douma WT (2016) The WTO and climate change. In: Farber DA, Peeters M (eds) Climate change law. Edward Elgar Publishing, Cheltenham/Northampton, pp 298–208

Eliason A (2019) Using the WTO to facilitate the Paris Agreement: a tripartite approach. Vanderbilt J Transnatl Law 52(3):545–575

Espa I, Marín Durán G (2018) Renewable energy subsidies and WTO law: time to rethink the case for reform beyond Canada – renewable energy/fit program. J Int Econ Law 21(4):621–653

Farah PD, Cima E (2015) The World Trade Organization, renewable energy subsidies, and the case of feed-in tariffs: time for reform toward sustainable development. Georgetown Int Environ Law Rev 27(4):515–537

Frey C (2016) Tackling climate change through the elimination of trade barriers for low-carbon goods: multilateral, plurilateral and regional approaches. In: Mauerhofer V (ed) Legal aspects of sustainable development. Springer, Berlin/Heidelberg, pp 449–468

Gelosso Grosso M (2007) Regulatory principles for environmental services and the general agreement on trade in services. ICSTD Issue Paper No. 6

Hoekman B, Mavroidis PC (2017) MFN clubs and scheduling additional commitments in the GATT: learning from the GATS. Eur J Int Law 28(2):387–407

Hoffmeister F (2015) Modernising the EU's trade defence instruments: mission impossible? In: Herrmann C, Simma B, Streinz R (eds) Trade policy between law, diplomacy and scholarship. Liber Amicorum in memoriam Horst G. Krenzler. Springer, Cham, pp 365–376

Horlick G (2013) Trade remedies and development of renewable energy. In: E15 Expert Group on Clean Energy Technologies and the Trade System (ed) Clean energy and the trade system: proposals and analysis. ICTSD/WEF, Geneva, pp 69–73

Howse R (2013) Securing policy space for clean energy under the SCM agreement: alternative approaches. In: E15 Expert Group on Clean Energy Technologies and the Trade System (ed) Clean energy and the trade system: proposals and analysis. ICTSD/WEF, Geneva, pp 47–51

Kampel K (2017) Options for disciplining the use of trade remedies in clean energy technologies. ICTSD Issue Paper

Kasteng J (2013) Trade remedies on clean energy: a new trend in need of multilateral initiatives. In: E15 Expert Group on Clean Energy Technologies and the Trade System (ed) Clean energy and the trade system: proposals and analysis. ICTSD/WEF, Geneva, pp 60–68

Kennedy KC (2009) The status of the trade-environment-sustainable development triad in the Doha Round negotiations and in recent U.S. trade policy. Indiana Int Comp Law Rev 19(3):529–552

Kommerskollegium (2013) Eliminating anti-dumping measures in regional trade agreements, the European Union example. National Board of Trade, Sweden

Kotsiubska V (2011) Public interest consideration in domestic and international antidumping disciplines. World Trade Institute Thesis

Lee J (2016) Green subsidies and countervailing duty investigations: some implications from recent examples of Korea. In: Park DY (ed) Legal issues on climate change and international trade law. Springer, Cham, pp 197–218

Lester S, Watson KW (2013) Free trade in environmental goods: the trade remedy problem. Free Trade Bulletin No. 54

Lima-Campos A, Vito A (2004) Abuse and discretion. The impact of anti-dumping and countervailing duty proceedings on Brazilian exports to the United States. J World Trade 38(1):37–68

Limenta M (2020) Palm oil for fuels: WTO rules and environmental protection. Global Trade Cust J 15(7):321–339

Liu HW, Maughan J (2012) China's rare earths export quotas: out of the China-raw materials gate, but past the WTO's finishing line? J Int Econ Law 15(4):974–1005

Matsushita M, Schoenbaum T, Mavroidis P, Hahn M (2015) The World Trade Organization, law, practice, and policy, 3rd edn. Oxford University Press, Oxford

Mavroidis PC, de Melo J (2015) Climate change policies and the WTO: greening the GATT, revisited. In: Barrett S, Carraro C, de Melo J (eds) Towards a workable and effective climate regime. CEPR Press, London, pp 225–236

Mavroidis PC, Neven DJ (2019) Greening the WTO environmental codes agreement, tariff concessions, and policy likeness. J Int Econ Law 22(1):373–388

Meléndez-Ortiz R (2016) Enabling the energy transition and scale-up of clean energy technologies: options for the global trade system. E15 Expert Group on Clean Energy Technologies and the Trade System, Policy Options Paper

Melin Y (2016) Users in EU trade defence investigations: how to better take their interests into account, and the new role of Member States as user champions after comitology. Global Trade Cust J 11(3):88–121

Merlo D (2021) Climate change and trade remedies. Fieldfisher Insight. https://www.fieldfisher.com/en/insights/climate-change-and-trade-remedies. Accessed 224 June 2023

Müller W, Khan N, Scharf T (2009) EC and WTO anti-dumping law. A handbook, 2nd edn. Oxford University Press, Oxford

Niels G (2000) What is antidumping policy really about? J Econ Surv 14(4):476–526

Potts J (2008) The legality of PPMs under the GATT. Challenges and opportunities for sustainable trade policy. IISD, Winnipeg

Rubini L (2012) Ain't wasting time no more: subsidies for renewable energy, the SCM Agreement, policy space, and law reform. J Int Econ Law 15(2):525–579

Shadikhodjaev S (2015) Renewable energy and government support: time to 'Green' the SCM Agreement? World Trade Rev 14(3):479–506

Sinnaeve A (2007) The 'community interest test' in anti-dumping investigations: time for reform? Global Trade Cust J 2(4):157–181

Steenblik R (2005) Environmental goods: a comparison of the APEC and OECD lists. OECD Trade and Environment Working Paper No. 2005-04

Steenblik RP, Droege S (2019) Time to ACCTS? Five countries announce new initiative on trade and climate change. IISD blog. https://www.iisd.org/articles/insight/time-accts-five-countries-announce-new-initiative-trade-and-climate-change. Accessed 24 June 2023

Sugathan M (2013) Lists of environmental goods: an overview. ICTSD Information Note

Teh R, Prusa TJ, Budetta M (2009) Trade remedy provisions in regional trade agreements. In: Estevadeordal A, Suominen K, Teh R (eds) Regional rules in the global trading system. Cambridge University Press, Cambridge, pp 166–248

UNCTAD (2014) Trade remedies: targeting the renewable energy sector. UNCTAD, Geneva

Van Bael & Bellis (2019) EU anti-dumping and other trade defence instruments, 6th edn. Wolters Kluwer, Alphen aan den Rijn

Van den Bossche P, Zdouc W (2017) The law and policy of the World Trade Organization. Text, cases and materials, 4th edn. Cambridge University Press, Cambridge

Van der Loo G (2016) The EU-Ukraine Association Agreement and deep and comprehensive free trade area. A new legal instrument for EU integration without membership. Brill/Nijhoff, Leiden/Boston

Van Vaerenbergh P (2018) The role of trade defence instruments in EU trade agreements: theory versus practice. Zeitschrift für Europarechtliche Studien 21(2):217–236

Vermulst E (2005) The WTO Anti-Dumping Agreement. Oxford University Press, Oxford

Vermulst E, Sud JD (2018) The new rules adopted by the European Union to address "significant distortions" in the anti-dumping context. In: Bungenberg M, Hahn M, Herrmann C, Müller-Ibold T (eds) The future of trade defence instruments. Global policy trends and legal challenges. Springer, Cham, pp 63–87

Vikhlyaev A (2004) Environmental goods and services: defining negotiations or negotiating definitions? J World Trade 38(1):93–122

Voon T (2010) Eliminating trade remedies from the WTO: lessons from regional trade agreements. Int Comp Law Q 59(3):625–667

Wellhausen M (2001) The community interest test in antidumping proceedings of the European Union. Am Univ Int Law Rev 16(4):1027–1082

Wouters J, Raina A, Hegde V (2020) The future of global economic governance: the European Union, the World Trade Organization and the crisis of multilateralism. Leuven CGGS Working Paper No. 219

Wu M (2014) Why developing countries won't negotiate: the case of the WTO Environmental Goods Agreement. Trade Law Dev 6(1):93–176

Wu M, Salzman J (2014) The next generation of trade and environment conflicts: the rise of green industrial policy. Northwest Univ Law Rev 108(2):401–474

Zhang Z (2013) Trade in environmental goods, with focus on climate-friendly goods and technologies. In: Prévost D, Van Calster G (eds) Research handbook on environment, health and the WTO. Edward Elgar Publishing, Cheltenham/Northampton, pp 673–699

Chapter 5
Low Environmental Standards and the ASCM Rules

5.1 Introduction

Government policies and standard-setting on environmental protection have an impact on producers' cost of production. Key among the government policies which would be categorised as subsidies conferring a benefit to producers are "lax" environmental standards as well as the provision of resources at less than their full value.[1] Some may argue that, in certain cases, low levels of regulation may even confer a subsidy to producers. *Doelle*, for instance, suggested that "[r]ecognition of failure to address environmental costs as a form of subsidy would actually set a precedent that could lead to a much more progressive relationship between trade and environment, by giving countries that are willing to take the lead in addressing an environmental issue a tool to do so without being economically disadvantaged by having to compete with countries who fail to internalise environmental costs in the price of the goods they produce."[2] If countries want to countervail such implicit subsidies granted to imported goods, this shall be in accordance with the rules of the ASCM.

Beyond the question whether environmental standards as such could be qualified as a countervailable subsidy, another question arises whether environmental standards may play a role in the determination of the appropriate (market) benchmark to determine the amount of any subsidy conferred. Several scholars have proposed to rely on the CVD instrument to equal out environmental cost internalisation efforts. Most notably, *Stiglitz* has proposed to impose carbon duties on the unfair subsidy the US is granting in comparison to the EU by not applying energy taxes and emission cuts.[3] He opines that not paying the full cost of production, *in casu* not

---

[1] Patterson (1992), p. 105.

[2] Doelle (2004), p. 102.

[3] Stiglitz (2006), p. 2.

paying the full price of the damage done to the environment, is a subsidy that should be offset by a high tax or CVD.[4] *Espa/Rolland* similarly develop on including environmental costs in CVD calculations and argue that "[s]o long as the same environmental costs are taken into account on both sides of the equation, calculations adjusted for environmental costs might pass muster under the ASCM."[5]

Accordingly, this chapter investigates environmental considerations in the law on countervailing measures. Several legally distinct legal questions arise in this exercise. First, whether the constituent criteria in the definition of a subsidy could be applied to a situation where low environmental standards impact the cost of production (Sect. 5.2). Second, whether the situation would be different for so-called dual pricing schemes, in which different levels of the price of raw materials may lead to below-cost exports (Sect. 5.3). Third, this chapter focuses on the benefit calculation and considers environmental costs in the market benchmarks used to determine the amount of benefit and ultimately the level of CVD (Sect. 5.4). This chapter concludes that the current rules do not permit CVDs to become an instrument to ensure environmental cost internalisation, suggesting that legislative drafting or differential interpretation of the rules would be necessary (Sect. 5.5).

5.2   Low Environmental Standards as Subsidies

5.2.1   The 'Invisible' Subsidy of Low Environmental Standards

Countries may argue that imported goods benefitted from an 'invisible' subsidy of cost externalisation in countries that do not impose environmental standards on their producers. The underlying unfairness is that certain industries in certain countries benefit from weak or unenforced environmental laws and regulations which do not require a sufficient level of environmental cost internalisation. Thus, the emissions externalisation grants an implicit subsidy to energy producers, consumers, and downstream goods.

According to some, the failure to internalise carbon costs may be qualified as a government failure, or a so-called 'regulatory failure subsidy',[6] which refers to governments conferring a benefit to producers in the form of the cost which is saved by companies for the fact that they do not have to comply with (international minimum) environmental standards, creating a difference between the actual cost and the higher cost for environmental compliance they would have incurred. As such, the question arises whether this subsidy could be countervailed through the imposition of anti-subsidy duties to bring the price of imported goods on the level of internalisation of environmental costs.

---

[4] *Ibid.*

[5] Espa and Rolland (2015), p. 10.

[6] See, for instance, Barceló (1994), p. 19; Patterson (1992).

Concrete proposals to impose eco-duties have been advanced by scholars and US elected officials in the 1990s on both sides of the Atlantic. Amongst the most famous proposals is the one advanced by US House of Representatives Majority Leader *Gephardt* to push for a Green 301 provision permitting eco-duties on imports not produced under conditions meeting US environmental standards.[7] Also Senator *Baucus* called for commodities on imported products to offset economic advantages achieved through less stringent environmental protection regulations,[8] and Senator *Boren* pointed out the unfair advantage enjoyed by other nations exploiting the environment and public health for economic gain as opposed to US manufacturers who are required to spend up to 250% more on environmental controls than other countries.[9] In the congressional debate on the 1990 US Clean Air Act amendments, the Senate discussed a proposed resolution urging that special tariffs be imposed on imported goods produced under air quality standards that do not comply with the standards under the Clean Air Act.[10]

Also in Europe, discussions on eco-duties emerged in the 1990s. The European Parliament adopted a resolution in 1992 calling on the GATT to forbid environmental dumping.[11] Yet at the same time, the Commission had labelled the possibility of environmental dumping duties non-negotiable.[12] Rather, a 1992 proposal included the plan to impose a tax on carbon emissions and energy.[13]

More recently, the debate on eco-duties has regained traction. In 2006, for instance, French Prime Minister *de Villepin* referred to eco-dumping in his pledge that the EU should act against countries that do not adhere to carbon emission standards—particularly non-Parties to the Kyoto Protocol—as a justification for a proposed eco-tax.[14] In addition, in December 2020, the US submitted a draft Ministerial Decision to the WTO that proposed to treat the lack of environmental protection as a subsidy.[15]

---

[7] Reported by Esty (1994), p. 155, fn. 1.

[8] Reported by Esty (1994), p. 163, fn. 14.

[9] International Pollution Deterrence Act of 1991. Statement of Senator David L. Boren, Senate Finance Committee, 25 October 1991.

[10] See S. Amend. 1321, 101st Cong. 2nd Session, 136 Cong. Record S3000. This so-called Gorton amendment was defeated 52 to 47.

[11] Reported by Esty (1994), p. 164. See Resolution A3-0329/92.

[12] GATT Group on Environmental Measures and International Trade, Submission by the European Community, The GATT and Trade Provisions of Multilateral Environmental Agreements, TRE/W/5, 17 November 1992.

[13] European Commission, Proposal for a Council Directive Introducing a Tax on Carbon Emissions and Energy, COM(92) 226 final, 30 June 1992. Reported by *Esty* (1994), p. 164.

[14] Kempf (2006).

[15] General Council, Draft Ministerial Decision, Advancing Sustainable Development Goals Through Trade Rules to Level the Playing Field, WT/GC/W/814, 17 December 2020. For a detailed analysis, see Sect. 8.3.1 below.

5.2.2 *Low Environmental Standards as Actionable Subsidies Under the ASCM*

Four prerequisites in Art. 1 and 2 of the ASCM define what constitutes an counter-vailable subsidy: (1) a financial contribution, (2) by a government, (3) conferring a benefit, and (4) such subsidy must be specific.[16] To determine whether lax environ-mental standards qualify as a subsidy, difficulties arise particularly in arguing the criteria of the financial contribution by a government (Sect. 5.2.2.1), benefit con-ferred (Sect. 5.2.2.2) and specificity (Sect. 5.2.2.3). Moreover, subsidies must be prohibited (i.e. export or import contingent) or actionable (*i.e.* causing adverse effects) as a further prerequisite for countervailing measures to be imposed (Sect. 5.2.2.4). For a successful argument concerning low environmental standards as a subsidy, all prerequisites would have to be fulfilled.

5.2.2.1 Financial Contribution (Art. 1.1(a) ASCM)

Qualifying the non-enactment or non-enforcement of environmental laws as a finan-cial contribution is the first requirement under Art. 1 ASCM. DSB rulings so far would suggest that the lack of government regulation setting emission reduction standards in the exporting country does not amount to a financial contribution and is therefore not to be qualified as a subsidy.[17] In fact, the Panel in *US – Export Restraints* confirmed that the term "financial contribution" was precisely included in the ASCM to prevent that any government measure conferring a benefit would be considered a subsidy.[18]

Nonetheless, arguments could be raised under certain subparagraphs of the defi-nition. Art. 1.1(a)(1) ASCM lists four exhaustive cases in which there are financial contributions by a government: (i) a direct transfer of funds, (ii) forgone govern-ment revenue that is otherwise due, (iii) the provision or purchase of goods by a government, or (iv) any of these functions carried out by a funding mechanism or through entrustment or direction of a private body. In addition, Art. 1.1(a)(2) ASCM also defines a subsidy as any form of income or price support in the sense of Art. XVI GATT. In the case of a failure to adequately regulate environmental protection in the exporting country, the second, fourth, and last type may be of relevance.

First, one could argue that a lack of sufficient environmental standards consti-tutes government revenue foregone, otherwise due as a subsidy in the sense of Art. 1.1(a)(1)(ii) ASCM. Early arguments raised in this regard pointed in the direction that penalties for non-compliance not being imposed constitute forgone revenue.[19]

---

[16] See Sects. 3.2.2.2 and 3.2.3.2.2 above.

[17] Müller (2017), p. 14.

[18] Panel report, *United States – Measures Treating Export Restraints as Subsidies*, WT/DS194/R, adopted 23 August 2001, para. 8.65 and 8.73.

[19] See Esty (1994), p. 164.

However, the criterion of government revenue foregone or not collected is predominantly aimed to deal with for instance fiscal incentives such as tax credits—not general or environmental regulatory levels in a country. Situations falling under this criterion usually take the form of a special domestic law on taxation, or an amendment to domestic customs law.[20] It thereby touches upon the sovereign fiscal powers of the national governments—which the WTO does not regulate—and thus merely foresees that subsidies disciplines must be respected when exercising these powers.[21] Two principal WTO cases on this provision concerned a rent tax treatment for income from foreign and domestic sales of US companies (*US – FSC*) and an exemption from payment of an MFN import duty that would otherwise apply to imports, conditional upon domestic production requirements (*Canada – Autos*).[22] A tax which is not due does not automatically fulfil the requirement of "otherwise due" under the financial contribution aspect of Art. 1.1 ASCM.[23] As soon as the tax is created and is lower for domestic producers than for imported products, it might constitute a revenue forgone that is otherwise due.[24]

Accordingly, this provision may be considered when the domestic level of a carbon tax does not match the taxation level of imports of like products, for instance. However, it is far from clear in how far differentiated taxation based on carbon footprint may constitute a financial contribution by a government. Only in very explicit cases, where for instance a country applies a general carbon tax, but not collects such tax in a certain sector, the definition of a financial contribution would be fulfilled under this criterion.[25] In any case, the prevailing domestic standard would be the relevant benchmark under the test of "government revenue that is otherwise due forgone or not collected", rather than the standard in the importing market or an internationally agreed upon standard.[26]

Moreover, even if it could be assumed that environmental regulation would fall under this criterion, the benchmark against which the Appellate Body compares the regulatory measures is the prevailing domestic standard.[27] Hence, a comparison to the local standard in the importing country or an internationally agreed upon standard cannot be considered in this type of financial contribution. Therefore, absent a

---

[20] Adamantopoulos (2008a), Art. 1 ASCM, para. 31.

[21] *Ibid*, para. 32.

[22] *Condon* (2009), p. 901. See Appellate Body Report, *United States – Tax Treatment for 'Foreign Sales Corporations' (Article 21.5 – EC)*, WT/DS108/AB/RW, adopted 29 January 2002; Appellate Body Report, *Canada – Certain Measures Affecting the Automotive Industry*, WT/DS139/AB/R, adopted 19 June 2000.

[23] Appellate Body report, *Brazil – Export Financing Programme for Aircraft*, WT/DS46/AB/R, adopted 20 August 1999, para. 156.

[24] Condon (2009), p. 902.

[25] Tarasofsky (2008), p. 14; Condon (2009), p. 901.

[26] Pauwelyn (2013), p. 471.

[27] Appellate Body report, *United States – Tax Treatment for "Foreign Sales Corporations"*, WT/DS108/AB/R, adopted 20 March 2000, para. 90 (emphasis added).

general policy of environmental protection, foreign exports that fail to internalise environmental costs cannot be called a subsidy.[28]

Second, the case law on government intervention in the form of export restraints may be considered. The Panels in *US – Export Restraints* and *Korea – Commercial Vessels* underlined that government intervention (or a regulatory failure) in the market is very different than entrusting or directing a private body in the sense of Art. 1.1(a)(1)(iv) ASCM.[29] Further case law on export restraints by a government confirms that a simple government intervention or exercise of general regulatory powers on the market which creates the by-product of an advantage does not suffice to meet the standard of Art. 1.1(a)(1)(iv) ASCM.[30] The financial contribution aspect foreclosed the possibility to treat any government action that incurs a benefit as a subsidy.[31] Similarly, in *China – GOES*, the Panel affirmed this position when deciding that higher prices paid by US steel purchasers as a result of a government measure in the form of a voluntary export restraint agreement were not entrusted and directed, even though it comes with a side-effect of higher prices.[32] By extension, the broader exercise of government powers—including the absent adoption of legislation for environmental and social protection—may not be qualified as a financial contribution and hence a subsidy.

Finally, in theory, it could be attempted to argue that low environmental standards or the absence of carbon emission mitigation measures are a "form of income or price support" to domestic producers which compete with other countries that do pay this cost.[33] However, given the absence any jurisprudential guidance on this residual category of Art. 1 ASCM, an argument that insufficient environmental legislation falls under this category is hard to sustain.[34]

5.2.2.2   Benefit (Art. 1.2 ASCM)

As a second requirement in the definition of a subsidy, Art. 1.1(b) ASCM requires the financial contribution, *in casu* in the form of lower or insufficiently enforced environmental regulation, confers a benefit to the recipient of the subsidy. The

---

[28] Pauwelyn 2013), p. 472.

[29] Panel report, *United States – Measures Treating Export Restraints as Subsidies*, WT/DS194/R, adopted 3 August 2001, para. 8.31; Panel report, *Korea – Measures Affecting Trade in Commercial Vessels*, WT/DS273/R, adopted 11 April 2005, para. 7.374–7.735; confirmed by Appellate Body report, *United States – Countervailing Duty Investigation on Dynamic Random Access Memory Semiconductors (DRAMS) from Korea*, WT/DS296/AB/R, adopted 20 July 2005, para. 114.

[30] Müller (2017), pp. 109–110.

[31] Panel report, *United States – Measures Treating Export Restraints as Subsidies*, WT/DS194/R, adopted 3 August 2001, para. 8.38 and 8.40.

[32] Panel report, *China – Countervailing and Anti-Dumping Duties on Grain-Oriented Flat-Rolled Electrical Steel from the United States*, WT/DS414/R, adopted 16 November 2012.

[33] Art. 1.1(a)(2) ASCM.

[34] Pauwelyn (2013), p. 472.

determination of a benefit is a separate legal requirement from the existence of a financial contribution.[35] The ASCM does not define what constitutes a "benefit" for the purposes of Art. 1.1(b) ASCM.[36] The commonly referred to definition was formulated in the case law, whereby a benefit exists "the financial contribution makes the recipient better off than it would otherwise have been, absent that contribution" and this can be "identified by determining whether the recipient has received a financial contribution on terms more favourable than those available to the recipient in the market."[37] The market benchmark acts as a filter to exclude normal conduct of the government under commercial circumstances from the scope of the ASCM, because such conduct is deemed not to be trade-distorting.[38]

One concern that could be raised is that the level of environmental protection set by government regulation does not come at a cost for the state. In *Canada – Aircraft*, the Appellate Body explicitly held that the cost to the government is irrelevant for determination of existence of a subsidy under Art. 1 ASCM.[39] The actual benefit is relevant and not the potential benefit, because the focus is on the recipient of the subsidy and not the government.[40] A beneficial government policy that does not have a cost for the government may therefore nonetheless benefit a recipient as it amounts to an economic advantage. This is particularly relevant for regulatory measures such as environmental regulation, which do not necessarily come at a price for the government (not) adopting them.

The use of a market benchmark for the determination of a benefit is problematic when the very market has been created by the government. In *Canada – Renewable Energy & Feed-In Tariff Program*, the Appellate Body needed to determine whether a benefit was conferred by Feed-In Tariffs (FITs) paid by the Ontario Power

---

[35] Appellate Body report, *Brazil – Export Financing Programme for Aircraft*, WT/DS46/AB/R, adopted 20 August 1999, para. 156–157; Panel report, *United States – Measures Treating Export Restraints as Subsidies*, WT/DS1994/R, adopted 23 August 2011, para. 8.20; Appellate Body report, *United States – Final Countervailing Duty Determination with respect to certain Softwood Lumber from Canada*, WT/DS257/AB/R, adopted 17 February 2004, para. 51.

[36] Panel report, *Mexico – Definitive Countervailing Measures on Olive Oil from the European Communities*, WT/DS341/R, adopted 21 October 2008, para. 7.151 ff.

[37] Appellate Body report, *Canada – Measures Affecting the Export of Civilian Aircraft*, WT/DS70/AB/R, adopted 20 August 1999, para. 157; confirmed in Appellate Body report, *European Communities and Certain member States – Measures Affecting Trade in Large Civil Aircraft*, WT/DS316/AB/R, adopted 1 June 2011, para. 705, 832 and 849; Appellate Body report, *Japan – Countervailing Duties on Dynamic Random Access Memories from Korea*, WT/DS336/AB/R, adopted 17 November 2007, para. 173 and 225; Appellate Body report, *Canada – Certain Measures Affecting the Renewable Energy Generation Sector*, WT/DS412/AB/R, adopted 24 May 2013, para. 5.163 and 5.165; Appellate Body report, *United States – Countervailing Duty Measures on Certain Products from China*, WT/DS437/AB/R, adopted 16 January 2015, para. 4.44.

[38] Müller (2017), p. 126.

[39] Appellate Body report, *Canada – Measures Affecting the Export of Civilian Aircraft*, WT/DS70/AB/R, adopted 20 August 1999, para. 149.

[40] Adamantopoulos (2008a), Art. 1 ASCM, para. 93.

Authority to producers of wind power and solar energy.[41] Considering that the ASCM provides that "prevailing market conditions" are to be considered, the Appellate Body decided that the relevant market was the renewable energy market rather than the wholesale electricity market. The Appellate Body thereby drew a difference between government interventions that create markets that would otherwise not exist, and government interventions in support of certain market players in existing markets. If government intervention creates a market, it cannot be said that it distorts the market. In the determination, not only demand-side but also supply-side factors can be relevant, as also supply-side factors can show the significance of government intervention in the market.[42] The solar and wind power energy market only existed by virtue of the Government of Ontario's measures imposing an energy supply mix on electricity distribution companies and would otherwise not be economically viable. At the Panel stage, one Panellist issued a dissenting opinion in favour of using the competitive wholesale market for electricity in Ontario.[43]

This Appellate Body analysis has been criticised for being motivated by environmental and climate change policy considerations, namely the promotion of renewable energy.[44] These findings give governments policy space to correct market distortions by creating new markets—but the pursuit of legitimate objectives is not a precondition as such.[45] It has spurred a debate whether green goods may justify a differentiated interpretation of WTO rules, and even proposals to codify these benefit criteria from the renewable energy cases, particularly that measures compensating the difference in production costs between conventional and renewable energy products are presumed not to confer a benefit.[46] This jurisprudence is advantageous for the protection of renewable energy and may have consequences in other government-created markets for environmental goods.[47]

5.2.2.3 Specificity (Art. 2 ASCM)

Arguing the specificity requirement is arguably very challenging in relation to environmental regulation because environmental protection standards apply horizontally by definition to the whole market/sector. Presuming that the existence or maintenance of low environmental standards may be qualified as a financial

---

[41] Appellate Body report, *Canada – Certain Measures Affecting the Renewable Energy Generation Sector*, WT/DS412/AB/R, adopted 24 May 2013; Appellate Body report, *Canada – Measures Relating to Feed-In Tariff Program*, WT/DS426/AB/R, adopted 24 May 2013.

[42] *Ibid*, para. 5.169 and 5.197.

[43] Panel report, *Canada – Certain Measures Affecting the Renewable Energy Generation Sector*, WT/DS412/AB/R, adopted 24 May 2013; Panel report, *Canada – Measures Relating to Feed-In Tariff Program*, WT/DS426/AB/R, adopted 24 May 2013, para. 9.1–9.23.

[44] See, for instance, Coppens (2014), pp. 463–468.

[45] *Ibid*, p. 461; Müller (2017), p. 136.

[46] Meléndez-Ortiz (2016), p. 10.

[47] See Sect. 5.4.1.1 below.

contribution conferring a benefit in the sense of Art. 1 ASCM, Art. 2 ASCM requires additionally subsidies to be specific to be countervailable. According to Art. 2.1 ASCM, specific subsidies are those that are granted to a specific enterprise or industry or group of enterprises or industries within the jurisdiction of the granting authority. Panels and the Appellate Body will assess whether access to a subsidy was limited to a particular class of recipients.[48] Generally, government contributions that are available for all economic players are not countervailable on account of not being specific (*e.g.* country-wide economic programs, social aid, or infrastructure grants). [49] Therefore, low environmental standards are available to all companies in all industries alike and in principle not specific.

The Appellate Body clarified that Art. 2 ASCM is characterised by a two-tier structure: first, the chapeau of Art. 2.1 ASCM and second, the scenarios enumerated in Art. 2.1(a) to (c) ASCM.[50] Art. 2 ASCM lists situations of *de jure* specificity (where access to the subsidy is explicitly limited to certain enterprises, or access to the subsidy is regulated through objective criteria or conditions which are not applied automatically or not strictly adhered to) and *de facto* specificity (where the subsidy program is used by certain enterprises, predominantly used by certain enterprises, disproportionately large amounts of the subsidy used by certain enterprises, or the granting authority has used its discretion towards certain enterprises). However, only for pollution-intensive industries, such as for instance the steel industry, it may amount to an actual benefit, which may arise to a *de facto* specific subsidy.[51] Such stance would require argumentation that the subsidy in the form of lax environmental standards is predominantly used by certain sectors, for instance energy-intensive sectors, or disproportionately large amounts of the subsidy are granted to certain sectors.

Beyond that, Art. 2.1(b) ASCM on *de jure* specificity outlines that objective criteria or conditions that are applied automatically and strictly adhered to shall prevent a finding of specificity. Objective criteria and conditions are those which are neutral, do not favour certain enterprises over others, are economic in nature, and horizontal in application.[52] Environmental considerations would be seen as "objective criteria or conditions" governing the eligibility for, and amount of, a subsidy under Art. 2.1(b) ASCM, preventing a finding of specificity.[53] One proposal to overcome this burden may be to create an interpretative note on what "objective criteria

---

[48] Appellate Body report, *United States – Countervailing Duty Measures on Certain Products from China*, WT/DS437/AB/R, adopted 16 January 2015, para. 4.169; 7 Appellate Body report, *Appellate Body report, United States – Countervailing Measures on Certain Products from China, Recourse to Article 21.5 of the DSU by China*, WT/DS437/AB/RW, adopted 15 August 2019, para. 5.228.

[49] Pauwelyn (2013), p. 472.

[50] Appellate Body report, *United States – Anti-Dumping and Countervailing Duties on Certain Products from China*, WT/DS379/AB/R, adopted 25 March 2011, para. 36–37 and 380–401.

[51] Barceló (1994), p. 11.

[52] Art. 2.1 ASCM, fn. 2.

[53] Pauwelyn (2013), pp. 472–473.

and conditions" means for the definition of *de jure* specificity in the field of clean energy subsidies.[54] In sum, it seems unlikely that a government policy of low environmental standards would pass the muster of the specificity requirement.

Amongst others, two types of subsidies exempted from the specificity requirement are export subsidies under Art. 2.3 ASCM and Chinese subsidies predominantly granted to SOEs under Sect. 10.2 CAP. Export subsidies are exempted from the specificity requirement as they are deemed to be specific by virtue of Art. 2.3 ASCM. *Pauwelyn* has argued that an (unlikely) finding *de facto* export contingency would exist when the subsidy is granted to provide an incentive to the recipient to export in a way that is not simply reflecting market forces of supply and demand in the domestic and export markets.[55]

In addition, Chinese subsidies to SOEs are subject to an additional legal provision in China's Accession Protocol (CAP), which in Sect. 10.2 CAP contains a specificity presumption for subsidies granted to Chinese SOEs:

> For the purposes of applying Articles 1.2 and 2 of the SCM Agreement, subsidies provided to State-owned enterprises will be viewed as specific if, inter alia, state-owned enterprises are the predominant recipients of such subsidies or state-owned enterprises receive disproportionately large amounts of subsidies.[56]

The circumstance that SOEs or state-controlled enterprises are (i) predominant recipients of a subsidy, or (ii) receive disproportionately large amounts of subsidies will suffice for a finding of *de facto* specificity. State ownership becomes therefore a relevant criterion of specificity in case of Chinese subsidies.[57] Investigating authorities may therefore focus on state ownership of the recipients of the subsidies, rather than on the factors for *de facto* specificity under Art. 2.1(c) ASCM.[58]

In sum, the specificity requirement will be a significant obstacle when arguing specificity of the 'subsidy' granted by government that maintains low environmental standards. In exceptional cases, where the specificity requirement is presumed or inapplicable, this hurdle may be overcome.

5.2.2.4 Adverse Effects and Serious Prejudice (Art. 5–6 ASCM)

Save the case where subsidies are outright prohibited, Art. 5 ASCM prescribes that subsidies are only actionable by means of imposition of CVDs when they cause adverse effects to the interests of other WTO Members. Subsidies falling in the category of actionable subsidies are the most important category for the imposition

---

[54] Meléndez-Ortiz (2016), p. 10.

[55] Pauwelyn (2013), p. 473. See Appellate Body report, *European Communities and Certain Member States – Measures Affecting Trade in Large Civil Aircraft*, WT/DS316/AB/R, adopted 1 June 2011, para. 1045.

[56] Sect. 10.2 CAP (emphasis added).

[57] Qin (2004), p. 891; Yamaoka (2013), p. 128.

[58] *Ibid.*

of CVDs. Accordingly, countries must also furnish grounds why imports of goods that do not internalise environmental costs cause 'serious prejudice to the domestic industry'.[59] Serious injury is defined in Art. 6.3 ASCM as situations where the subsidy has the effect of (a) displacing or impeding imports of the like product into the market of the subsidising Member, (b) displacing or impeding exports of the like product of another Member from a third country market, (c) significant price undercutting, price suppression, or loss in sales in the same market, (d) increasing the world market share of the subsidising Member.

Moreover, countries could also launch a claim directly under Art. 6 ASCM. Such claim is distinct from a CVD claim, in that is relates to the allowability of the imposition of a CVD rather than the CVD itself. Art. 6.7 ASCM includes a defence for WTO Members in DSB procedures,[60] which allow to point out reasons why displacement and impedance shall not arise, *i.e.* reasons other than the subsidy in question why exports of a complaining member may be negatively affected.[61] They include "failure to conform to standards and other regulatory requirements in the importing country" under Art. 6.7(f) ASCM. This could be argued to include environmental regulatory standards in the importing country. The standards and regulatory requirements may include any requirement regarding characteristics, process or production methods, including measures falling under the scope of Art. III:4 GATT, Annex 1(2) TBT Agreement standards and Annex A(1) SPS Agreement regulatory requirements.[62] The value of this provision is the mere finding that a product is unable to enter a market because of its failure of standards, irrespective of WTO consistency or these measures and irrespective of whether a subsidy has the effect of displacement or impeding the product.[63]

Therefore, investigating authorities will also have to prove that the low environmental standards cause serious prejudice to the domestic industry before imposing a CVD.

5.2.3 Rethinking the Scope of WTO Subsidies Disciplines

Given the obstacles in qualifying low environmental standards as countervailable subsidies, this section highlights proposals to rethink the scope of the subsidy disciplines. Since the options for the judiciary to interpret the relevant provisions under Art. 1 and 2 ASCM is limited (Sect. 5.2.3.1), multilateral (Sect. 5.2.3.2) or bilateral

---

[59] Art. 5(c) ASCM.

[60] Panel report, *United States – Subsidies on Upland Cotton*, WT/DS267/R, adopted 21 March 2005, para. 7.1405, fn. 1503.

[61] Müller (2017), p. 288.

[62] Piérola (2008), Art. 6 ASCM, para. 120–122.

[63] *Ibid*, para. 123–124.

negotiations (Sect. 5.2.3.3) may become a way to broaden the scope of anti-subsidy measures.

5.2.3.1 Interpretation of ASCM Rules

The requirements of financial contribution and the specificity requirement are most problematic for insufficient environmental regulatory standards to be qualified as an actionable subsidy. Panels or the Appellate Body could provide a facilitating interpretation of the existing rules.

In relation to the financial contribution requirement, absent possibilities under the current definition, one proposed solution that has not yet been explored in the jurisprudence is that access to a natural resource (*in casu* the atmosphere) may be qualified as a financial contribution.[64] Moreover, the Appellate Body could also have the opportunity to discuss the specific situation where the Paris Agreement tax is created and is lower for domestic producers than for imported products, it might constitute a revenue forgone that is otherwise due.[65]

Regarding the specificity criterion, relaxations of the requirement for energy/raw materials under the idea of environmental protection or climate change mitigation. Moreover, an argument could be developed regarding an interpretation of "objective criteria" as a ground for *de jure* specificity.

Nonetheless, given the criticism surrounding the creative interpretation of new markets in the *Canada FIT* cases, it is to be awaited whether a Panel or the Appellate Body would take a hard stance on including an activist interpretation of the subsidy rules in relation to environmental protection.

5.2.3.2 Amendments to the ASCM

The introduction of environmental considerations in the ASCM traditionally surrounds discussions on greening subsidies rules rather than the rules on countervailing duties. On the one hand, the permission of subsidies that would otherwise be prohibited invoking the ground that the subsidy will have considerable beneficial environmental consequences, and on the other hand, the prohibition of subsidies that would otherwise be allowed on the ground that the subsidised activities may be particularly harmful to the environment.[66] These aspects have been researched at length and will not be the focus of this section.[67] Instead, this section focuses on green considerations specifically in the CVD disciplines.

---

[64] Howse and Eliason (2009), p. 75.

[65] Condon (2009), p. 902.

[66] Sands and Peel (2018), p. 895.

[67] See, for instance, Rubini (2012); Farah and Cima (2015); Shadikhodjaev (2015); Shadikhodjaev (2013); Laurenza and Simões (2014); Espa and Marín Durán (2018); Cosbey and Mavroidis (2017); Cima (2018); Bigdeli (2011); Raslan (2018).

Particularly, a broader scope of the CVD disciplines that may include the possibility to countervail imported products that have enjoyed indirect subsidies through low environmental standards could be considered. However, in its current conception, the ASCM is not meant to capture the injurious effects of insufficient environmental regulation on domestic markets. Modifications of the ASCM may be considered to broaden the spectrum of government actions capable of being countervailed if they cause injurious effects. The recent US proposal[68] offers the Ministerial Conference an opportunity to re-open the debate on greening the ASCM from an unconventional perspective. It is expected that the long-standing opposition between developed countries who fear their own environmental efforts and competitive position versus developing countries who opine that such proposals are 'green protectionism' or 'eco-imperialism' imposing developed countries' preferences and values on developing countries, at the expense of the latter's ability to develop.[69] Although developed countries will see the adoption of duties as an effective way to level the playing field, developing countries see them as a disapproval of the country's environmental standard-setting.[70]

Apart from the adoption of a broader concept of a subsidy as a subset of government measures (or inaction) in the market, specific alternative proposals have been formulated for the promotion of renewable energy, for instance the proposal to explicitly include an obligation to internalise environmental costs incurred during the life-cycle of the products.[71] Art. 1 ASCM could also clarify which energy subsidies fall within the scope of subsidies disciplines, or at least include a detailed classification of generation, production, and supply of clean energy equipment and services subject to its subsidies disciplines, or prohibited subsidies category, or exceptions from Art. XX GATT or Art. 8.2(c) ASCM.[72] A contrary approach may also be chosen, where measures investigated that 'promote' environmentally harmful activities could also be considered countervailable by means of a presumption in the exception categories. An illustrative list could be modelled after the illustrative list of export subsidies which are prohibited.[73] In addition, the category of prohibited subsidies under Art. 3 ASCM could be expanded for other motives, including environmentally motivated ones.[74]

Temporary waivers could authorise discriminatory measures for climate change mitigation under Art. XI:3 and 4 WTO. *Howse* proposed that a clean energy waiver be conditioned on the removal of any discriminatory elements of a subsidy (for example, local content requirements) and of any other policies that may be in

---

[68] General Council, Draft Ministerial Decision, Advancing Sustainable Development Goals Through Trade Rules to Level the Playing Field, WT/GC/W/814, 17 December 2020. For a detailed analysis, see Sect. 8.3.1 below.

[69] Cima and Mbengue (2021), p. 4.

[70] *Ibid*, p. 5.

[71] Doelle (2004), p. 100.

[72] See Sect. 4.5.1 above. See also Espa and Rolland (2015), p. 12.

[73] Patterson (1992), p. 105.

[74] Horlick and Clarke (2017), pp. 681 ff.

contradiction with the purpose the waiver aims to fulfil (such as climate change mitigation or environmental costs internalisation), as well as contain an introductory clause similar in language to the chapeau of Art. XX GATT.[75]

In addition to difficulties in decision-making requirements at the WTO level,[76] changing the basic concept of a subsidy embodied in the ASCM would structurally affect the core of the agreement, which is not mandated under the DDA.[77] Whereas a clarification and improvement of existing disciplines is envisaged, WTO Members vouched to leave the basic principles of the trade remedy agreements intact.

5.2.3.3 Regional Trade Agreements

Willing partners may also find each other in negotiations on the bilateral or regional level to prevent competitive advantages from imposing higher or lower environmental standards. The recent EU-UK TCA is an example of a modern approach where sustainable development and environmental protection have been linked to a competitive, level playing field approach.[78] This agreement appears to set a workable definition of environmental standards in the context of trade disciplines, but the application in practice is to be awaited.[79]

5.3 Dual Pricing Schemes as Actionable Subsidies Under the ASCM

The possibility to counter the effects of dual pricing schemes for raw materials and energy have raise specific legal questions when discussing mitigation measures under the ASCM rules. Challenging dual pricing schemes has been motivated not only by trade considerations, but also by environmental considerations (Sect. 5.3.1). However, the WTO rules on the definition of a subsidy and the requirements to offset input subsidisation are limited in scope and are not capable in the current state to effectively capture dual pricing practices (Sect. 5.3.2). Scholars have therefore explored avenues to suppress input dumping schemes under the ASCM, but these have not yet led to a bullet-proof remedy, thus necessitating changes to the legislative framework and concrete proposals (Sect. 5.3.3).

---

[75] Howse (2013), p. 53; Espa and Rolland (2015), p. 12.

[76] Art. X WTO Agreement requires consensus on the need to reform and 2/3 majority on the new text.

[77] Doha Development Agenda, para. 28.

[78] EU-UK TCA, Title XI: Level Playing Field for Open and Fair Competition and Sustainable Development.

[79] See Sect. 8.3.3 below.

5.3.1 Environmental Impacts of Dual Pricing Schemes

Dual pricing schemes have been investigated from the perspective of their trade-distorting effects, but also their environmentally harmful consequences have been documented.[80] Energy dual pricing is a practice where a resource-endowed state, for instance through their monopolistic state-trading enterprises, sell their energy resources at significantly lower prices on the domestic market compared to the prices on the export market and/or the prevailing global market prices.[81] Particularly, such schemes promote wasteful consumption of fossil fuels, foster energy-intensive industries that profit from energy inputs below price, and discourage investment in the development of clean energy technology and innovation of energy-efficient production processes.[82] Such policies run counter to the polluter-pays principle, which promotes environmental cost internalisation.[83] Dual pricing schemes, by setting domestic prices of energy artificially low, fail to encourage internalisation of carbon emissions into the price of goods. It is viewed as unsustainable where government policies provide such cheap energy to encourage unfettered waste of energy, as this results in increased carbon emissions, water, and air pollution, etc. As such, maintaining dual pricing schemes also obstructs the achievement of SDG Goal 7.2, which targets to increase substantially the share of renewable energy in the global energy mix by 2030. More broadly, the maintenance of fossil fuel subsidies is linked to reasons of energy security supply, industrial policy, protectionism, economic benefit, protection of employment in labour-intensive industries, and access to energy.[84]

Capturing dual pricing practices under the ASCM rules requires a focus on the trade-distorting effects of these trade practices and the price levels of goods put on the international market. Considering that dual pricing is often associated with the provision of low-cost energy or raw material inputs to domestic producers of energy-intensive products, the ASCM disciplines have often been discussed as an adequate tool to combat the practice. Under the ASCM, issues related to "input subsidisation" may arise where subsidies are granted on the upstream level affecting prices of downstream products.[85] The phenomenon of input subsidisation occurs for both the provision of energy and raw materials.

First, certain industries are characterised by the fact that energy costs comprise a large share of the production costs, as is for instance the case in the production of products from steel, petrochemical, or fertilizer industries such as aluminium, silicon and ferrosilicon, potassium chloride, seamless pipes and tubes, and urea and

---

[80] See, for instance, Pogoretskyy (2011), pp. 184 ff.; Marhold (2017); Behn (2007).

[81] Marhold (2017), p. 1.

[82] *Ibid*, p. 2.

[83] Schwartz (2015), p. 437.

[84] Marhold (2017), p. 3.

[85] For an analysis of the legal implications, see Sect. 5.3.2 below.

ammonium nitrate.[86] The steel sector serves as particularly relevant example in this regard. According to the OECD, the environmental impact of the steel sector may be reduced in two manners: energy-efficient production of steel (short term) and low-carbon steel production (long term). As such, the OECD Steel Committee contributes to monitoring the environmental performance of the steel sector, particularly on account of the use of energy.[87] Energy is a major input in the price of steel production (contributing 20–40% of the total cost),[88] and therefore, energy prices impact the production cost of steel heavily.

Second, industries processing natural resources may equally be affected by the prices of the main raw material inputs. For example, the paper industry relies heavily on the key input of pulp (made from timber), accounting for up to 80% of the cost of raw materials.[89] The sector is under increased scrutiny for GHG emissions, environmental impact of the production process, struggles with land-right uses, and a high extent of illegal logging have been documented across the globe.[90] Where governments facilitate or subsidise domestic timber and pulp industries, the price of paper (the final product) will be affected heavily. Another example is the production of biodiesel is heavily reliant on the input of the raw material of soybeans, accounting for up to 75–80% of the cost of production.

Accordingly, when the production of goods benefit from cheap inputs in the form of electricity or raw materials, they may cause injurious effects on the market of the importing country. Importing countries may seek recourse to the ASCM rules to discipline this type of trade-distortive conduct. As the inputs—which make out a significant proportion of the cost of production—are made available domestically at prices below global market prices, it could be argued that these states grant an unfair advantage to their energy-intensive industries, which can be remedied via the anti-subsidy rules—if the legal requirements are fulfilled.

---

[86] Tietje et al. (2011), p. 1076.

[87] See OECD, Environmental performance of the steel sector, available at https://www.oecd.org/sti/ind/steel-environment-energy-efficiency.htm (last accessed 22 June 2023).

[88] World Steel Association, Fact sheet: Energy use in the steel industry, April 2019, available at https://www.worldsteel.org/en/dam/jcr:f07b864c-908e-4229-9f92-669f1c3abf4c/fact_energy_2019.pdf (last accessed 22 June 2023).

[89] See, for instance, Australian Dumping Committee, Report No. 341, A4 Copy paper – Brazil, China, Indonesia and Thailand. Australian Government, Department of Industry, Innovation and Science; Environmental Paper Network, The State of the Global Paper Industry – Shifting Seas: New Challenges and Opportunities for Forests, People and the Climate, 2018, p. 28.

[90] See Eliason and Fiorini (2020), p. 1.

5.3.2   Dual Pricing Schemes as Input Subsidies Under the ASCM

An anti-subsidy investigation generally targets end-products at the downstream level that have been exported into the jurisdiction of the investigating authority. In the case of dual pricing schemes, however, investigating authorities must consider both the upstream level (raw material or energy input) and the downstream level (end-product or good). Neither the WTO rules, nor WTO jurisprudence gives conclusive guidance to investigating authorities for the investigation of such situations of indirect subsidisation. The Appellate Body's jurisprudence did, however, hint in the direction that a subsidy determination must be made both at the level of the upstream and the downstream level.[91] The criteria under Art. 1 ASCM apply on both levels,[92] and may lead to specific legal issues in the investigations on input subsidies and dual pricing schemes.

This section focuses on the particularities of the downstream level investigation.[93] Particularly, this section outlines the financial contribution requirement (Sect. 5.3.2.1), the benefit and benefit pass-through analysis (Sect. 5.3.2.2), and the specificity requirement (Sect. 5.3.2.3). Moreover, it discusses possible grounds mandating countervailing measures: export contingency (Sect. 5.3.2.4) and adverse effects/serious prejudice (Sect. 5.3.2.5).

5.3.2.1   Financial Contribution (Art. 1.1(a) ASCM)

The first requirement of the ASCM is to prove the existence of a financial contribution by a government.[94] Two out of the four possible forms of financial contributions in Art. 1.1 ASCM may be relevant for input subsidy investigations, namely the provision of goods or services by the government and financial contributions through private bodies.

First, the provision of inputs of energy and raw materials may be qualified as government provision of goods and services in the sense of Art. 1.1(a)(1)(iii) ASCM. Excluding general infrastructure, this provision foresees that a government purchase or sale at below market prices can be considered a financial contribution. Such situation may occur in cases where governments directly provide energy inputs at preferential rates, or when the government depresses energy prices in such

---

[91] Appellate Body report, *United States – Final countervailing Duty Determination with Respect to Certain Softwood Lumber from Canada*, WT/DS257/AB/R, adopted 17 February 2004, para. 142.

[92] See Sect. 3.2.2.2 above.

[93] General environmental considerations that may arise in the upstream level investigation have been discussed in the previous section. See Sect. 5.2 above.

[94] Art. 1 ASCM.

a way that some energy-intensive industries are *de facto* provided with a financial contribution.[95]

Second, given that dual pricing schemes are frequently carried out through SOEs, the debate on whether SOEs can be captured as the subsidy-granting body arises. On the one hand, contributions from certain SOEs may be excluded from the definition of a subsidy. The Appellate Body provided that a public body within the meaning of Art. 1.1(a)(1) ASCM must be an entity that "possesses, exercises or is vested with governmental authority."[96] Mere ownership and control by the government are not sufficient to constitute a public body.[97] On the other hand, Art. 1.1(a)(iv) ASCM may capture other SOEs via the notion of provision of a financial contribution through a funding mechanism or a private body. However, as clarified by the Panel in *US – Export Restraints*, Art. 1.1(a)(1)(iv) ASCM requires investigating authorities to prove that a private body is executing a particular government policy.[98] The mere regulation of energy price ceilings does not suffice.[99] Although this may put an extra link in the investigated chain of companies, namely a private body between the government entity and the downstream subsidy recipient, this must not affect the relevance of the subsidy pass-through test as such.[100]

In addition, Art. 1 ASCM also includes "any form of income or price support" as a subsidy, but practice on this aspect is so scarce that its relevance to energy dual pricing is uncertain.[101]

5.3.2.2 Benefit (Art. 1.1(b) ASCM)

5.3.2.2.1   Indirect Subsidies Under the ASCM

Under the 'standard' situation of subsidisation, a governmental entity or a public body directly grants a financial contribution to an enterprise or industry, which accordingly receives a benefit.[102] The ASCM, however, also foresees the possibility to countervail indirect subsidies under Art. VI:3 GATT and Art. 10, fn. 36

---

[95] Pogoretskyy (2011), p. 201.

[96] Appellate Body report, *United States – Definitive Anti-Dumping and Countervailing Duties on Certain Products from China*, WT/DS379/AB/R, adopted 25 March 2011, para. 317–318.

[97] For a discussion, see Zhou et al. (2019), pp. 1017–1019; Chiang (2018), p. 873; Wu (2016), pp. 301–305; Ding (2014), pp. 173–174; Cartland et al. (2012), p. 1002. See also Van Vaerenbergh (2019), pp. 9 ff.

[98] Panel report, *United States – Measures Treating Export Restraints as Subsidies*, WT/DS194/R, adopted 23 August 2001, para. 8.28.

[99] Appellate Body report, *United States – Countervailing Duty Investigation on Dynamic Random Access Memory Semiconductors (DRAMS) from Korea*, WT/DS296/AB/R, adopted 20 July 2005, para. 108.

[100] Shadikhodjaev (2012), p. 638.

[101] Pogoretskyy (2011), p. 202. See also Sect. 5.2.2.1 above.

[102] Art. 1 ASCM.

ASCM. The footnote clarifies that a countervailing duty shall be understood to mean a levy to offset any subsidy bestowed directly or indirectly upon the manufacture, production, or export of any merchandise.[103] The Appellate Body, in *US – Softwood Lumber IV* quoted this provision as one of the relevant legal bases for dealing with subsidised inputs.[104]

One form of indirect subsidisation is included in the definition of a subsidy: Art. 1.1(a)(iv) ASCM addressed subsidies which are provided through payments in a funding mechanism or through entrustment or direction of a private body to grant financial contributions (see Fig. 5.1). Other forms of indirect subsidies include situations where an upstream producer sells an input to a downstream producer which therefore also received the benefit occurring through the upstream subsidy, cases where a privatisation takes place,[105] or situations—outside the CVD context—where a serious prejudice claim under Art. 5 ASCM is raised.[106] In the context of dual pricing, the effect of the provision of subsidised inputs on downstream products is targeted.

Indirect subsidisation cases affect the benefit analysis for investigating authorities. In cases of indirect subsidisation through raw material provision, in addition to the existence of the benefit, investigating authorities must prove that the benefit received by the upstream producer has "passed-through" to the downstream producer.[107] This means an additional step for investigating authorities to determine whether and to what extent a subsidy has passed-through from the upstream to the downstream level.

The legal requirements for the subsidy pass-through test have been developed in the jurisprudence of the Appellate Body. The relevant case law has dealt with, for instance, cases concerning Canadian subsidies for live swine indirectly subsidising Canadian pork,[108] subsidies for harvesting timber as input subsidy for softwood

---

[103] Art. 10 ASCM, fn. 36 (emphasis added).

[104] Appellate Body report, *United States – Final Countervailing Duty Determination with Respect to Certain Softwood Lumber from Canada*, WT/DS257/AB/R, adopted 17 February 2004, para. 140–141.

[105] In such case, a subsidy to a formerly related company may have been passed through to a now independent company. For an analysis, see Diamond (2008). See Appellate Body report, *United States – Imposition of Countervailing Duties on Certain Hot-Rolled Lead and Bismuth Carbon Steel Products Originating in the United Kingdom*, WT/DS138/AB/R, adopted 7 June 2000; Appellate Body report, *United States – Countervailing Measures Concerning Certain Products from the European Communities*, WT/DS212/AB/R, adopted 8 January 2003.

[106] For an analysis, see Müller (2017), pp. 268–269. See also the dispute *United States – Subsidies on Upland Cotton*, WT/DS267.

[107] Adamantopoulos (2008b), Art. VI GATT, para. 24.

[108] GATT Panel report, *United States – Countervailing Duties on Fresh, Chilled and Frozen Pork from Canada*, DS7/R, adopted 11 July 1991, BISD 38S/30, para. 4.1–4.10.

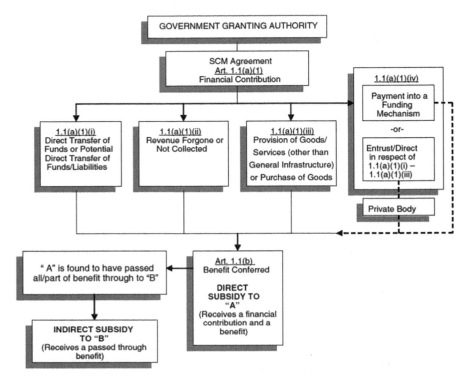

Fig. 5.1 Subsidy pass-through. Source: WTO Negotiating Group on Rules, Benefit Pass-Through, Communication from Canada, TN/RL/GEN/7, 14 July 2004

lumber,[109] and subsidised Mexican olives affecting olive oil prices.[110] In *US – ADD and CVD (China)*, China challenged CVD measures imposed by the US on steel products, pipes and tubes, and tyres bought by downstream producers from SOEs through private trading companies.[111] As such, the issue of input dumping is prevalent in both cases of raw material distortions as well as energy-related dual pricing schemes.

---

[109] Panel report, *United States – Final Countervailing Duty Determination with Respect to Certain Softwood Lumber from Canada*, WT/DS257/R, adopted 17 February 2004, para. 7.91 and 7.99; Appellate Body report, *United States – Final Countervailing Duty Determination with Respect to Certain Softwood Lumber from Canada*, WT/DS257/AB/R, adopted 17 February 2004, para. 140–141.

[110] Panel report, *Mexico – Definitive Countervailing Measures on Olive Oil from the European Communities*, WT/DS341/R, adopted 21 October 2008, para. 7.145–7.169.

[111] Appellate Body Report, *United States – Definitive Anti-Dumping and Countervailing Duties on Certain Products from China*, WT/DS379/AB/R, adopted 25 March 2011, para. 277–359.

5.3.2.2.2 Benefit and Benefit Pass-Through (Art. 1.1(b) ASCM)

Anti-subsidy investigations of indirect subsidisation in terms of cheap energy or raw material inputs face a significant hurdle in the benefit and benefit pass-through analysis. A subsidy benefit pass-through analysis is carried out, in case of input subsidies, where a subsidy is given to a producer of an input which is subsequently used in the downstream production of another product.[112] The analysis of the benefit pass-through logically follows the determination whether the direct recipient of a financial contribution itself has received a benefit, which is then passed through.[113] As such, investigating authorities must investigate the fulfilment of the subsidy criteria equally for the upstream and the downstream producer. The standard order of assessment is first the upstream benefit and then the downstream benefit.[114] Arguing otherwise may lead to an unwanted conclusion that an inexistent financial contribution conferring a benefit at the upstream level was passed through to the downstream level. The benefit analysis on the upstream level is a standard benefit analysis, which has been dealt with above.[115]

On the downstream level, investigating authorities confronted with dual pricing schemes in anti-subsidy investigations must examine the benefit pass-through. In practical terms, the pass-through test comprises of two separate phases: first, *whether* and second, t*o what extent* the benefit has passed through (two-step analysis).[116] This follows from Art. 19.1 ASCM, which allows the imposition of a CVD when investigating authorities determined the existence and the amount of subsidy.

Subsidised inputs cannot automatically be considered to confer a benefit to downstream producers of end-products. In a first step, domestic authorities carry out a pass-through examination of the benefit, especially for unrelated producers, whether arm's-length prices have been paid.[117] DSB jurisprudence confirms that carrying out a pass-through analysis is necessary only if (1) the input producer and the downstream producer are unrelated (*i.e.* transactions take place at arm's length), and (2) only the downstream product is covered by the CVD investigation.[118] This established the relevant determinations to be made by the investigating authority. First, transactions at arm's length between the recipient of the subsidy and the recipient of the benefit are a prerequisite for the pass-through test. What constitutes an

---

[112] *Müller* (2017), pp. 143 and 373 ff.

[113] Panel report, *United States – Definitive Anti-Dumping and Countervailing Duties on Certain Products from China*, WT/DS379/R, adopted 25 March 2011, para. 12.1–12.4 and 12.36.

[114] Shadikhodjaev (2012), p. 639.

[115] See Sect. 5.2.2.2 above.

[116] Appellate Body report, *United States – Final Countervailing Duty Determination with Respect to Certain Softwood Lumber from Canada*, WT/DS257/AB/R, adopted 17 February 2004, para 140.

[117] Panel report, *United States – Preliminary Determinations with Respect to Certain Softwood Lumber from Canada*, WT/DS236/R, adopted 1 November 2002, para. 7.71–7.74.

[118] Panel report, *United States – Final Dumping Determination on Softwood Lumber from Canada*, WT/DS264/R, adopted 31 August 2004, para. 388.

arm's length transaction is controversial in the case law.[119] Sales between unrelated parties necessitate a pass-through analysis, irrespective of whether such sales were at arm's length or not.[120] Second, by way of exception, when both the upstream and the downstream producer are subject to the same CVD investigation, no pass-through test must be carried out.

Not only must the investigating authority analyse whether the benefit is passed through entirely or only partially, it must also secure quantification of the benefit on the level of the downstream producer. Therefore, in a second step, the investigating authority assesses whether the benefit has passed through entirely or only to a specific amount.[121]

A pass-through analysis can also have a specificity dimension when the subsidised (energy) input is widely available on the market. In such cases, downstream manufacturers will likely not be considered 'certain enterprises' in the sense of Art. 2 ASCM.[122]

5.3.2.3   Specificity (Art. 2 ASCM)

Only subsidies that are 'specific' can be subject to the unilateral and multilateral actions. After establishing the existence of a financial contribution and a benefit that is passed through to the downstream level, investigating authorities shall determine that the input subsidy is specific in the sense of Art. 2 ASCM.[123] That is, only if the dual pricing schemes are not considered prohibited subsidies, for which the specificity is presumed.[124] In energy-intensive goods, dual pricing of energy and raw material inputs may lead to below-cost prices upon exportation. It does not appear, however, that the mere supply of low-priced energy to domestic energy-intensive industries (regardless export performance) constitutes a prohibited export subsidy, not even *de facto*.[125]

In case of indirect subsidies, the question arises at which level specificity must be determined. WTO law is silent in this regard. Some scholars argue that specificity at the downstream level should be required.[126] Pointing to the fact that a specific subsidy to for instance power generators on the upstream level may be passed on to a wide range of energy-intensive industries, others argue that second level specificity is not necessary, especially given the test of pass-through of the benefit and

---

[119] See Shadikhodjaev (2012), pp. 634–636.

[120] Panel report, *United States – Final Dumping Determination on Softwood Lumber from Canada*, Recourse by Canada to Art. 21.5 of the DSU, WT/DS257/RW, adopted 20 December 2005, para. 4.58–4.82 and 4.88.

[121] See Sect. 5.4 below.

[122] Müller (2017), p. 378. See Sect. 5.3.2.3 below.

[123] See also Sect. 5.2.2.3 above.

[124] Art. 2.3 ASCM. See also Sect. 5.3.2.4 below.

[125] Pogoretskyy (2011), p. 209.

[126] Selivanova (2008), p. 143.

arm's-length of the transactions in the benefit analysis effectively replace such specificity necessity on the downstream level.[127] If specificity must be determined on both the upstream and the downstream level and given that both analyses would not affect one another, reasons of efficiency demand the determination on the downstream level to be addressed first.[128]

As set out above, dual pricing schemes are in principle available to all producers to benefit from and would therefore generally not be considered specific subsidies to certain enterprises in the sense of Art. 2 ASCM.[129] In practice, the focus would lie on the determination whether certain enterprises had *de facto* preferential access to the financial contribution.[130] It could be argued that specificity exists as a subsidy for the energy industry or industries that have an intensive input of energy and are heavily reliant on the input of energy (e.g. fertilizer producers).[131] Especially in countries where only one or a few predominant users of an energy resource is present, this could amount to an argumentation that a subsidy was available in "disproportionately large amounts" to these industries. However, at this junction, a differentiation must be made between energy inputs and inputs of raw materials. The Panel in *US – Softwood Lumber IV* held that, for energy inputs (oil, gas, but also water, for instance), the input is available to an indefinite number of industries, and therefore specificity of an input subsidy cannot simply be assumed.[132] Dual pricing schemes for gas and other energy inputs would therefore likely fail the specificity analysis before a DSB Panel.[133] Whether, in the latter case, inputs of specific raw materials (e.g. wood) may be considered specific, was not answered conclusively by the Panel. In any case, it would not be automatic.

Finally, it merits mention that a separate specificity test on the level of the downstream product can be avoided when the benefit relates to the same industrial sector on both levels.[134]

---

[127] Pogoretskyy (2011), p. 214.

[128] Shadikhodjaev (2012), p. 642.

[129] Panel report, *China – Countervailing and Anti-Dumping Duties on Grain-Oriented Flat-Rolled Electrical Steel from the United States*, WT/DS414/R, adopted 16 November 2012, para. 7.135.

[130] Art. 2.1(c) ASCM.

[131] Selivanova (2007), pp. 29–30.

[132] Panel report, *United States – Final Dumping Determination on Softwood Lumber from Canada*, WT/DS264/R, adopted 31 August 2004, para. 7.116.

[133] Selivanova (2007), p. 30.

[134] Shadikhodjaev (2012), p. 640. See, for instance, Panel report, *United States – Final Dumping Determination on Softwood Lumber from Canada*, WT/DS264/R, adopted 31 August 2004, para. 7.106–7.125; Panel report, *United States – Measures Affecting Trade in Large Civil Aircraft – Second Complaint*, WT/DS353/R, adopted 31 March 2011, para. 7.196 and 7.205.

5.3.2.4 Export Contingency (Art. 3 ASCM)

Art. 3.1(a) ASCM establishes a prohibition of subsidies contingent in law or in fact upon export performance. Such subsidies are deemed to be specific and consequently fulfil the requirement of countervailability under the ASCM.[135] Energy dual pricing schemes are unlikely to fall under the definition of *de jure* prohibited subsidies but could in some circumstances constitute *de facto* export subsidies.[136] This standard is met when the granting of a subsidy is tied to actual or anticipated exportation or export earnings.[137] The Panel in *Australia – Automotive* observed that the facts together must demonstrate that the grant or maintenance of a subsidy is conditioned upon actual or anticipated exportation earnings and cannot be deemed to be fulfilled merely because the enterprise receiving the subsidy exports.[138] The Appellate Body specified that although exportation by the enterprise receiving the subsidy cannot constitute the sole consideration, but may be taken into account as a relevant fact.[139] Based on this reading, the mere supply of a two-tiered pricing scheme for energy or raw material inputs does not constitute a *de facto* export subsidy.

5.3.2.5 Adverse Effects and Serious Prejudice (Art. 5–6 ASCM)

Art. 5(c) ASCM prescribes that "serious prejudice" to the interests of other WTO Members must be proven for a subsidy to be actionable.[140] It relates to negative effects on another Member's trade interests regarding a particular product.[141] Serious prejudice is defined in Art. 6 ASCM: loss of import or export volume or market share, adverse price effects, or both, in the relevant market is targeted. In theory, energy dual pricing schemes may trigger any of the adverse effects foreseen in Art. 5 ASCM.[142] Accordingly, this criterion would be fulfilled for the imposition of CVDs on imports from low-standard countries.

---

[135] Art. 2.3 ADA.

[136] Pogoretskyy (2011), p. 208.

[137] See Art. 3 ASCM, fn. 4.

[138] Panel report, *Australia – Subsidies Provided to Producers and Exporters of Automotive Leather*, WT/DS126/R, adopted 16 June 1999, para. 9.57.

[139] Appellate Body report, *Canada – Measures Affecting the Export of Civilian Aircraft*, WT/DS70/AB/R, adopted 20 August 1999, para. 166.

[140] See Sect. 5.2.2.4 above.

[141] Panel report, *Korea – Measures Affecting Trade in Commercial Vessels*, WT/DS273/R, adopted 11 April 2005.

[142] Pogoretskyy (2011), p. 210.

5.3.3 Strengthening WTO Subsidy Disciplines for Dual Pricing

Although anti-subsidy rules may capture some forms of dual pricing as indirect subsidies, other environmentally harmful dual pricing schemes fall outside the ambit of the ASCM. Improving disciplines for dual pricing schemes under the CVD rules can take the form of multilateral negotiations (Sect. 5.3.3.1) as well as bilateral initiatives (Sect. 5.3.3.2).

5.3.3.1 Amendments to the ASCM

Discussions on dual pricing are far from new in the framework of the WTO. It was discussed already in the GATT 1947 era that the sale of raw materials in domestic markets below export prices could be a potential target for trade remedy duties.[143] Since the Tokyo Round, taking place in the verge of the oil crises of the 1970s, discussion on tackling dual pricing through GATT/WTO disciplines have been ongoing. Energy-endowed states have resisted the inclusion of legally binding rules on trade over natural resources, both under the GATT as well as under the ASCM.[144] The issue was addressed and discussed again in the Uruguay Round, but further clarification and improvement of rules and remedies in the area are further warranted.[145] The close link between preferential natural resource pricing and considerations of state sovereignty, however, make WTO negotiations a sensitive and delicate undertaking.[146]

Regulating input subsidies would grant investigating authorities a secure remedy against environmentally impactful energy or raw material dual pricing schemes. For instance, input subsidies may be considered as an addition to the list of prohibited subsidies in Art. 3 ASCM.[147] Since this would render input subsidies arising out of dual pricing schemes automatically actionable under the ASCM, investigating authorities do not have to prove specificity anymore.[148] In 2018, the US-EU-Japan trilateral group proposed to qualify subsidies that lower input prices domestically in comparison to prices of the same goods when destined for export as prohibited subsidies because of the difficulties in proving their actionable nature.[149] Their harmful

---

[143] Wüstenberg (2019), p. 410.

[144] Marhold (2017), p. 6.

[145] *Ibid.*

[146] See, for instance, Negotiating Group on Rules, Subsidies Disciplines Requiring Clarification and Improvement, Communication from the United States, TN/RL/W/78, 19 March 2003.

[147] See, for instance, Marhold (2017), p. 16; Espa and Rolland (2015), p. 11. See also, for instance, Expanding the Prohibited "Red Light" Subsidy Category, Proposal by the United States, WTO/RL/GEN/94, 16 January 2006; Negotiating Group on Rules, Subsidies, Submission of the European Communities, WTO/TN/RL/GEN/135, 24 April 2006.

[148] See Art. 2.3 ASCM.

[149] Joint Statement on Trilateral Meeting of the Trade Ministers of the United States, Japan, and the European Union, 31 May 2018, available at https://ustr.gov/about-us/policy-offices/press-office/

effect would justify a reversal of the burden of proof.[150] Proposals to expand Art. 3.1 ASCM have not succeeded in the past, but an explicit link between input subsidies and the achievement of SDG goals may provide a good momentum for change.[151] This is furthermore evidenced by the negotiations on a multilateral fisheries subsidies agreement, which is driven by environmental concerns and an explicit call in the SDGs for the WTO to take action.[152] These proposals have not gained general consensus among WTO Members.

Furthermore, an amendment of Art. 1 or 14 ASCM to provide specific rules on how to calculate the amount of subsidy or benefit passed through may also be considered. This would include codified rules for the calculation of input subsidies. The WTO Negotiation Group on Rules presented a proposal for a new Art. 14.2 ASCM, detailing out the market benchmark for input subsidy calculation. Analysing this proposal, *Shadikhojaev* suggested to redraft this proposal as a footnote in Art. 1.1(b) ASCM, rather than a new Art. 14.2 ASCM.[153]

> [W]here a subsidy is granted in respect of an input used to produce the product under consideration, and the producer of the product under consideration is <u>not the same entity as</u> the producer of the input, no benefit from the subsidy in respect of the input shall be attributed to the product under consideration unless a determination has been made that, <u>as a result of this subsidy</u>, the producer of the product under consideration obtained the input on terms more favourable than otherwise would have been commercially available to that producer in the market.[154]

The original proposal could not find consensus amongst WTO Members and was therefore not adopted.

Despite the unsuccessful attempts to establish multilateral binding rules on input dumping, dual pricing schemes have been addressed in accession negotiations to the WTO. The EU tabled the issue in the accession negotiations with Saudi Arabia and Russia.[155] In the former case, Saudi Arabia confirmed that prices for petroleum and natural gas would not vary depending on whether the users were Saudi or foreign owned.[156] In the latter case, Russia even tied some of its export duties on energy products apart from making commitments on dual pricing schemes.[157] Although not entirely successful, these examples illustrate that dual pricing schemes are a topic that can be subject to negotiation in the WTO framework, which will even become

---

press-releases/2018/may/joint-statement-trilateral-meeting (last accessed 22 June 2023).

[150] Li and Tu (2020), pp. 863–864.

[151] Marhold (2017), p. 16.

[152] See Sect. 8.3.2.1 below.

[153] Shadikhodjaev (2012), p. 645.

[154] *Ibid* (emphasis added).

[155] Panel report, *United States – Final Dumping Determination on Softwood Lumber from Canada*, WT/DS264/R, adopted 31 August 2004, para. 577.

[156] Report from the Working Party on the Accession of the Kingdom of Saudi Arabia to the World Trade Organization, WT/ACCC/SAU/61, 1 November 2005, para. 28.

[157] Report of the Working Party on the Accession of the Russian Federation to the World Trade Organization, WT/ACC/RUS/70, 17 November 2011, para. 120; Marhold (2017), p. 7.

a more expanded topic during the process of accession of a number of acceding countries which are energy-exporting.[158] What can be agreed upon can also be taken from recent practice on energy and raw material dual pricing schemes in the context of bilateral negotiations.

5.3.3.2   Regional Trade Agreements

Dual pricing schemes may also be part of negotiations of bilateral or regional trade agreements. For instance, the issue was part of the (meanwhile halted) TTIP negotiations. The EU had included a clause preventing Parties from adopting or maintaining higher prices for exports of goods than prices charged for the same goods on the domestic market.[159] In the same vein, the EU had included a "GATT-plus" prohibition on dual pricing in the EU-Ukraine Association Agreement.[160] Although such provisions do not link dual pricing explicitly to (indirect) subsidies, at the very least, this proves that inclusion of dual pricing provisions is possible between willing trade partners.[161]

5.4   Benefit Calculation and Environmental Costs of Production

Besides the option to qualify low environmental standards or dual pricing schemes as countervailable subsidies, the ASCM rules on benefit calculation could also be used to capture the cost advantage of not having to adhere to environmental regulations. In the case of such implicit subsidies, the amount of subsidy—and therefore potentially the amount of CVD—would equal the value of the cost savings resulting from the "lax" environmental standards or under-priced resources.[162] This section outlines the applicable law and jurisprudence on calculating the amount of benefit under Art. 14 ASCM (Sect. 5.4.1) and the China-specific rules contained in Sect. 15(b) CAP (Sect. 5.4.2), and outlines potential avenues to allow for a more relaxed approach to deal with distorted costs and prices under the applicable legal framework (Sect. 5.4.3).

---

[158] See, for instance, Algeria, Azerbaijan, Iran, Iraq, Libya, and Sudan are all energy-producing and -exporting countries currently in the process of acceding to the WTO.

[159] TTIP, Art. XXX (Export Pricing).

[160] Art. 270(1) EU-Ukraine AA.

[161] Marhold (2017), p. 18.

[162] Patterson (1992), p. 106.

5.4.1 ASCM Rules on Benefit Calculation (Art. 14 ASCM)

Under WTO law, the amount of subsidy is calculated in terms of benefit conferred to the recipient, which occurs generally by comparing the export price with an appropriate benchmark. The market of the exporting Member is the appropriate benchmark for determining the existence and the amount of benefit. Investigation authorities may encounter two different scenarios: reliance on the market benchmark (Sect. 5.4.1.1) and reliance on alternative, in-country benchmarks (Sect. 5.4.1.2).

5.4.1.1   Market Benchmarks in the Country of Production

The default situation under the ASCM is reliance on market benchmarks in the country of production. The benefit is calculated by comparing the export price with the market benchmark price in the country of production. The Appellate Body has confirmed that to determine whether a financial contribution and a benefit exist, a comparison between the market price and the amount of government contribution must be carried out.[163] Already in *Canada – Aircraft*, the Panel held that "the only logical basis for determining the position the recipient would have been in absent the financial contribution is the market."[164]

Accordingly, when the market benchmark includes a full internalisation of environmental costs of production, then the benefit will be larger, and the CVD may be considered to internalise environmental costs. Figure 5.2 illustrates how environmental costs can be considered on both the price of the goods on the importing market, as well as on in the price of the like product destined for sale or consumption in the export market. This would result in a higher amount of subsidy and consequently a higher CVD duty, which accounts for environmental costs of production.

However, such argument would require that a perfect, undistorted market benchmark be used where the market forces are deemed to have realised a cost internalisation of the environmental damages into the price of the traded goods. In relation to government distortions to prices, however, the question is whether the benchmark comparator is the market as it is or a hypothetical market, free of any distortion created by the financial contribution at issue?[165] In other words, do investigating authorities identify the price of the benefit in the existing market in the country at issue, or those in an alternative 'undistorted' market?[166] The ASCM is based on the former interpretation: Investigating authorities do not search for the perfect market

---

[163] Crowley and Hillman (2018), p. 206.

[164] Panel report, *Canada – Measures Affecting the Export of Civilian Aircraft*, WT/DS70/R, adopted 20 August 1999, para. 9.112.

[165] Zheng (2010), pp. 21 ff.

[166] Beaulieu and Prévost (2020), p. 222.

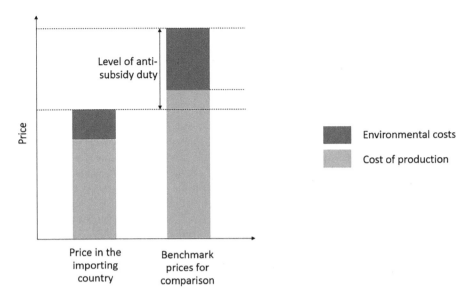

Fig. 5.2 Including environmental costs in amount of subsidy calculations. Source: Author's own creation

benchmark. *Zheng* notes, in that regard, that a perfect, undistorted market as the benchmark would be uncontroversial from an economic theoretical point of view because undistorted markets allocate resources efficiently and subsidies can be measured through deviations.[167] According to free market theory, such hypothetical undistorted market benchmarks would fully internalise the environmental costs. Nonetheless, the ASCM disciplines are based on the market benchmark as-is.

According to Art. 14 ASCM, investigating authorities may develop any method of calculation of the amount of subsidy in terms of the benefit conferred to the recipient of the subsidy.[168] Generally, the amount of benefit in CVD investigations is calculated in terms of commercial benchmarks.[169] Comparable private transactions on the market are the relevant benchmark for investigating authorities to compare the government financial contribution to.[170] The Appellate Body in *US – Carbon Steel (India)*, in furtherance of the general principle of market orientation underlying Art. 14 ASCM, has defined 'market' and 'prevailing market conditions' as the

---

[167] Zheng (2010), p. 36.

[168] See Sect. 3.2.3.2.2 above.

[169] Appellate Body report, *European Communities – Imposition of Countervailing Duties on Certain Hot-Rolled Lead and Bismuth Carbon Steel Products Originating in the United Kingdom*, WT/DS138/AB/R, adopted 7 June 2000, para. 57–74; Panel report, *Brazil – Export Financing Programme for Aircraft – Second Recourse to Art. 21.5 DSU by Canada*, WT/DS46/RW2, adopted 23 August 2001, para. 5.29.

[170] Durling (2008), Art. 14 SCMA, para. 9.

area of economic activity in which buyers and sellers come together and the forces of supply and demand interact to determine prices.[171] As such, under the anti-subsidy rules, the comparison of the price of allegedly subsidised goods in the export markets against the market benchmarks in the country of production.

The subparagraphs of Art. 14 ASCM include principles for benefit calculation for four types of subsidies: government provision of equity capital, loans by a government, loan guarantees by a government, and provision of goods or services or purchase of goods by a government. For these types of financial contributions, no benefit is conferred, unless granted under conditions that deviate from market practices. With regard to equity capital, the provision sets the benchmark as "the usual investment practice (including for the provision of risk capital) of private investors"; for loans, the comparable commercial loan which the firm could actually obtain on the market"; for loan guarantees, the "comparable commercial loan absent the government guarantee"; and for provision of goods, "adequate remuneration" to be determined "in relation to prevailing market conditions [...] (including price, quality, availability, marketability, transportation and other conditions of purchase or sale)."[172] Turning to the text of Art. 14(d) ASCM specifically, the provision lists exemplary factors that shall be considered in the analysis of the prevailing market conditions, which does not include regulatory aspects under which environmental standards could be considered.

If these benchmark prices existing of, or at least considering, the environmental protection standards, the amount of CVD may reflect an internalisation of environmental costs in accordance with the polluter-pays principle. Broadly speaking, when market benchmarks will be used, the comparison does not include environmental costs in the market comparator.

5.4.1.2   Government Distortions, Alternative Benchmarks and Environmental Cost Internalisation

The market benchmark may not be an appropriate standard for comparison, especially in case of government distorted prices. Therefore, alternative, out-of-country benchmarks may be more relevant to be used in CVD calculations. When relying on alternative benchmarks, investigating authorities take charge of determining the benchmark and could theoretically have more freedom to consider environmental regulation and calculate environmental costs in the benchmark price. However, significant limitations exist both related to the situations in which market benchmarks may be disregarded, as well as the various alternative methods to determine the benchmarks. These make it unlikely domestic authorities could introduce significant environmental costs in the benchmark prices.

---

[171] Appellate Body report, *United States – Countervailing Measures on Certain Hot-Rolled Carbon Steel Flat Products from* India, WT/DS436/AB/R, adopted 19 December 2019, para. 4.150.
[172] Art. 14(a)-(d) ASCM.

The government is the sole or predominant player on the market in certain energy and natural resources markets, where government distortions are frequently linked to environmental regulation—particularly in non-market economies but also in many market economies. The definition of the market and prevailing market conditions under Art. 14 ASCM do not achieve clarity in such cases of sole or predominant government ownership.[173] According to the 'circularity problem', "[a]s the government is the sole, or predominant, supplier of a good, to compare the remuneration for the good to the market price prevailing in the country would be circular, since the market price would be the price of the good charged by the sole or predominant provider – the government."[174] Both in case the government is the sole player on the market and in case the government sets prices because of its market power, a comparison between the government price and the market price is useless.

Hence, to avoid this circularity problem, investigating authorities have relied, for benefit comparisons, on alternative benchmark prices. The Appellate Body allows the use of surrogate market prices for inputs in CVD investigations in cases where government intervention distorts the relevant market.[175] In *US – Softwood Lumber IV*, the Appellate Body accepted the possibility of deviation from domestic prices in relation to subsidies in the form of provision of goods or services or purchased of goods by a government in the sense of Art. 14(d) ASCM.[176] In subsequent reports, this approach was confirmed and extended. In *US – ADD and CVD (China)*, for example, the Appellate Body decided—and thus confirmed the Panel—that Art. 14(b) ASCM also includes the possibility to disregard interest rates in China as benchmarks for loans from state-owned banks in the sense of Art. 14(b) ASCM.[177] Although the Appellate Body already hinted in the direction that similar reasoning may apply to the other paragraphs of Art. 14 ASCM,[178] no definitive decisions on the other paragraphs have been delivered. There may be sufficient links between loans and loan guarantees to rely on the jurisprudence on Art. 14(b) ASCM in relation to loan guarantees.[179] Therefore, in all subparagraphs of Art. 14 ASCM, reliance on alternative benchmarks could be accepted.

Environmental costs can be included in alternative benchmarks since they have as point of view the cost structures outside the country under investigation. This discussion of market benchmarking in government monopolies has mostly been developed in the jurisprudence under Art. 14(d) ASCM. Importantly, the Appellate

---

[173] Qin (2018), p. 582.

[174] Beaulieu and Prévost (2020), p. 221.

[175] See Bungenberg and Van Vaerenbergh (2020), p. 280.

[176] Appellate Body report, *United States – Final Countervailing Duty Determination with Respect to Certain Softwood Lumber from Canada*, WT/DS257/AB/R, adopted 17 February 2004, para. 167–168.

[177] Appellate Body report, *United States – Definitive Anti-Dumping and Countervailing Duties on Certain Products from China*, WT/DS379/AB/R, adopted 25 March 2011, para. 446 and 483 ff.

[178] *Ibid*, para. 10.122.

[179] Panel report, *Canada – Export Credits and Loan Guarantees for Regional Aircraft*, WT/DS222/R, adopted 19 February 2002, para. 7.345.

Body in *US – Softwood Lumber IV* held that when the government is the predominant supplier in a country, domestic prices are likely to be distorted as private suppliers will align their prices with those of the government, justifying reliance on out-of-country benchmarks.[180] The Appellate Body seemed to have fundamentally changed that stance in *US – Carbon Steel (India)*, where it held that government prices may be market-determined and should therefore not be *ipso facto* excluded for the determination of market benchmarks, even if the prices were set in the pursuit of public policy objectives rather than profit maximalisation.[181] It noted that a price may be relied upon as a benchmark under Art. 14(d) ASCM if it is a market-determined price reflecting prevailing market conditions in the country of provision.[182] Further jurisprudence in for instance *US – Countervailing Measures (China)* confirmed that government-set prices are not necessarily distorted,[183] and that "the selection of a benchmark for the purposes of Article 14(d) cannot, at the outset, exclude consideration of in-country prices from any particular source, including government-related prices other than the financial contribution at issue."[184] In *US – Countervailing Measures (21.5 – China)*, the Appellate Body recalled and confirmed its jurisprudence, and outlined the obligations of the investigating authorities to investigate whether prices are market-determined.[185] Only as such, investigating authorities can provide sufficient explanation as to how prices have been distorted as a result from government intervention in the market.[186] Most recently, in *US – Coated Paper (Indonesia)*, after examining the previous case law, the Panel recognised that predominant government ownership is not sufficient in itself to justify not using in-country prices for the 'benefit' determination.[187] Finally, the Panel in *US – Softwood Lumber VII* held that adjustments are not only not preferred when relying on external proxies, but also not in case of in-country prices under different prevailing market conditions.[188] Accordingly, the Panel considered a regionality requirement before market before external sources to be used, illustrating the strong tendency in jurisprudence to stay as close to the market conditions as possible.

---

[180] Appellate Body report, *United States – Final Countervailing Duty Determination with respect to certain Softwood Lumber from Canada*, WT/DS257/AB/R, adopted 17 February 2004, para. 100–102.

[181] Appellate Body report, *United States – Countervailing Measures on Certain Hot-Rolled Carbon Steel Flat Products from India*, WT/DS436/AB/R, adopted 19 December 2014, para. 4.170.

[182] *Ibid*.

[183] Appellate Body report, *United States – Countervailing Duty Measures on Certain Products from China*, WT/DS437/AB/R, adopted 16 January 2015, para. 4.46.

[184] *Ibid*, para. 4.64.

[185] Appellate Body report, *United States – Countervailing Duty Measures on Certain Products from China (Article 21.5 – China)*, WT/DS437/AB/RW, adopted 15 August 2019, para. 5.155.

[186] *Ibid*, para. 4.160–5.161.

[187] Panel report, *United States – Anti-Dumping and Countervailing Measures on Certain Coated Paper from Indonesia*, WT/DS491/R, adopted 22 January 2018.

[188] Panel report, *United States – Countervailing Measures on Softwood Lumber from Canada*, WT/DS533/R, circulated 24 August 2020, para. 7.28.

As such, when there is no free marketplace benchmark available, prices will be determined based on a proxy third-country benchmark,[189] where environmental costs may play a role in case they refer to out-of-country costs and prices. Certain calculation methods make use of purely external prices.[190] The former is accepted by the Appellate Body in *US – Softwood Lumber IV*, where the Appellate Body accepted reliance on out-of-country benchmarks for the determination of the adequate remuneration under Art. 14(d) ASCM, if it is not possible to rely on similar goods sold by private suppliers in arm's length transactions in the country of provision.[191] The latter was merely considered by the Panel in *US – ADD and CVD (China)* as the approach from the US with respect to Chinese land, but has not been examined by the Appellate Body.[192] In case of dual pricing, the recipients of the inputs pay "less than adequate remuneration" for their gas, oil or other natural resources. Although the domestic market conditions in the country of production shall constitute the primary reference point, other benchmarks may be determined on a case-by-case basis, including for instance prices on world markets or constructed values based on production costs. When it comes to the first benchmark, world prices for energy and natural gas do not exist.[193] It is problematic that it is commonly accepted that there is no global price for natural gas or electricity that could serve as market benchmark.[194] In the latter case, investigating authorities shall endeavour to define a benchmark that corresponds to the prevailing market conditions in the country of provision of the alleged subsidy. As such, the chosen benchmark must reflect the prevailing market conditions in the country of provision of the alleged subsidy and must consider relevant comparative advantages existing in that country.[195]

However, as discussed above, regardless the alternative method chose by investigating authorities, out-of-country benchmarks do not replicate the price that would prevail in an undistorted market in the country under investigation, but should rather reflect the market as it is.[196] As a general principle, external benchmark prices must be close to the prevailing market conditions in the country and must be as in Art. 14(d) ASCM.[197] Thus, even when external benchmarks are used, the investigating authority must explain how the chosen benchmark relates to the prevailing market

---

[189] Benitah (2009), pp. 577–578.

[190] See Qin (2018), pp. 602–603.

[191] Appellate Body report, *United States – Final Countervailing Duty Determination with respect to certain Softwood Lumber from Canada*, WT/DS257/AB/R, adopted 17 February 2004, para. 90.

[192] *Ibid*, para. 167–168.

[193] IEA, Energy Prices and Taxes (2022); Energy Charter Secretariat Report (2021).

[194] Pogoretskyy (2011), p. 203.

[195] *Ibid*, p. 213.

[196] Zheng (2010), p. 40.

[197] Müller (2017), p. 463; see Appellate Body Report, *United States – Final Countervailing Duty Determination with Respect to Certain Softwood Lumber from Canada*, WT/DS257/AB/R, adopted 17 February 2004, para. 103 and 106.

conditions in the country of provision and how it reflects the price, quality, availability, marketability, transportation and other conditions of purchase or sale.

The approach of the Appellate Body to stay as close as possible to the market situation in the country of production, even when relying on alternative benchmarks must also be situated in the discussion on comparative advantages for developing countries stemming from their level of environmental regulation.[198] Provision of natural resources is the one of the most prominent examples, because it is the most basic type of comparative advantage in trade and often linked to public policies on environmental protection and sustainable development.[199] Reliance on out-of-country prices *without adjustment* has been criticised by *Qin* as depriving the subsidising country "of any comparative advantage it may have in the good in question," which does not accord with the aim of CVDs under ASCM.[200] Also the Appellate Body considers the protection of comparative advantages and does not envisage adjustments to nullify comparative advantages.[201] Hence, the tendency is to protect the standard-setting power in countries regulating natural resources and environmental and sustainability planning—even regarding the use of external benchmarks.

In sum, in all cases discussed, the orientation lies on the market of production, which may be considered not internalising environmental costs. The ASCM does not search for the undistorted market when determining the amount of benefit to the recipient of the financial contribution. Doing so would mean that investigating authorities have a very broad discretion to disregard in-country prices and rely on other benchmarks leading to inflated benefit determinations and higher CVDs.[202] This wide flexibility undermines the security and predictability that the disciplines on the use of CVDs are intended to provide.[203] This is particularly true in the case of natural resources where the government typically regulates the extraction and use of resources and thereby distort the market.[204] The jurisprudence displays clear tendencies that steer away from the possibility for investigating authorities to inflate market benchmarks and ultimately CVDs.

---

[198] See also Sects. 2.4.2.1 and 5.3.1 above.

[199] Qin (2018), p. 580.

[200] *Ibid*, p. 605.

[201] Appellate Body report, *United States – Final Countervailing Duty Determination with respect to certain Softwood Lumber from Canada*, WT/DS257/AB/R, adopted 17 February 2004, para. 108–109.

[202] Beaulieu and Prévost (2020), p. 223.

[203] *Ibid*.

[204] *Ibid*.

5.4.2 China-Specific Methodology (Sect. 15 CAP)

In relation to Chinese imports, the applicable legal framework in Art. 14 ASCM for countervailing measures is complemented by provisions of the CAP. As a *lex specialis* rule to Art. 14 of the ASCM,[205] Sect. 15(b) CAP allows reliance on benchmarks outside the Chinese market,[206] and foresees that:

> [...] if there are <u>special difficulties</u> [...], the importing WTO Member may then use methodologies for identifying and measuring the subsidy benefit which take into account the possibility that prevailing terms and conditions in China may not always be available as appropriate benchmarks. In applying such methodologies, where practicable, the importing WTO Member should <u>adjust</u> such prevailing terms and conditions before considering the <u>use of terms and conditions prevailing outside China</u>.[207]

This provision seems to loosely follow the patterns of the second *Ad* Note to Art. VI:1 GATT which allows for NME methodologies in anti-dumping investigations.[208] It provides a more favourable legal basis for the imposition of countervailing measures: if special difficulties exist in the application of Art. 14 ASCM, an importing Member may disregard the domestic prices and resort to out-of-country benchmarks.

This unexplored methodology may allow investigating authorities in countries making use of this provision to disregard domestic prices in favour of external benchmark prices which reflect environmental costs appropriately. The legal standard is that investigating authorities have "special difficulties" in the application of the sub-paragraphs of Art. 14 ASCM.[209] To date, no jurisprudence exists with regard to Sect. 15(b) CAP, so there is no definition of the term special difficulties.[210] Investigating authorities have a broad discretion in the definition of special difficulties. What is clear is that the evidentiary burden should be lower than for applying Art. 14 ASCM, which contains carefully crafted conditions interpreted by the Appellate Body.[211] Special difficulties may for instance be argued to include the existence of state-distorted markets in China. Proposals to make use of this latitude in language to include environmental costs may be considered. Such argument would then lie in the absence of a sufficient level of environmental regulation that ensures internalisation of environmental costs of production on the Chinese market.

In case such argument can be sustained, investigating authorities may resort to external benchmarks, which open the door to include environmental costs in the determination of the normal value. Two methodologies foreseen in Sect. 15(b) CAP

---

[205] In the first half-sentence, Sect. 15(b) CAP confirms the applicability of the SCM Agreement, and particularly Art. 14(a), 14(b), 14(c) and 14(d).

[206] Vietnam accepted the same commitment upon accession. See Report of the Working Party on the Accession of Viet Nam, WT/ACC/VNM/48, 27 October 2006, para. 255.

[207] Sect. 15(b) CAP (emphasis added).

[208] Qin (2004), pp. 891–892. See also Sect. 3.2.4 above.

[209] Bungenberg and Van Vaerenbergh (2020), pp. 282 ff.

[210] Müller (2018), pp. 77 ff.

[211] Zhou et al. (2019), pp. 1014–1017.

are (i) adjustments of the prevailing terms and conditions inside China, and (ii) external benchmarks may be used, *i.e.* terms and conditions prevailing outside China. The Appellate Body has already considered that normal or classical modes of adjustments are not always practicable and therefore not preferred.[212]

This country-specific methodology may therefore constitute a ground for targeting true external benchmarks based on costs and prices outside China, namely market economy benchmarks which may then be chosen to include a sufficient level of environmental standard. If such argument stands under Sect. 15(b) CAP, investigating authorities have a strong legal basis to challenge any type of government distortions on the Chinese market. Given the fact that the provision of "special difficulties" is unexplored, it is doubtful that an investigating authority would make an argument based on government distortion on account of environmental regulation to resort to alternative benchmark methodologies foreseen in the provision.

5.4.3 Remodelling ASCM Benchmarking Rules

5.4.3.1 Multilateral Negotiations on Art. 14 ASCM

Several options have been discussed for amendments to Art. 14 ASCM to deal with government distorted prices of natural resource inputs and market distortions in non-market economies. If investigating authorities would have the possibility to consider distortions or government monopolies, a more flexible determination of applicable benchmarks could include costs reflecting higher environmental standards.

Interestingly, the initial draft of ASCM anticipated the problem of dual pricing and included a paragraph (e) to Art. 14 ASCM, preventing a finding of benefit when the government is the sole provider or purchaser of goods or services, unless the government discriminates among users or providers:

> (e) When the government is the sole provider or purchaser of the good or service in question, the provision or purchase of such good or service shall not be considered as conferring a benefit, unless the government discriminates among users or providers of the good or service. Discrimination shall not include differences in treatment between users or providers of such goods or services due to normal commercial considerations.[213]

The draft provision arguably reflects concern with respecting government policy choices regarding ownership of resources and the comparative advantage arising therefrom.[214]

---

[212] Appellate Body report, *United States – Final Countervailing Duty Determination with Respect to Certain Softwood Lumber from Canada*, WT/DS257/AB/R, adopted 17 February 2004. See also Benitah (2009), pp. 20 and 144.

[213] Revised Draft Text by the Chairman of the Negotiation Group on Subsidies and Countervailing Measures, GATT Doc. MTN/GNG/NG10/W/38/Rev.2, 2 November 1990 (emphasis added).

[214] Beaulieu and Prévost (2020), p. 222.

Moreover, a WTO proposal tabled for the creation of a new Art. 14.2 ASCM talks about benefit quantification on the basis of "terms more favourable than otherwise would have been commercially available to that producer in the market."[215] This provision would point in the direction of the market benchmark discussion.[216] In addition, the proposal clarified in footnote that when prices are found to be distorted, other sources, such as world market prices may be used. This is remarkable, because it only refers to world prices and do not foresee adjustments to reflect the market prices. Accordingly, in the context of dual pricing schemes, the establishment of an appropriate benchmark remains a difficult challenge for investigating authorities. On top of the challenge to practically meet the legal standard, investigating authorities may suffer a lack of sufficient information about the actual costs of energy resources and a lack of cooperation of energy producers or energy security issues.[217]

Furthermore, *Müller* also drafted an Art. 14.3 ASCM for conduct on NMEs, including a methodology to determine NMEs and an explicit inclusion of an alternative benchmark for NME situations:

> 14.3 In non-market-economy situations, the use of alternative benchmark methodologies is expressly permitted for the purpose of benefit calculation in anti-subsidy investigations. A non-market-economy situation is defined as a situation, where no market prices of a certain product exist on the in-country market at all, or where the existing in-country price for a certain product is distorted by government influence, so that the market situation in the country under investigation resembles a monopoly (market distortion).
>
> 14.3.1 For the determination of market distortion, a market distortion analysis shall be conducted.
>
> [...]
>
> 14.3.2 The <u>minimum allowable import price</u> shall be used as alternative benchmark in the benefit calculation. The minimum allowable import price is defined as the <u>lowest average price of all market economy producers of a like product in sales to in-country purchasers</u>.[218]

An important challenge in the determination of an appropriate benchmark is how to reflect the comparative advantage in the assessment of prevailing market conditions in the country of subsidisation. Investigating authorities must find balance between the two positions: on the one hand, whether selling energy inputs below cost already is an expression of the comparative advantage and on the other hand, whether it can be expected from energy-endowed countries to sell their energy resources at the same price as industrialised net energy-importing countries.[219] This is a delicate balance that investigating authorities and/or WTO Panels are yet to fully define.

---

[215] See WTO Negotiating Group on Rules, Draft Consolidated Chair Texts of the AD and SCM Agreements, TN/RL/W/213, 30 November 2007; WTO Negotiating Group on Rules, New Draft Consolidated Chair Texts of the AD and SCM Agreements, TN/RL/W/236, 19 December 2008.

[216] For the parallel discussion in anti-dumping investigations, see Sect. 6.3 below.

[217] Pogoretskyy (2011), p. 207.

[218] Müller (2018), p. 221 (emphasis added).

[219] Pogoretskyy (2011), p. 207.

5.4.3.2 Putting Sect. 15(b) CAP to Practice

As outlined above, Sect. 15(b) CAP gives investigating authorities a strong legal basis to rely on alternative benchmarks in anti-subsidy investigations on goods from China. The provision has several advantages, most notably the fact that there is no explicit expiration date on the provision—contrary to the parallel provision on anti-dumping which lapsed in December 2016.[220] However, the substantive condition of "special difficulties" in the application of the rules of Art. 14 ASCM is undefined. Investigating authorities may need to explore the possibilities to argue on the basis of this provision in cases of government-distorted markets, including markets in which insufficient environmental regulation led to distorted costs of production.[221] Although this is a theoretical possibility, investigating authorities have been reluctant to rely on this legal basis.

5.5 Chapter Summary

Countries may argue that imported goods benefitted from an 'invisible' subsidy of cost externalisation in countries that do not impose environmental standards on their producers. In such cases, the rules on countervailing measures embodied in the ASCM may be used to provide a remedy. Key among the government policies which would be categorised as subsidies conferring a benefit to producers are "lax" environmental standards as well as the provision of resources at less than their full value. In the former case, industries benefit from weak or unenforced environmental laws and regulations that do not require a sufficient level of environmental cost internalisation. In the latter case, energy or raw material inputs sold at below-cost prices on the domestic market create a subsidising effect on the downstream products. Not only do dual pricing schemes have harmful trade-distorting effects, but they also have environmentally harmful consequences as they promote wasteful energy and raw material consumption on domestic markets.

Qualifying lax environmental standards as countervailable subsidies is, however, not a straightforward task. Subsidies in the form of low environmental standards undoubtedly confer a benefit to producers, but qualification as a subsidy under the ASCM is problematic, particularly on account of the criterion of a financial contribution and the specificity requirement. In the case of dual pricing schemes, additional legal problems relating to the financial contribution, government criterion for public bodies and benefit pass-through arise. It is unlikely that a strong argument can be made under the current rules. Thus, legislative amendments would be necessary to broaden the subsidy concept to any kind of regulatory (in)action by a

---

[220] Müller (2018), p. 219. See, https://archive.org/stream/AgreementOnMarketAccess/Us-chinaBilateralAgreementProtocols (last accessed 22 June 2023).

[221] See Bungenberg and Van Vaerenbergh (2020).

government, or to include specific exceptions for instance related to environmental cost internalisation or specifically for the renewable energy sector.

Beyond the question whether environmental standards as such could be qualified as a countervailable subsidy, the question arises whether environmental standards may play a role in the determination of the appropriate (market) benchmark to determine the amount of any subsidy conferred. The benchmarking techniques developed by several WTO Members have been curtailed by the Appellate Body to resemble as closely as possible the situation on the market in the country of production. Even though the jurisprudence has accepted several techniques of alternative benchmarks—including out-of-country benchmarks—the aim is to reconstruct as closely as possible the domestic market benchmark in the country of production. Moreover, should reliance on world prices be allowed, this may not provide a sufficient solution in case of dual pricing schemes, absent of internationally accepted prices for oil, natural gas, and electricity, for instance. Further legislative drafting to endow more flexibility on investigating authorities to insert non-distorted costs and prices which fully internalise environmental impacts of production would be necessary. In relation to China, a largely unexplored legal basis exists to rely on out-of-country prices exists.

References

Adamantopoulos K (2008a) Art. 1 ASCM. In: Wolfrum R, Stoll PT, Hestermeyer H (eds) Max Planck commentaries on world trade law, WTO – trade in goods. Brill, Leiden

Adamantopoulos K (2008b) Art. VI GATT. In: Wolfrum R, Stoll PT, Hestermeyer H (eds) Max Planck commentaries on world trade law, WTO – trade in goods. Brill, Leiden

Barceló JJ III (1994) Countervailing against environmental subsidies. Can Bus Law J 23(1):3–22

Beaulieu E, Prévost D (2020) Subsidy determination, benchmarks, and adverse inferences: assessing 'benefit' in *US – Coated Paper (Indonesia)*. World Trade Rev 19(2):216–231

Behn D (2007) The effect of dual pricing practices on trade, the environment, and economic development: identifying the winners and the losers under the current WTO disciplines. http://ssrn.com/abstract=1151153. Accessed 22 June 2023

Benitah M (2009) The WTO law of subsidies: a comprehensive approach. Kluwer Law International, Alphen aan den Rijn

Bigdeli SZ (2011) Resurrecting the dead? The expired non-actionable subsidies and the lingering question of 'green space'. Manch J Int Econ Law 8(2):2–37

Bungenberg M, Van Vaerenbergh P (2020) Countervailing Measures und das Chinesische Beitrittsprotokoll zur WTO. Zeitschrift für Europarechtliche Studien 23(2):267–293

Cartland M, Depayre G, Woznowski J (2012) Is something going wrong in the WTO Dispute Settlement? J World Trade 46(5):979–1016

Chiang TW (2018) Chinese state-owned enterprises and WTO's anti-subsidy regime. Georgetown J Int Law 46(2):845–877

Cima E (2018) Promoting renewable energy through FTAs? The legal implication of a new generation of trade agreements. J World Trade 52(4):663–696

Cima E, Mbengue MM (2021) 'Kind of Green'. The U.S. proposal to advance sustainability through trade rules and the future of the WTO. ESIL Reflect 10(1):1–9

Condon BJ (2009) Climate change and unresolved issues in WTO law. J Int Econ Law 12(4):895–926

Coppens D (2014) WTO disciplines on subsidies and countervailing measures. Balancing policy space and legal constraints. Cambridge University Press, Cambridge

Cosbey A, Mavroidis PC (2017) A turquoise mess: green subsidies, blue industrial policy and renewable energy: the case for redrafting the subsidies agreement of the WTO. EUI Working Papers RSCAS 2014/17

Crowley MA, Hillman JA (2018) Slamming the door on trade policy discretion? The WTO appellate body's ruling on market distortions and production costs in *EU-Biodiesel (Argentina)*. World Trade Rev 17(2):195–213

Ding R (2014) 'Public body' or not: Chinese state-owned enterprise. J World Trade 48(1):167–190

Doelle M (2004) Climate change and the WTO: opportunities to motivate state action on climate change through the World Trade Organization. Rev Eur Comp Int Environ Law 13(1):85–103

Durling JP (2008) Art. 14 ASCM. In: Wolfrum R, Stoll PT, Hestermeyer H (eds) Max Planck commentaries on world trade law, WTO – trade in goods. Brill, Leiden

Eliason A, Fiorini M (2020) *Australia – Anti-Dumping Measures on A4 Copy Paper*: opening a door to more anti-dumping investigations. EUI Working Paper RSCAS 2020/87

Espa I, Marín Durán G (2018) Renewable energy subsidies and WTO law: time to rethink the case for reform beyond *Canada – Renewable Energy/Fit Program*. J Int Econ Law 21(4):621–653

Espa I, Rolland SE (2015) Subsidies, clean energy, and climate change. E15 Initiative Think Piece

Esty DC (1994) Greening the GATT. Trade, environment, and the future. Institute for International Economics, Washington

Farah PD, Cima E (2015) The World Trade Organization, renewable energy subsidies, and the case of feed-in tariffs: time for reform toward sustainable development. Georgetown Int Environ Law Rev 27(4):515–537

Horlick G, Clarke PA (2017) Rethinking subsidy disciplines for the future: policy options for reform. J Int Econ Law 20(3):673–703

Howse R (2013) Securing policy space for clean energy under the SCM agreement: alternative approaches. In: E15 Expert Group on Clean Energy Technologies and the Trade System (ed) Clean energy and the trade system: proposals and analysis. ICTSD/WEF, Geneva, pp 47–51

Howse R, Eliason AL (2009) Domestic and international strategies to address climate change: an overview of the WTO legal issues. In: Cottier T, Nartova O, Bigdeli SZ (eds) International trade regulation and the mitigation of climate change. World Trade Forum. Cambridge University Press, Cambridge, pp 48–93

Kempf H (2006) M. de Villepin Propose une Taxe sure CO_2 des Produits Importés. Le Monde

Laurenza EC, Simões BG (2014) How Canada – renewable energy supports the use of the alternative 'commercial reasonableness' standard in future feed-in tariff disputes. Global Trade Cust J 9(3):104–122

Li S, Tu X (2020) Reforming WTO subsidy rules: past experiences and prospects. J World Trade 54(6):853–888

Marhold A (2017) Fossil fuel subsidy reform in the WTO: options for constraining dual pricing in the multilateral trading system. ICTSD Issue Paper

Meléndez-Ortiz R (2016) Enabling the energy transition and scale-up of clean energy technologies: options for the global trade system. E15 Expert Group on Clean Energy Technologies and the Trade System, Policy Options Paper

Müller W (2017) WTO agreement on subsidies and countervailing measures: a commentary. Cambridge University Press, Cambridge

Müller S (2018) The use of alternative benchmarks in anti-subsidy law. A study on the WTO, the EU and China. Springer, Cham

Patterson E (1992) GATT and the environment. Rules challenges to minimize adverse trade and environmental effects. J World Trade 26(3):99–109

Pauwelyn J (2013) Carbon leakage measures and border tax adjustments under WTO law. In: Prévost D, Van Calster G (eds) Research handbook on environment, health and the WTO. Edward Elgar Publishing, Cheltenham/Northampton, pp 448–506

Piérola F (2008) Art. 6 ASCM. In: Wolfrum R, Stoll PT, Hestermeyer H (eds) Max Planck commentaries on world trade law, WTO – trade in goods. Brill, Leiden

Pogoretskyy V (2011) Energy dual pricing in international trade: subsidies and anti-dumping perspectives. In: Selivanova Y (ed) Regulation of energy in international trade law: WTO, NAFTA and Energy Charter. Kluwer Law International, Alphen aan den Rijn, pp 181–228

Qin JY (2004) WTO regulation of subsidies to state-owned enterprises (SOEs) – a critical appraisal of the China Accession Protocol. J Int Econ Law 7(4):863–919

Qin JY (2018) Market benchmarks and government monopoly: the case of land and natural resources under global subsidies regulation. Univ Pa J Int Law 43(3):575–642

Raslan RAA (2018) Green subsidies and WTO trade rules: a 'conflict of values' or a 'conflict of norms'? J World Trade 52(6):917–942

Rubini L (2012) Ain't wasting time no more: subsidies for renewable energy, the SCM agreement, policy space, and law reform. J Int Econ Law 15(2):525–579

Sands P, Peel J (2018) Principles of international environmental law, 4th edn. Cambridge University Press, Cambridge

Schwartz P (2015) Principle 16: The Polluter-Pays Principle. In: Viñuales JE (ed) The Rio Declaration on Environment and Development. A commentary. Oxford University Press, Oxford, pp 427–450

Selivanova Y (2007) The WTO and energy: WTO rules and agreements of relevance to the energy sector. ICTSD Issue Paper No. 1

Selivanova Y (2008) Energy dual pricing in the WTO: analysis and prospects in the context of Russia's Accession to the World Trade Organization. Cameron May, London

Shadikhodjaev S (2012) How to pass the pass-through test: the case of input subsidies. J Int Econ Law 15(2):621–646

Shadikhodjaev S (2013) First WTO judicial review of climate change subsidy issues. Am J Int Law 107:864–878

Shadikhodjaev S (2015) Renewable energy and government support: time to 'Green' the SCM agreement? World Trade Rev 14(3):479–506

Stiglitz J (2006) A new agenda for global warming. Economists' Voice

Tarasofsky RG (2008) Heating-up international trade law: challenges and opportunities posed by efforts to combat climate change. Carbon Climate Law Rev 2(1):7–17

Tietje C, Kluttig B, Franke M (2011) Cost of production adjustments in anti-dumping proceedings: challenging raw material inputs dual pricing systems in EU anti-dumping law and practice. J World Trade 45(5):1071–1102

Van Vaerenbergh P (2019) EU trade defence policy against unfair trade from Chinese SOEs: unilateral or multilateral approaches? Geneva Jean Monnet Working Papers 01/2019

Wu M (2016) The "China, Inc." challenge to global trade governance. Harv Int Law J 57(2):261–342

Wüstenberg M (2019) Anti-dumping off the rails: the European Union's practice to alleged input dumping. Global Trade Cust J 14(9):407–416

Yamaoka T (2013) Analysis of China's accession commitments in the WTO: new taxonomy of more and less stringent commitments, and the struggle for mitigation by China. J World Trade 47(1):105–157

Zheng W (2010) The pitfalls of the (perfect) market benchmark: the case of countervailing duty law. Minn J Int Law 19(1):1–54

Zhou W, Gao H, Bai X (2019) Building a market economy through WTO-inspired reform of state-owned enterprises in China. Int Comp Law Q 68(4):977–1022

Chapter 6
Low Environmental Standards and the ADA Rules

6.1 Introduction

To ensure an appropriate balance between environmental policies and trade policies, it is critical that the costs and prices on which trade rules are vested duly reflect environmental costs. This balance may also become relevant under the anti-dumping rules. If the price of goods does not reflect the environmental costs incurred during the production process, charges of 'environmental dumping' or 'eco-dumping' may be raised when such goods are put on international markets.[1] According to the argument, since countries have no or insufficient legislation in place that ensures environmental cost internalisation, the price of imported goods does not reflect the cost of environmental harm, which renders the imports 'dumped' on the importing market and allows the importing country to impose ADDs to offset the dumping margin to a price level that includes the environmental costs.

However, the GATT concept of dumping is limited to price dumping and is not aimed at countering other forms of dumping such as eco-dumping.[2] Accordingly, the anti-dumping instrument can in principle not be used as a tool to combat the failure to internalise environmental costs. Only if the requirements of dumping under the ADA are met because of the lack of internalisation of environmental costs, the anti-dumping rules could become an instrument to counter eco-dumping practices.

Accordingly, this chapter focuses on the role of environmental costs and low environmental standards in the anti-dumping investigation. Government regulation which fails to ensure the internalisation of environmental costs into the price of

---

[1] See Sands and Peel (2018), p. 899. See also Charnovitz (1993), pp. 31–32; Esty (1994), p. 163, fn. 13; Rauscher (1994), pp. 823–825; Lothe (2001); Pauwelyn (2013), pp. 465 ff.

[2] See Sect. 3.2.2.1 above.

© The Author(s), under exclusive license to Springer Nature Switzerland AG 2023
P. Van Vaerenbergh, *Greening Trade Remedies*, EYIEL Monographs - Studies in European and International Economic Law 31,
https://doi.org/10.1007/978-3-031-38172-0_6

exported goods may be qualified as a government distortion on the market relevant to the anti-dumping rules (Sect. 6.2). If environmental costs are calculated equally in the normal value and in the export price, an interpretation in the direction of including environmental costs in the dumping margin calculation can be permissible in theory. This chapter discusses environmental costs in the normal value calculation methodologies (Sect. 6.3) and environmentally motivated adjustments to the dumping margin (Sect. 6.4). Against that background, it also sheds light on certain recent developments that aim to ensure environmental cost internalisation in the anti-dumping legal framework (Sect. 6.5).

6.2   Environmental Regulation and Government-Distorted Costs and Prices

Environmental regulation affects the price at which companies can produce goods and place these goods on the international market. Charges of eco-dumping are, despite the terminology used, frequently targeted against an activity performed by the government and not by an individual firm.[3] Formulating a policy response under international trade rules can therefore also be considered under the WTO anti-subsidy disciplines.[4] Nonetheless, the issue of government-distorted prices and the calculation of ADDs has been centre-stage in law, practice, and dispute settlement on anti-dumping. Government-distorted prices may result from a wide array of governmental regulations, including environmental regulation. The applicable standard of environmental protection, lax enforcement thereof, or insufficient implementation may influence the cost of production of certain industries.

Although the GATT and ADA are already mindful that certain market situations may render prices inappropriate for the comparison, the anti-dumping rules do not comprehensively foresee how to deal with the issue of government-distorted costs and prices in the calculation of ADDs. WTO anti-dumping rules are vested on a comparison between the export price and the normal value of goods whereby dumping exists if the export price is lower than the normal value of a good according to Art. VI:1 GATT and Art. 2.1 ADA.[5] Contrary to the subsidies and safeguards rules, the argument to include environmental standards and costs under the anti-dumping rules does not relate to constitutive elements but rather on how to include environmental costs in the price of good in comparison to the price these goods should have been. Rather, for anti-dumping rules, the impact of environmental standards would be visible in the comparison between the price of the goods on the export market versus the price of the goods on the domestic market.

---

[3] Rauscher (1994), pp. 823–825.

[4] See Chap. 5 above.

[5] Art. VI:1 GATT and Art. 2.1 ADA.

Figure 6.1 illustrates how environmental costs impact the dumping margin—and hence the level of ADD—in the comparison between export price and normal value. If the environmental costs included in the benchmark price (the normal value) is higher than the environmental costs included in the price of the dumped goods, then the ADD can be seen as addressing the issue of eco-dumping.

Investigating authorities can influence the benchmark price to include government-distorted costs in two manners. First, by increasing the benchmark prices (normal value) by ensuring that costs and prices used in alternative calculation methodologies, particularly the CNV method and the NME methodologies, properly include environmental costs. Second, by making adjustments to the dumping margin at the stage of fair comparison to reflect environmental costs. If adjustments are made to the export price and/or normal value, there must be proof that export prices have been affected to a different degree than the normal value in order for the dumping margin to be affected. Both methods lead to inflated dumping margins and higher ADDs at a level of environmental protection that reflects full internalisation of environmental costs of production.

Scholars have argued in favour of amending the ADD calculation methodologies to address government-distorted costs and prices arising from low environmental standards. *Choi/Lee*, for instance, have defended the use of a modified anti-dumping mechanism that ensures achievement of sustainable development goals through

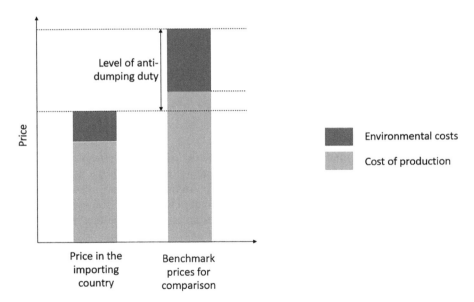

Fig. 6.1 Including environmental costs in dumping margin calculations. Source: Author's own creation

inclusion of carbon costs in the dumping margin determination.[6] Moreover, *Patterson* has proposed to amend the anti-dumping rules to allow for 'anti-eco-dumping' actions: if environmental costs are not accurately reflected in prices of goods in international trade practices, then trade of such goods must be considered dumped.[7] In the broader discussion on market distortions, *Shadikhodjaev* has argued that the ADA should be amended to allow market-oriented adjustments to input costs and other normal value elements, as long as parallel adjustments are made to the export price.[8] However, the pathway to implement such argument in practice is filled with obstacles from the jurisprudential interpretations on the normal value and the price comparability requirement of Art. 2 ADA.

6.3 Environmental Cost Distortions and Normal Value Calculations

The ADA does not contain a definition of the 'normal value' of a good.[9] The normal value in the country of production is the relevant benchmark price which investigating authorities use to determine whether goods have been sold at dumping prices. Art. 2 ADA contains between different methodologies to determine the normal value of goods. In principle, the domestic prices in the exporting country will be used (Sect. 6.3.1). Alternatively, alternative methodologies are available under the conditions of Art. 2.2 ADA (Sect. 6.3.2) or Art. 2.7 ADA in connection with the second *Ad* Note to Art. VI GATT (Sect. 6.3.3). These provisions are relevant to assess whether environmental costs can be included in the normal value of a good.

6.3.1 Market Economies: Standard Methodology (Art. 2.1 ADA)

Under the standard methodology under the ADA, which is applicable to market economies, environmental costs can in principle not be added to the normal value calculation of an imported good. Also *Pauwelyn* argues that using anti-dumping as an instrument to level the carbon or environmental playing field is impossible under the WTO rules on dumping.[10] At the core of his argument lies the fact that the normal value is oriented at the exporting market.[11]

---

[6] Choi and Lee (2017).

[7] Patterson (1992), p. 104.

[8] Shadikhodjaev (2019), pp. 104–106.

[9] Stewart and Mueller (2008), Art. 2 ADA, para. 43.

[10] Pauwelyn (2013), pp. 466 ff.

[11] *Ibid.*

According to Art. VI:1 GATT and Art. 2.1 ADA, the normal value of a good in principle refers to the "price, in the ordinary course of trade, for the like products when destined for consumption *in the exporting country*."[12] In other words, the benchmark price for comparison is not domestic prices which do internalise environmental costs, but rather the 'normal' prices in the country of the producer or exporter. As a result, the point of reference for the anti-dumping rules is the ordinary course of trade in the domestic market of the exporting country. Export prices are not compared to domestic market price levels in markets where environmental or carbon measures apply—or even a hypothetical, ideal price level that fully internalises environmental costs—but rather the price level in the country of export itself, where prices will not include the cost of environmental protection measures. As a result, differences in environmental protection levels in the exporting as opposed to the importing country would not add to a finding of dumping.

Governments that want to offset the harmful effects of environmental dumping on the domestic markets in the form of additional duties on imports from countries that have not implemented environmental protection regulations could therefore in principle not rely on the anti-dumping rules under Art. 2.1 ADA.

6.3.2 Market Economies: Alternative Methodologies (Art. 2.2 ADA)

The alternative methodologies to determine the normal value of goods grant investigating authorities more flexibility to consider certain (environmental) costs in the normal value of goods. This section reiterates on the two-step structure of Art. 2.2 ADA (Sect. 6.3.2.1) before considering the lack of environmental protection standards as a ground to disregard domestic prices (Sect. 6.3.2.2) and under the methodologies to determine the normal value (Sect. 6.3.2.3).

6.3.2.1 The Structure of Art. 2.2 ADA

Art. 2.2 ADA also foresees two alternative methodologies to determine the normal value of products, upon a finding that domestic prices shall not serve as the benchmark for comparison with the export prices charged by foreign producers or exporters on the market of the importing WTO Member.[13] These two alternative methodologies are only available if an investigating authority proves that domestic prices in the country of export are not adequate as a benchmark for comparison to the export price.[14]

---

[12] Art. 2.1 ADA (emphasis added).

[13] De Baere et al. (2021), para. 135.

[14] *Ibid.*

When there are <u>no sales of the like product in the ordinary course of trade</u> in the domestic market of the exporting country <u>or</u> when, <u>because of the particular market situation</u> or the low volume of the sales in the domestic market of the exporting country, <u>such sales do not permit a proper comparison</u>, the margin of dumping shall be determined by comparison with a comparable price of the like product when exported to an appropriate third country, provided that this price is representative, or with the cost of production in the country of origin plus a reasonable amount for administrative, selling and general costs and for profits.[15]

Art. 2.2 ADA presents investigating authorities with a two-step obligation in investigations. First, proof of the grounds for disregarding domestic prices must be furnished, before, second, reliance on the alternative methodologies for determination of normal value may be used. The consideration that the exporting country does not internalise environmental costs in the prices and costs may influence both steps.

First, the question arises whether low environmental standards, or the insufficient enforcement thereof, can amount to a ground for disregarding domestic prices. Art. 2.2 ADA lists three grounds:

- there are no sales in the ordinary course of trade;
- domestic sales do not permit a proper comparison because of the particular market situation in the domestic market of the exporting country;
- domestic sales do not permit a proper comparison because of the low volume of sales in the domestic market of the exporting country.

Second, investigating authorities may consider the impact of environmental regulations on the cost determination in the alternative methodologies. Art. 2.2 ADA foresees two alternative methods to determine normal value benchmarks:

- a comparable price of the like product when exported to an appropriate third country, provided that the price is representative, or
- the cost of production of the product in the country of origin, plus a reasonable amount for administrative, selling, and general costs and for profits (CNV method).

Investigating authorities have free choice to rely on the CNV method or choose prices from an analogue country.[16] Whereas export prices to representative third countries are not frequently used because it cannot be excluded that such exports are also dumped into those third country markets, the CNV method is more popular among investigating authorities.[17]

---

[15] Art. 2.2 ADA (footnote omitted, emphasis added).

[16] Stewart and Mueller (2008), Art. 2 ADA, para. 53. See, more recently, Panel report, *United States – Anti-Dumping Measures on Certain Oil Country Tubular Goods from Korea*, WT/DS488/R, adopted 12 January 2018, para. 7.18.

[17] Vermulst (2005), p. 33. The EU, for instance, has not relied on export prices to a third country in the last 20 years to determine the normal value with reference to the fact that these prices might also be made at dumping prices. See Van Bael & Bellis (2019), pp. 88–89. The US, on the other hand, has used export prices to other countries on a regular basis.

However, it must be underlined that the aim for investigating authorities determining the normal value is to construct the prices still as if they were produced *in the country of origin*.[18] The normal value would thus include in principle the same environmental costs in the export price and the domestic prices in the country of origin. Even when resorting to external benchmarks, the aim for investigating authorities is to recreate the price benchmarks as if the goods were produced and/or sold in the market of exportation. No additional environmental costs can be introduced by investigating authorities in computing the normal value of goods because the aim of this exercise is precisely determining the cost of the good as reflected in the country of production—*i.e.* for instance, before any carbon taxes charged at the domestic level are calculated.[19] However, particularly the CNV method leaves investigating authorities considerable discretion leading to generally higher dumping margins.

6.3.2.2 Grounds to Disregard Domestic Prices (Art. 2.2 ADA)

The failure of a government to adopt, maintain, implement, and effectively enforce environmental regulations that ensure cost internalisation could be used as a ground for disregarding domestic prices in anti-dumping investigations. Government-distorted prices are not separately considered in Art. 2.2 ADA. Therefore, this section assesses whether a lack of environmental regulation could be argued to amount to a 'particular market situation' (Sect. 6.3.2.2.1) or 'sales outside the ordinary course of trade' (Sect. 6.3.2.2.2).

6.3.2.2.1 Insufficient Environmental Regulations as a Particular Market Situation (Art. 2.2 ADA)

Investigating authorities may disregard domestic prices because a particular market situation in the domestic market in the exporting country renders domestic sales inutile for a proper comparison.[20] As the provision has already been used and discussed in NME-like situations, a WTO Member could therefore argue that the non-application of proper environmental protection standards constitutes a PMS. The PMS test is applied in two distinguished parts: First, the existence of a PMS must be established, and second that PMS must make a comparison with domestic market prices inappropriate.[21] The DSB thereby clarified that the phrases "particular market

---

[18] In relation to the CNV method, see explicitly, Panel report, *Thailand – Anti-Dumping Duties on Angles, Shapes and Sections of Iron or Non-Alloy Steel and H Beams from Poland*, WT/DS122/R, adopted 5 April 2001, para. 7.127.

[19] Pauwelyn (2013), p. 467.

[20] Art. 2.2 ADA, second ground.

[21] De Baere et al. (2021), para. 143.

situation" and "permit a proper comparison" in Art. 2.2 ADA operate together to establish when domestic market sales can be disregarded.[22]

6.3.2.2.1.1 Existence of a PMS

The first question is whether unfit environmental protection standards may be qualified as creating a PMS. In the current practice, most cases where the PMS method was used related to government intervention on the market.[23] A danger exists that such interpretation where government intervention on the market is challengeable through anti-dumping duties is applied overlapping with the sphere of application of the ASCM, which expressly regulates injurious government behaviour through subsidisation. Despite this concern, there exists no prohibition to address government action with anti-dumping remedies. In *US – Offset Act (Byrd Amendment)*, the Appellate Body already carried out a harmonious interpretation of Art. 18.1 ADA and Art. 32.1 ASCM and their respective footnotes, interpreting that "an action that is not "specific" within the meaning of Art. 18.1 of the Anti-Dumping Agreement and of Art. 32.1 of the SCM Agreement, but is nevertheless related to dumping or subsidisation, is not prohibited by Art. 18.1 of the Anti-Dumping Agreement or Art. 32.1 of the SCM Agreement."[24] The Panel clarified that a situation which might be qualified as a subsidy should it be examined under the ASCM does not preclude an examination under the PMS—however, adding a *caveat* that such qualification is not a necessary precondition for the case-by-case analysis under the PMS.[25] Moreover, investigating authorities should also consider the prohibition of Art. VI:5 GATT to impose ADDs and CVDs on the same product for the same situation of dumping and/or subsidisation.

Whether government policies on environmental protection and climate change may be interpreted in the concept of a PMS is not yet dealt with in the WTO jurisprudence. Notably, jurisprudence regarding the scope of the PMS is scarce. The GATT dispute *EEC – Cotton Yarn* dealt with an exchange rate freeze and high inflation on the domestic market, and the question whether this must be factored in the normal value and whether this impacted only export prices or also domestic prices.[26] The Panel did not explicitly reject external factors such as government macroeconomic policies or exchange rate policies as grounds on which the PMS can be

---

[22] Panel report, *Australia – Anti-Dumping Measures on A4 Copy Paper*, WT/DS529/R, adopted 4 December 2019, para. 7.27.

[23] Lesmana and Koesnaidi (2019), pp. 415–416.

[24] Appellate Body report, *United States – Continued Dumping and Subsidy Offset Act of 2000*, WT/DS217/AB/R, adopted 27 January 2003, para. 262.

[25] Panel report, *Australia – Anti-Dumping Measures on A4 Copy Paper*, WT/DS529/R, adopted 4 December 2019, para. 7.50.

[26] See GATT Panel report, *European Economic Community – Imposition of Anti-Dumping Duties on Imports of Cotton Yarn from Brazil*, BISD 42S/17, adopted 30 October 1995.

invoked.[27] Therefore, at least, it is not expressly excluded that government failure to implement environmental obligations could qualify as a PMS.

In the first WTO dispute on the term PMS, the Panel in *Australia – A4 Copy Paper* considered the Australian investigating authority's finding that the Indonesian Government's influence on the timber market (through subsidies and export restrictions) constituted a PMS.[28] The Panel confirmed the GATT Panel's finding and added that that the term PMS did not have to be interpreted in a manner to envisage all possible situations which would prevent a proper comparison between domestic and export prices.[29]

The Panel further addressed two situations brought about by Indonesia that would allegedly be excluded from the scope of a PMS, namely situations arising from government actions and situations that distort input costs. Both grounds are relevant in relation to a potential argument on low environmental standards.

First, regarding situations arising from government actions, the Panel in *Australia – A4 Copy Paper* confirmed that situations arising from government action are not necessarily disqualified from constituting a PMS. In principle, low environmental standards can therefore be considered as a government (in)action in the sense of the provision. However, the Panel found that an investigation whether distortions affect market sales and/or export prices is to be handled under the proper comparison requirement.[30] In addition, the Panel in *EU – Cost Adjustment Methodologies (Russia)* later rejected Russia's argument that the PMS concept is exclusively related to the concept in the second *Ad* Note to Art. IV:1 GATT where a country has a complete or substantially complete monopoly.[31] Therefore, insufficient environmental protection for both market economies and non-market economies could be considered under the PMS test.

Second, regarding situations that distort input costs, the Panel in *Australia – A4 Copy Paper* rejected the argument that input dumping situations must be distinguished from PMS based on an argument on the legislative history (input dumping specifically discussed but not included, by contrast PMS explicitly discussed and included) concluded that the input dumping situations must not necessarily be excluded from the PMS situations.[32] The Panel considered that the issue of input dumping is to be addressed in the interpretation of the wording "because of" rather than the definition of PMS. As discussed above, dual pricing schemes for energy

---

[27] *Yun* (2017), p. 238.

[28] Kim and Bohanes (2020), p. 481; De Baere et al. (2021), para. 145–148.

[29] Panel report, *Australia – Anti-Dumping Measures on A4 Copy Paper*, WT/DS529/R, adopted 4 December 2019, para. 7.21.

[30] *Ibid*, para. 7.37.

[31] Panel report, *European Union – Cost Adjustment Methodologies and Certain Anti-Dumping Measures on Imports from Russia – (Second complaint)*, WT/DS494/R, circulated 24 July 2020, para. 7.186.

[32] Panel report, *Australia – Anti-Dumping Measures on A4 Copy Paper*, WT/DS529/R, adopted 4 December 2019, para. 7.28–7.29.

and raw material inputs have grave environmental impacts.[33] Such injurious input dumping schemes may thus also be considered as a PMS in the sense of Art. 2.2 ADA.

Finally, the Panel in *Australia – A4 Copy Paper* considered for the first time the meaning of "particular" in the PMS concept. It found that it meant "distinct, individual, single, specific", which necessarily calls for a case-by-case analysis.[34] By contrast, Indonesia had argued that circumstances must be "exceptional" whereas Australia held that circumstances must be "distinguishable and not general".[35] The Panel disregarded the interpretation set out by Indonesia and found that the market situation must "be distinct, individual, single, specific but that does not necessarily make it unusual or out of the ordinary – *i.e.* exceptional."[36]

In sum, the term PMS also covers situations in which distortions are based on government action and a PMS may also exist for market economies in situations where input costs are distorted, regardless of whether the distortions not only affect domestic market sales (*i.e.* the normal value) but also affect the export price.[37] This hypothetically opens the door for an argument that low environmental standards to constitute a PMS too. However, a necessary precondition is that that such situation renders the sales themselves unfit to permit a proper comparison.

6.3.2.2.1.2   Proper Comparison

The second condition under Art. 2.2 ADA to apply the PMS exception is that the nature of the PMS should render the sales unfit for comparison.[38] Investigating authorities must prove that because of the PMS, a proper comparison between export price and normal value is impossible.

The Panel in *Australia – A4 Copy Paper* found that investigating authorities under Art. 2.2 ADA, must "determine whether domestic sales of the like product in the ordinary course of trade do not permit a proper comparison between the export price and the domestic sales price because of the particular market situation or the low volume."[39] This requires a qualitative assessment focussing on the relative effect of the PMS on the domestic versus the export prices, hence how the PMS affects the domestic price in relation to how it affects the export price—if at all—and ultimately how the comparison between the two is affected.[40] This means that where

---

[33] See Sect. 5.3.1 above.

[34] Panel report, *Australia – Anti-Dumping Measures on A4 Copy Paper*, WT/DS529/R, adopted 4 December 2019, para. 7.21.

[35] *Ibid*, para. 7.22.

[36] *Ibid*.

[37] Müller-Ibold (2020), p. 250.

[38] This is a distinct legal obligation than the fair comparison requirement under Art. 2.4 ADA. See Sect. 6.4.2.1.2 below.

[39] Panel report, *Australia – Anti-Dumping Measures on A4 Copy Paper*, WT/DS529/R, adopted 4 December 2019, para. 7.74.

[40] *Ibid*, para. 7.75–7.76.

domestic sales prices, found to be distorted, will nevertheless permit a proper comparison with export prices because export prices are equally affected by the PMS, thereby failing the PMS test as a whole and giving a ground for the investigating authority to use the distorted domestic prices nonetheless as normal value. The Panel reiterated that a relative comparison is necessary due to the requirement of "because of".

In effect, the Panel read a requirement of 'even-handedness' into the proper comparison under Art. 2.2 ADA.[41] Only if the PMS affects the domestic price to a larger extent than the export price or exclusively affects the export price, then a proper comparison is affected and the use of the alternative CNV method is mandated.[42] *Zhou/Percival* described this finding as a welcome development, but one that must still be further developed in practice.[43] At the same time, it can be criticised that an even-handedness approach where both the export price and the normal value must be adapted at the level of the PMS cannot rely on the legal basis in Art. 2.2 ADA, which exclusively applies to the normal value and can consequently not affect the export price. Following this logic, a PMS would automatically affect the proper comparison under Art. 2.4 ADA. Focusing on the effect on the domestic industry, a more appropriate comparison would be the deflated export price and the constructed normal value. The discussion on price comparability and related adjustments to the normal value and export price is detailed out below.[44]

Consequently, if the Panel's interpretation would be applied, investigating authorities would have to prove that low environmental standards must influence the price of the domestic goods. The Panel did not consider that an effect on domestic and export prices is necessarily the same (and therefore permits comparison), but rather that a thorough examination of the factual background must be carried out, because many factors may influence how such low-cost inputs affect the price.[45] Investigating authorities must establish that price distortions have impacted on normal value and export price asymmetrically.[46] Such difference in effect is possible, even if the distortions concern costs that are incurred indiscriminately for domestic and export products. In *Australia – A4 Copy Paper*, the salient aspect for the determination was the price of the pulp which directly affected the price of the paper.[47]

---

[41] Zhou and Peng (2021), p. 99.

[42] By contrast, the Panel noted earlier that a situation impacting domestic and export sales alike is not excluded from the scope of a particular market situation. See Panel report, *Australia – Anti-Dumping Measures on A4 Copy Paper*, WT/DS529/R, adopted 4 December 2019, para. 7.37 and 7.39.

[43] Zhou and Peng (2021), p. 99.

[44] See Sect. 6.4 below.

[45] Panel report, *Australia – Anti-Dumping Measures on A4 Copy Paper*, WT/DS529/R, adopted 4 December 2019, para. 7.80–7.81.

[46] Zhou and Peng (2021), p. 99.

[47] Panel report, *Australia – Anti-Dumping Measures on A4 Copy Paper*, WT/DS529/R, adopted 4 December 2019, para. 7.88.

Sustaining an asymmetric impact of environmental regulation on domestic good versus export goods will therefore be very difficult.

6.3.2.2.2 Environmental Standards and Sales Outside the Ordinary Course of Trade (Art. 2.2 ADA)

It could also be argued that goods produced without effective environmental cost internalisation are goods sold outside the ordinary course of trade (OCT). Art. 2.2 ADA mandates disregarding domestic prices when no domestic sales of the like product in the 'ordinary course of trade' exist. A finding that there are no sales in the ordinary course of trade suffices as such to disregard the domestic prices and rely on the alternative methodologies for determining normal value under Art. 2.2 ADA.

The ADA does not exclude considering environmental standards in relation to the ordinary course of trade. The ADA does not define the term under Art. 2.1 ADA.[48] One example of sales outside the OCT is included in Art. 2.2.1 ADA, where the ADA provides that sales of the like product at prices below per unit costs of production plus SG&A costs are qualified as sales outside the OCT. Since the Uruguay Round, this provision clarifies that national anti-dumping authorities may disregard such sales as the standard for comparison if such sales are made at prices that would make recovery of costs impossible,[49] over an extended period of time[50] and in substantial qualities.[51] However, the Appellate Body does not consider that this provision purports to exhaust the range of methods for determining whether sales are in the OCT.[52] Therefore, the OCT concept leaves freedom for considering distorted prices.

Although state intervention may be indicative for sales not being in the OCT, they cannot satisfy the condition by itself.[53] In *US – Hot Rolled Steel*, the Appellate Body clarified that the OCT test is a test whether practices are in line with the normal market practices.[54] This relates to whether business transactions are made in accordance with the arm's-length principle, rather than whether the prices were

---

[48] Stewart and Mueller (2008), Art. 2 ADA, para. 47.

[49] Art. 2.2.1 ADA.

[50] The extended period of time should normally be one year but shall in no case be less than six months. See Art. 2.2.1 ADA, fn. 4.

[51] Sales below per unit costs are made in substantial quantities when the authorities establish that the weighted average selling price of the transactions under consideration for the determination of the normal value is below the weighted average per unit costs, or that the volume of sales below per unit costs represents not less than 20 per cent of the volume sold in transactions under consideration for the determination of the normal value. See Art. 2.2.1 ADA, fn. 5.

[52] Appellate Body report, *United States – Anti-Dumping Measures on Certain Hot-Rolled Steel Products from Japan*, WT/DS184/AB/R, adopted 23 August 2001, para. 147.

[53] Zhou (2018), p. 628.

[54] Appellate Body report, *United States – Anti-Dumping Measures on Certain Hot-Rolled Steel Products from Japan*, WT/DS184/AB/R, adopted 23 August 2001, para. 140.

government-distorted, and it includes not only prices but also other terms and conditions of transactions.[55] Therefore, *Zhou* argued that there is no place for a test of state-distorted prices under the OCT test and that state intervention cannot have an influence on the OCT test.[56]

On the other hand, the OCT test may be read as involving the consideration of the reasonableness of the purchase price of inputs. Accordingly, *Zhou* acknowledges that the OCT criterion may become relevant for instances of input dumping on the level of raw materials.[57] Similarly, *Pogoretskyy* notes that situations of input dumping or energy dual pricing could be qualified as situations "not in the ordinary course of trade" if a broad interpretation of the concept of OCT is upheld.[58]

Therefore, it is undecided whether low environmental standards in a country can render sales outside the OCT. The ground is largely unexplored and may therefore be the next battleground for the DSB to provide further clarifications as to the utility for government-distorted prices and input dumping practices.[59]

6.3.2.3   Alternative Methodologies to Determine the Normal Value (Art. 2.2 ADA)

If investigating authorities have been successful in establishing a ground for disregarding the domestic prices of the exporting country (be it on the basis of an argument that low environmental standards do not permit proper comparison or any other reason), they may resort to the CNV method (Sect. 6.3.2.3.1) and the third country method (Sect. 6.3.2.3.2) to determine the normal value of the products under investigations. These alternative methodologies grant investigating authorities more discretion to ensure environmental costs of production are included in the normal value of the goods.

6.3.2.3.1   Environmental Costs in the Constructed Normal Value (Art. 2.2, 2.2.1.1 and 2.2.2 ADA)

In line with to Art. 2.2 ADA, the CNV method instructs investigating authorities to compute the normal value by adding a reasonable amount of SG&A costs (Sect. 6.3.2.3.1.2) and a reasonable profit margin to the cost of production (Sect. 6.3.2.3.1.1).

---

[55] *Ibid*, para. 141–143.

[56] Zhou (2018), p. 628. See also Noël and Zhou (2016), pp. 563–565; Noël (2016), pp. 302–304.

[57] *Ibid.*

[58] See, for instance, Vermulst (2005), pp. 20 ff; Pogoretskyy (2011), p. 218 and fn. 158.

[59] See also Sect. 6.5.2 below.

6.3.2.3.1.1 Cost of Production (Art. 2.2 ADA)

The relevant provision of the ADA is Art. 2.2.1.1, which reads in its first sentence:

> For the purpose of paragraph 2, costs shall normally be calculated on the basis of records kept by the exporter or producer under investigation, provided that such records are in accordance with the generally accepted accounting principles of the exporting country and reasonably reflect the costs associated with the production and sale of the product under consideration.[60]

Two central questions arise: Can government intervention in the market, *in casu* through low environmental standard setting, be a reason to leave the producers' records aside (Sect. 6.3.2.3.1.1.1), and can cost adjustments for environmental costs on a basis other than data from the country of origin included in the constructed normal value (Sect. 6.3.2.3.1.1.2)? In addition, this section also highlights the specific situation of start-up costs under Art. 2.2.1.1 ADA (Sect. 6.3.2.3.1.1.3).

6.3.2.3.1.1.1 Can a Lack of Environmental Costs Be a Reason to Leave the Producers' Costs Aside? (Art. 2.2.1.1 ADA)

Prices which do not reflect the environmental costs of production could be argued not to reasonably reflect the costs of production and sale. According to some, the inclusion of environmental costs based on a reasonableness test included in this provision would not be accepted by a Panel, because it goes beyond the regulatory context of the exporting country.[61] Others argue that the environment would be a legitimate objective that can allow prices to be reasonably included.[62]

In principle, as foreseen in Art. 2.2.1.1 ADA, the records kept by the party under investigation shall be the basis for the calculation of the costs. However, the provision also foresees that distorted prices will not always be 'reasonably' reflected in the producers' records. The plain language of Art. 2.2.1.1 ADA reveals that this reasonableness requirement relates to the producers' records and not the costs themselves—as such, if the requirements are met, it is irrelevant whether the costs are artificially low due to insufficient environmental regulation.

The DSB has confirmed this reading in disputes conducted under Art. 2.2.1.1 ADA dealing with the question whether the recorded costs reflected the actual costs associated with the production and sale of the product under investigation. The Panel in *Egypt – Steel Rebar* clarified that the test whether costs are reasonably reflected is "whether a particular cost element does or does not pertain, in that investigation, to the production and sale of the product in question in that case."[63]

---

[60] Art. 2.2.1.1, first sentence, ADA (emphasis added).

[61] See, for instance, Pauwelyn (2013), p. 468.

[62] See, for instance, Choi and Lee (2017), p. 48.

[63] Panel report, *Egypt – Definitive Anti-Dumping Measures on Steel Rebar from Turkey*, WT/DS211/R, adopted 1 October 2002, para. 7.39. See also Panel report, *European Communities – Anti-Dumping Measure on Farmed Salmon from Norway*, WT/DS337/R, adopted 15 January

This reading was confirmed by the Appellate Body in *EU – Biodiesel*, which has clarified that there is no place for a reasonableness test of the costs themselves in the word "reasonable" under Art. 2.2.1.1 ADA. It ruled that the 'reasonableness' test in the second condition of Art. 2.2.1.1 ADA is one whether the costs are reasonably captured, not if the costs themselves are reasonable as compared to hypothetical costs that should have been incurred.[64] Thus, Art. 2.2.1.1 ADA does not involve an examination of the reasonableness of the reported costs themselves. The reasonableness should refer to the reflection of the costs related genuinely to the production.[65] Distraught commentators such as *Crowley/Hillmann* observed that this restrictive interpretation meant "slamming the door" on trade policy discretion in anti-dumping.[66] It confines the possibility for investigating authorities to consider government-induced distortions of any kind under the anti-dumping rules (or, at least, the rules of the CNV methodology).

The Appellate Body in *Ukraine – Ammonium Nitrate* stated that it is not excluded to use other circumstances.[67] In addition, it further clarified that there are no open-ended "non-arm's-length transactions" or "other practices" "exceptions" in the conditions of the first sentence of Art. 2.2.1.1 ADA.[68]

Moreover, the Panel in *Australia – A4 Copy Paper* has confirmed that even if both conditions of Art. 2.2.1.1 ADA are fulfilled, there may still exist grounds to disregard domestic prices.[69] This position "opened the door" again on account of a reasonableness test in the word "normally" under the same provision. Art. 2.2.1.1 ADA holds that, for the purposes of Art. 2.2 ADA, costs of production will normally be calculated on the basis of the records kept by the exporter or producer under investigation, except where the twin conditions of GAAP and reasonably reflecting the costs are not met.[70] The Panel in *Australia – A4 Copy Paper* confirmed that the word "normally" constitutes a separate legal basis to disregard an exporter's records.[71] With regard to Art. 2.2.1.1 ADA, particularly, the Panel considered that

---

2008, para. 7.483; Panel report, *China – Anti-Dumping and Countervailing Duty Measures on Broiler Products from the United States*, WT/DS427/R, adopted 25 September 2013, para. 7.133.

[64] Panel report, *European Union – Anti-Dumping Measures on Biodiesel from Argentina*, WT/DS473/R, adopted 26 October 2016, para. 7.242; see also Appellate Body report, *European Union – Anti-Dumping Measures on Biodiesel from Argentina*, WT/DS473/AB/R, adopted 26 October 2016, para. 6.56.

[65] Appellate Body report, *European Union – Anti-Dumping Measures on Biodiesel from Argentina*, WT/DS473/AB/R, adopted 26 October 2016, para. 6.26.

[66] Crowley and Hillman (2018), pp. 206–208. See also Zhou (2018), pp. 627–628.

[67] Appellate Body report, *Ukraine – Anti-Dumping Measures on Ammonium Nitrate*, WT/DS493/AB/R, adopted 30 September 2019, para. 6.88.

[68] *Ibid*, para. 6.97.

[69] De Baere et al. (2021), para. 200–206.

[70] Panel report, *China – Anti-Dumping and Countervailing Duty Measures on Broiler Products from the United States – Recourse Under Article 21.5 of the DSU by the United States*, WT/DS427/RW, adopted 28 February 2018, para. 7.29.

[71] Panel report, *Australia – Anti-Dumping Measures on A4 Copy Paper*, WT/DS529/R, adopted 27 January 2020, para. 7.110 ff.

Australia's method of applying surrogate production costs was not based on the reasonably reflecting the costs, but rather on the reasonableness of the costs.[72] The question whether costs are competitive market costs associated with production is irrelevant.[73] As such, the Panel did not apply the test relevant in the *EU – Biodiesel* decision.[74] Shifting the debate whether certain environmental costs may be considered to have impacted the costs of production in the exporter's or producer's records to the 'normally' requirement, the Panel again "opened a door" to more anti-dumping investigations in the case of upstream subsidisation.[75] Any interpretation allowing upstream subsidies as a PMS would make the anti-dumping instrument very attractive as a remedy for importing countries, that may then impose ADDs at (higher) computed values.[76]

This view is at least not excluded by the Appellate Body in *Ukraine – Ammonium Nitrate*, where it held that there might be circumstances other than those in the two conditions in which costs of production may not be calculated on the basis of the records kept by the exporter or producer under investigation.[77] The Appellate Body held that "simply because parties to input transactions are considered to be unrelated does not mean that cost calculations should necessarily be based on records kept by the producer under the first sentence of Art. 2.2.1.1. In particular, as explained above, given the reference to 'normally' in the first sentence of Article 2.2.1.1, we do not exclude that there might be circumstances, other than those in the two conditions set out in that sentence, in which the obligation to base the calculation of costs on the records kept by the exporter or producer under investigation does not apply."[78] Therefore, if an investigating authority cannot provide a ground to disregard the reported costs under the second condition of Art. 2.2.1.1 ADA, it must rely on the costs as reflected in the records of the investigated producers.[79]

The Panel in *EU – Cost Adjustment Methodologies II (Russia)* addressed the issue again most recently.[80] The Panel did not consider the case on Russian imports to be distinguishable from the Argentinian and Ukrainian situation, thus not mandating deviation from the earlier jurisprudence.[81] Moreover, the Panel disagreed

---

[72] *Ibid*, para. 7.102.

[73] *Ibid*, para. 7.102.

[74] *Ibid*, para. 7.103–7.107.

[75] See Eliason and Fiorini (2020).

[76] *Ibid*, p. 5.

[77] Appellate Body report, *Ukraine – Anti-Dumping Measures on Ammonium Nitrate*, WT/DS493/AB/R, adopted 30 September 2019, para. 6.87.

[78] *Ibid*, para. 6.104–6.105.

[79] *Ibid*, para. 6.122.

[80] Panel report, *European Union – Cost Adjustment Methodologies and Certain Anti-Dumping Measures on Imports from Russia — (Second complaint)*, WT/DS494/R, circulated 24 July 2020.

[81] *Ibid*, para. 7.102.

with the arguments raised by the EU concerning the word "normally" in Art. 2(5) of the EU's BADR, which the Panel found nearly identical to Art. 2.2.1.1 ADA.[82]

In sum, the language of Art. 2.2.1.1 ADA contains grounds to disregard exporters' and producers' records when they do not properly take accord of environmental costs of production. Whereas the term "reasonably" relates to the records itself rather than the costs, the term "normally" constitutes a separate ground for investigating authorities to disregard records. Although this theoretically may be a basis to argue inclusion of environmental cost, future dispute settlement on Art. 2 ADA may alter that situation.[83]

It remains undecided whether a test of reasonableness of the cost in the producer's records may be carried out by investigating authorities—including on the issue of environmental costs.

6.3.2.3.1.1.2   Including Environmental Cost in the Cost of Production (Art. 2.2.1.1 ADA)

Art. 2.2.1.1 ADA does not prescribe any particular methodology for calculating cost of production.[84] Through the reference to paragraph 2, Art. 2.2.1.1 ADA foresees that the cost of production in the country of origin is meant, which translates into an obligation for investigating authorities to determine constructed normal value "in the country of origin".[85]

Environmental costs of production could be calculated in the construction of the costs of production but are not explicitly foreseen in Art. 2.2.1.1 ADA. The costs of production are the prices paid or to be paid to produce something within the country of origin.[86] Production costs comprise of the cost of materials, direct labour costs and other costs directly related to the production process. Cost of materials include all expenses incurred in obtaining the materials, including inland transport and duties; direct labour costs are those labour costs which can be identified with a particular product or process, and include pay, employee benefits and other employee-related expenses. Manufacturing overheads cover all expenses incidental to and necessary for the products, including for instance indirect labour costs, supervision, subcontractor fees, depreciation, rent, power, maintenance/repair, and accounting adjustments to inventory.

---

[82] *Ibid*, para. 7.105–7.106.

[83] See Sect. 6.5.2 below.

[84] See, for instance, Panel report, *United States – Final Dumping Determination on Softwood Lumber from Canada*, WT/DS264/R, adopted 31 August 2004, para. 7.311.

[85] The Panel and Appellate Body, in *Ukraine – Ammonium Nitrate*, held that costs used in the OCT test under Art. 2.2.1 ADA must be considered consistent with Art. 2.2.1.1 ADA, since Art. 2.2.1 is covered by the reference to paragraph 2 in Art. 2.2.1.1 ADA. See Appellate Body report, *Ukraine – Anti-Dumping Measures on Ammonium Nitrate*, WT/DS493/AB/R, adopted 30 September 2019, para. 7.116.

[86] Appellate Body report, *European Union – Anti-Dumping Measures on Biodiesel from Argentina*, WT/DS473/AB/R, adopted 26 October 2016, para. 6.69.

Moreover, information on environmental costs are frequently not available, including the costs of energy inputs. One problem surrounding the application of the CNV method in practice is the absence or unavailability of information on production costs in the exporting market. Art. 2.2 ADA and Art. VI:1(b)(ii) GATT do not specify precisely what evidence or information an investigating authority may resort to, but neither limits an investigating authority in the sources of information to be used for establishing the cost of production in the country of origin. However, the Appellate Body in *EU – Biodiesel* explains that if an investigating authority relies on information from outside the country of origin, such information shall be adapted as necessary to determine the cost of production in the country of origin.[87] Accordingly, a reservation made under the standard situation also applies for the second method where investigating authorities compute the normal value.[88] This jurisprudence was confirmed in the *Ukraine – Ammonium Nitrate (Russia)* case with findings on reliance on out-of-country evidence to calculate the cost of production of Russian gas which must be adapted to reflect the true costs in the country of origin.[89] The later Panel in *Australia – A4 Copy Paper*, however, seemingly disagreed and found that the Australian investigating authority acted inconsistently with the ADA by rejecting the records kept by exporters and using third-country export prices as a proxy for the exporters' costs.[90] The Panel in *EU – Cost Adjustment Methodologies II (Russia)* reiterated again the legal standard developed in *EU – Biodiesel* and *Ukraine – Ammonium Nitrate* and concluded reliance on out-of-country information is mandated if the investigating authority assesses whether such information shall be adapted to reflect the cost of production in the country of origin.[91] In that case, the Panel concluded that the Commission had insufficiently explained how the information used in the calculation was adapted to ensure it represented the cost of production in the country of origin.[92]

Before the landmark decision of the Appellate Body in *EU – Biodiesel*, the WTO had not addressed whether the mere existence of artificially low, subsidised prices of raw material costs in the producers' records allows investigating authorities to concluded that costs are not reasonably reflected.[93] The Panel in *Australia – A4 Copy Paper* seemed to qualify that stance, by holding that Art. 2.2 ADA requires the investigating authority to consider available alternatives for replacing recorded

---

[87] *Ibid*, para. 6.70–6.71; Panel Report, *Ukraine – Anti-Dumping Measures on Ammonium Nitrate*, WT/DS493/AB/R, adopted 30 September 2019, para. 7.99. See also Furculiță (2017), p. 364.

[88] See Sect. 6.3.1 above.

[89] Panel report, *Ukraine – Anti-Dumping Measures on Ammonium Nitrate*, WT/DS493/R, adopted 30 September 2019, para. 7.92, 7.99 and 7.103.

[90] Panel report, *Australia – Anti-Dumping Measures on A4 Copy Paper*, WT/DS529/R, adopted 27 January 2020, para. 7.132.

[91] Panel report, *European Union – Cost Adjustment Methodologies and Certain Anti-Dumping Measures on Imports from Russia – (Second complaint)*, WT/DS494/R, circulated 24 July 2020, para. 7.122–7.123.

[92] *Ibid*, para. 7.124 ff.

[93] Tietje et al. (2011), p. 1089.

costs "so as to use the costs that are unaffected by the distortion to the extent possible."[94] As such, adjustments are only to be made for those components of costs unaffected by government-caused distortions.[95] This would lead to a comparison between distorted export prices and undistorted CNV, which is an improper comparison.[96] In *EU – Biodiesel*, the Appellate Body criticised the EU for choosing outside-prices exactly for the reason that they did not reflect the Argentinian prices.[97]

Although the Appellate Body in *EU – Biodiesel* rejected the consideration of reasonableness of costs under the second condition of Art. 2.2.1.1 ADA, it did not interpret the wording of "normally".[98] Consequently, the Panel in *Australia – A4 Paper* filled that gap by holding that the term "normally" may provide some flexibility to consider reasonableness of costs, and the replacement of distorted costs of production with competitive benchmarks.[99] As such, the Panel read an exception into the basic rule, which is applicable upon considerations of reasonableness. Particularly, the Panel held that there may be circumstances in which benchmark costs are considered despite the fact that the two conditions of Art. 2.2.1.1 ADA are fulfilled.[100] However, investigating authorities can only disregard the costs reflected in the exporters' and producers' records on the basis of the word "normally" *after* it considers the two requirements of Art. 2.2.1.1 ADA and finds that they are both fulfilled.[101] Although the Panel did not detail further on the specific circumstances of such cases, it does give back some flexibility to investigating authorities. As such, the Panel restored the balance of the sentence and rightfully shifted the assessment of reasonableness from "reasonably reflect" to "normally".

6.3.2.3.1.1.3   The Issue of Start-Up Costs in the Renewable Energy Sector (Art. 2.2.1.1 ADA)

A particular issue in the case of clean energy is mainly to include costs over the whole product cycle, specifically start-up costs for new products and factories, which is very present in new and rapidly developing industries such as the solar panel industry. For instance, solar panel prices drop steadily because costs half every other year as a result of high start-up costs.[102] Because unit costs are usually higher during the start-up phase of a company, therefore they give rise to the need

---

[94] Panel report, *Australia – Anti-Dumping Measures on A4 Copy Paper*, WT/DS529/R, adopted 4 December 2019, para. 7.162.

[95] *Ibid*, para. 7.164.

[96] Zhou and Peng (2021), p. 100.

[97] Appellate Body report, *European Union – Anti-Dumping Measures on Biodiesel from Argentina*, WT/DS473/AB/R, adopted 26 October 2016, para. 6.81.

[98] Crowley and Hillman (2018), pp. 207–208.

[99] Zhou and Peng (2021), p. 99.

[100] Panel report, *Australia – Anti-Dumping Measures on A4 Copy Paper*, WT/DS529/R, adopted 4 December 2019, para. 7.110–7.115.

[101] *Ibid.*

[102] Horlick (2013), p. 69.

for specific rules comprising of a downward adjustment. Art. 2.2.1.1 and fn. 6 ADA foresee a downward adjustment regarding start-up costs, which was explicitly nego-tiated by WTO Members after anti-dumping practice took off in high-tech goods sectors, of which the solar panel industry may be a good example.[103] They have to reflect the costs at the end of the start-up period, or if that period extends beyond the period of investigation, the most recent costs which can reasonably be taken into account by the authorities during the investigation.[104]

Rules inspired on this provision may be considered, particularly provisions to ensure that the product cycle of clean energy technologies is considered in the cost methodologies used by authorities. This means a more proper enforcement of the existing rules under Art. 2.2.1.1 ADA in conjunction with footnote 6. However, the US and the EU have not fully made use of this provision. In the US, for instance, marketing costs are not part of the start-up costs.[105] Also the EU has equally proven reluctant to rely on this provision. The European Commission usually rejects adjust-ments for start-up operations,[106] although one successful example in the EU was *Hot-Rolled Coils from India.*[107]

Against that background, *Kampel* proposes a formulation based on Art. 6.2 of the Aircraft Agreement,[108] where parties are directed to consider certain types of costs when considering pricing:

> Signatories agree that pricing of civil aircraft should be based on a reasonable expectation of recoupment of all costs, including non-recurring programme costs, identifiable and pro-rated costs of military research and development on aircraft, components, and systems that are subsequently applied to the production of such civil aircraft, average production costs, and financial costs.[109]

A such formulation could be included in plurilateral or bilateral agreements on envi-ronmental goods at the EU, with the aim to consider pricing in light of certain types of costs—*in casu* environmental costs of production.

---

[103] Stewart and Mueller (2008), Art. 2 ADA, para. 49.

[104] Art. 2.2.1.1 ADA, fn. 6.

[105] See 19 USC Section [f][1][iii].

[106] Van Bael & Bellis (2019), p. 73.

[107] Commission Decision No 1357/2001/ECSC of 4 July 2001 amending Decision No 283/2000/ECSC imposing a definitive anti-dumping duty on imports of certain flat-rolled products of iron or non-alloy steel, of a width of 600 mm or more, not clad, plated or coated, in coils, not further worked than hot-rolled, originating, inter alia, in India, OJ 2001 L 182/27, rec. 21; Commission Decision No 841/2002/ECSC of 21 May 2002 amending Decision No 283/2000/ECSC imposing a definitive anti-dumping duty on imports of certain flat rolled products of iron or non-alloy steel, of a width of 600 mm or more, not clad, plated or coated, in coils, not further worked than hot-rolled, originating, inter alia, in India and accepting an undertaking, OJ 2002 L 134/11, rec. 21.

[108] Kampel (2017), pp. 27 and 36.

[109] Art. 6.2 Aircraft Agreement (emphasis added).

6.3.2.3.1.2   SG&A Costs (Art. 2.2.2 ADA)

Expenses to comply with environmental regulations could be considered part of the SG&A costs in the construction of the normal value. *Choi/Lee* argue that SG&A costs be considered to have to include an additional administrative cost equalling the CO_2 emissions per tonne of produced steel.[110] SG&A costs are costs that will normally affect all products produced or sold by a company.[111] They include all expenses, which are incurred in connection with the sales of the like product on the exporter's domestic market (*i.e.* not export sales[112]).

Again, a test of reasonableness could be considered when determining whether environmental costs could be included in the amount of SG&A costs.[113] A systemic interpretation of all three elements of the CNV under Art. 2.2 ADA would support this. As a consequence, it would mean that neither source of the CNV can incorporate distorted prices.[114] WTO jurisprudence, however, does not prescribe a separate reasonability test to be carried out.[115]

The Appellate Body in *EU – Biodiesel* has restricted the test of reasonableness of SG&A costs and profit to the OCT test.[116] Investigating authorities do not have unfettered discretion, but must consider normal business activities, providing no room for the use of benchmarks on the sole basis of state intervention and price distortions.[117] Accordingly, SG&A costs would have to be constructed in line with the prevailing market conditions, including government price distortions.

In sum, environmental costs could be classified as SG&A costs, but the language of Art. 2.2 ADA does not foresee an explicit reasonableness test which can serve as a basis for investigating authorities to include such costs in the normal value.

---

[110] Choi and Lee (2017), p. 43.

[111] Panel report, *United States – Final Dumping Determination on Softwood Lumber from Canada*, WT/DS264/R, adopted 31 August 2004, para. 7.263.

[112] See ECJ, *Nakajima All Precision Co Ltd v Council*, case C-69/89, judgment of 7 May 1991, ECLI:EU:C:1991:186, para. 64.

[113] Tietje et al. (2011), p. 1093.

[114] Zhou (2018), p. 629.

[115] Panel report, *Thailand – Anti-Dumping Duties on Angles, Shapes and Sections of Iron or Non-Alloy Steel and H Beams from Poland*, WT/DS122/R, adopted 5 April 2001, para. 7.122–7.128. See also De Baere et al. (2021), para. 260.

[116] Appellate Body report, *European Union – Anti-Dumping Measures on Biodiesel from Argentina*, WT/DS473/AB/R, adopted 6 October 201, para. 6.39 and fn. 172.

[117] Zhou (2018), p. 629.

6.3.2.3.2   Environmental Costs in Prices to Appropriate Third Countries (Art. 2.2 ADA)

The second alternative for competent authorities is determining the normal value on the basis of export prices from the country under investigation to appropriate third countries.[118] In this method, prices are not constructed on the basis of cost factors in the production process plus SG&A cost and a profit margin, but rather based on sales prices of the like product exported to another appropriate third country.

Export prices to third countries do not provide investigating authorities with an appropriate tool to challenge input dumping schemes or government-distorted prices. Not only can it be presumed that these export prices are equally not internalising environmental costs of production, but the aim of the exercise is to determine prices as if they would be in the country of production. The export price of these products exported from the country of production to third countries may equally be deemed distorted by the government regulation at the production stage, the schemes have become an inherent part of the product's cost structure, and the market benchmark is therefore rendered moot.[119]

6.3.3   Non-Market Economies: Alternative Methodologies (Art. 2.7 ADA + Second Ad Note)

The ADA allows the construction of the normal value not based on prices in the country of production. This could allow to bring environmental costs into the normal value. In the case of so-called non-market economies, Art. 2.7 ADA and the second *Ad* Note to Art. VI:1 GATT permit investigating authorities to resort to the surrogate country method to determine normal value for NMEs (Sect. 6.3.3.1). China, however, is subject to individual rules it agreed upon when acceding the WTO (Sect. 6.3.3.2). In addition, the law and practice in two of the most active users of anti-dumping is discussed (Sect. 6.3.3.3).

6.3.3.1   NME Methodologies (Art. 2.7 ADA + Second *Ad* Note)

The non-market economy rules contained in Art. 2.7 ADA in conjunction with the second *Ad* Note to Art. VI:1 GATT may play a key role in the discussion whether low prices due to low environmental standards may be tackled under the ADA rules. The second *Ad* Note to Art. VI:1 GATT and Art. 2.7 ADA consider that "in case of imports from a country which has a complete or substantially complete monopoly

---

[118] Art. 2.2 ADA, second alternative.
[119] Pogoretskyy (2011), pp. 218–219.

of its trade and where all domestic prices are fixed by the state", domestic prices may not be an appropriate benchmark for comparison. In practice, investigating authorities rely on NME provisions to disregard domestic prices and use prices of costs in other market economy countries as a basis for the normal value determination involving NMEs.[120] In such cases, it is explicitly mandated to deviate from the prices and costs in exporting countries and substitute those with costs incurred by producers in appropriate market economy countries. Accordingly, such methodologies determine the costs in the third country, as opposed to the methodologies under Art. 2.2 ADA, which attempt to reflect the costs and prices in the exporting country.

The third country method is the most commonly used method, replacing the prices from the NME with surrogate prices for the same product in a comparable market economy country.[121] Investigating authorities must justify the selection of an analogue country which, unlike the investigated country, displays a higher level of environmental protection and internalisation of environmental costs on its market. If the third country chosen does adhere to environmental standards, the corresponding costs can be presumed to have been internalised in the normal value, at least indirectly. However, the ADA does not contain guidance on how to determine or select the most appropriate third country.[122] As such, investigating authorities are free to rely on market structure (including level of trade), competition on the market, sales volumes, etc. to find an appropriate third country. In addition, the second *Ad* Note leaves more discretion to the investigating authority to find that a strict comparison between prices is not appropriate, than under the grounds listed in Art. 2.2 ADA.[123]

The normal value of goods based in third countries that do adhere to sufficient environmental standards internalise environmental costs and therefore have the effect that the ADD will equal out price environmental differences (at least partially).[124] Similarly, these provisions could be an adequate legal basis for challenging input dumping schemes. *Selivanova*, however, points out that investigating authorities rely on third-country data, which is problematic as normally costs of energy in these countries would be much higher.[125]

On a final note, the situation of complete or substantially complete state monopolies foreseen in the second *Ad* Note does not represent modern realities of a globalised world market anymore. The provision was drafted on a proposal of Czechoslovakia to overcome problems of price comparability in so-called state-trading countries or non-market economies, applicable to for instance transition economies in Eastern Europe, socialist countries such as China and Vietnam, and

---

[120] Vermulst (2005), pp. 44–45.

[121] Stewart and Mueller (2008), Art. 2 ADA, para. 123.

[122] *Ibid*, para. 58.

[123] Panel report, *European Union — Cost Adjustment Methodologies and Certain Anti-Dumping Measures on Imports from Russia — (Second complaint)*, WT/DS494/R, circulated 24 July 2020, para. 7.188.

[124] Pauwelyn (2013), p. 469.

[125] Selivanova (2008), p. 30.

CIS countries such as Russia and Ukraine, and North Korea.[126] After the break-up of the Soviet Union and the transition of Eastern European countries, China is now the major country which is still subject to NME methodologies given the finding by investigating authorities that prices are centrally-planned.[127] Although state monopolies controlling trade and all domestic prices are extremely rare now—especially among the WTO Membership—such methodologies are still widely used by industrialised countries to counter input dumping.[128] However, absent other provisions in the ADA, WTO Members would be left without sufficient instruments to tackle dumping in the situations of market distortions by a government intervention such as input dumping.[129] Several WTO Members have developed adjustment strategies to exporters' gas and electricity costs, which amount to a *de facto* NME treatment.[130]

6.3.3.2 China's Accession Protocol (Sect. 15 CAP)

For China, Vietnam and Tajikistan, the legal basis for NME methodologies and the inclusion of environmental costs into the dumping margin lies in specific accession commitments with relation to price comparability for anti-dumping procedures.[131] These countries accepted that methodologies not based on a strict comparison with domestic prices or inputs may be used for a period of 15 years after the accession date to the WTO. China's and Vietnam's transition periods ended in 2016 and 2018 respectively, whereas Tajikistan is subject to commitments until 2025.[132]

The CAP provides for a unique situation in WTO law: China has accepted to be treated automatically as a non-market economy for the purposes of anti-dumping duty calculation for a period of up to 15 years after its accession.[133] The wording of Sect. 15(a)(ii) CAP is inspired on the provision of the second *Ad* Note to Art. VI:1 GATT:

> The importing WTO Member may use a <u>methodology</u> that is <u>not based on</u> a strict comparison with <u>domestic prices or costs in China if</u> the producers under investigation can<u>not</u> clearly show that <u>market economy conditions prevail</u> in the industry producing the like product with regard to manufacture, production and sale of that product.[134]

---

[126] Polouektov (2002).

[127] Palmeter (1998), p. 117; Stewart and Mueller (2008), Art. 2 ADA, para. 125.

[128] See Sect. 6.3.3.3 below.

[129] Pogoretskyy (2011), p. 220.

[130] *Ibid.*

[131] Report of the Working Party on the Accession of Viet Nam, WT/ACC/VNM/48, 27 October 2006, para. 255; Report of the Working Party on the Accession of Tajikistan, WT/ACC/TJK/30, 6 November 2012, para. 164.

[132] See Sect. 3.2.4 above.

[133] See Yamaoka (2013), pp. 123–125.

[134] Sect. 15(a)(ii) CAP (emphasis added).

This legal presumption temporarily relieved investigating authorities from proving the Chinese domestic prices were distorted and allowed them to disregard domestic Chinese prices.[135] Alternative methodologies could be used when the investigating authority can "clearly show" that market conditions do not prevail, namely the surrogate country method, or the constructed normal value method.[136] In essence, it allowed investigating authorities to treat China as an NME by replacing domestic prices or costs with those in a third country market economy.

The difference between the NME assumption of Sect. 15 CAP and the PMS premise of Art. 2.2 ADA is that PMS does not handle a market distortion itself, as the CAP does, but rather the influence of a market distortion on the normal value.[137] Sect. 15 CAP relieves the investigating authority of its burden of proof; consequently, an effect of distortion of the normal value does not have to be proven by the investigating authority under Sect. 15(b) CAP, contrary to the requirement for arguing a PMS exists.[138] In that sense, it sets a higher threshold for the investigating authorities than under the expired Section 15 CAP—that is only in relation to distorted exports from China.[139]

6.3.3.3   Approaches by WTO Members

Several heavy users of anti-dumping measures have already developed policies in relation to Chinese dumped imports. After relying on a country-specific approach based on Sect. 15 of the CAP, the EU introduced a new purportedly country-neutral significant distortions methodology in 2017.[140] The US also amended the Trade Preferences Extension Act (TPEA) of 2015 in anticipation of the lapse of the CAP provision.[141] Australia had, as a precondition for the Australia-China FTA, accepted China as a market economy, thereby effectively ending the use of Sect. 15 CAP, but set a 'bad example' to the world by effectively continuing NME methodologies by relying on a falsely interpreted instrument of PMS when conducting investigations against Chinese imports.[142] Also Canada has recently amended its anti-dumping

---

[135] Appellate Body report, *European Communities – Definitive Anti-Dumping Measures on Certain Iron or Steel Fasteners from China*, WT/DS397/AB/R, adopted 28 July 2011, para. 287. See also Zhang (2011), pp. 876 ff.

[136] Appellate Body report, *European Communities – Definitive Anti-Dumping Measures on Certain Iron or Steel Fasteners from China*, WT/DS397/AB/R, adopted 28 July 2011, para. 268.

[137] See Sect. 6.3.2.2.1 above.

[138] Zhou and Percival (2016), p. 877.

[139] Vietnam and Tajikistan accepted the same commitments as embodied in Sect. 15(a) and (d) of China's Accession Protocol upon accession to the WTO. See Report of the Working Party on the Accession of Viet Nam, 27 October 2006, WT/ACC/VNM/48, para. 255; Report of the Working Party on the Accession of Tajikistan, 6 November 2012, WT/ACC/TJK/30, para. 164.

[140] See new Art. 2(6a) BADR.

[141] See Nicely and Gatta (2016).

[142] Zhou and Percival (2016), pp. 887 ff.

rules in the Special Import Measures Regulations to address input dumping and the particular market situation by allowing the CNV method.[143] The amended EU and US approaches will discussed in more detail below.

6.3.3.3.1   EU Significant Distortions Methodology

In 2017, the EU introduced a novel approach for dumping margin determination into the BADR,[144] as a response to the lapse of the provision which was used until then in the CAP. The old NME methodology compared Chinese domestic producers' sales prices and costs with domestic sales prices and costs of the like product in a third country market economy or analogue country. The new methodology foresees the application of the CNV method in case of existence of 'significant distortions'. The main changes are that the EU now employs a country-neutral approach for all WTO Members, that country reports will be made available for complaining industries, and that for the first time social and environmental criteria play a role in the anti-dumping procedures.[145]

This new methodology—which has been discussed at length on its compatibility with WTO rules[146]—has introduced environmental considerations for the first time in the legal framework of anti-dumping in the EU in at least two aspects for the normal value determination. This development is important because it foresees a possible ground to argue that environmental standards exist.

First, according to Art. 2(6a)(b) BADR, significant distortions are "those distortions which occur when reported prices or costs, including the costs of raw materials and energy, are not the result of free market forces because they are affected by substantial government intervention." In assessing whether significant distortions exist, the Commission can consider international standards, including International Labour Organisation (ILO) Conventions, as well as relevant multilateral environmental agreements (MEAs).[147] However, no direct legal provision within the BADR formally confirms this possibility. The six indicative criteria listed in Art. 2(6a)(b) BADR focus primarily on the structural links between the state and companies active in the market, and policies and active acts taken by the government influencing the market.[148] Environmental policies are not linked to the criteria for assessing the existence of significant distortions, but with the mention of distorted wage costs, at least one element of sustainable development is relevant. Overall, the consideration

---

[143] Tereposky & Derose (2019).

[144] See Sect. 3.3.2 above.

[145] See Reinhold and Van Vaerenbergh (2021).

[146] See, for instance, Hoffmeister (2021), pp. 338 ff.; De Baere (2021), pp. 356 ff.; Van Bael & Bellis (2019), p. 27; Noël and Zhou (2016), pp. 418 ff.; Müller (2018), pp. 57 ff.; Vermulst and Sud (2018), pp. 63 ff.; Tietje and Sacher (2018), pp. 91 ff.; Ruessmann and Beck (2014); Geraets (2018), p. 492; Antonini (2018), pp. 89 ff.

[147] Regulation (EU) 2017/2321, Recital 4.

[148] In detail, see Reinhold and Van Vaerenbergh (2021).

of social and environmental standards in this new methodology will lead to an increased level of duties imposed and will therefore enhance the market-closing effect of dumping measures.[149]

Moreover, the existence of significant distortions will be proven based on country-specific reports outlining the state of the market in selected exporting countries. A first such report was prepared by the Commission in December 2017 for the People's Republic of China,[150] and another report on the Russian Federation was published in October 2020.[151] These reports create an almost irrefutable presumption that distortions exist.[152] These reports also do not contain a specific reference to the standard of environmental regulation in the country as a relevant aspect for the determination of significant distortions.

Second, the new rules apply adherence to ILO Conventions and MEAs as a selection criterion to find representative third countries in both the significant distortions method (Art. 2(6a)(a) BADR) and listed non-WTO Members (Art. 2(7) subpara. 1 BADR).[153] The application is limited since it is only if there are several possible countries, preference shall be given to those countries which have "an adequate level of social and environmental protection". As such, the Commission has confirmed it is only a secondary criterion.[154] The new rules make it difficult to find a good reference country.[155] The practice of the Commission focusses not only on prices and costs in the appropriate third country, but takes into account all data concerning the market.[156] The Regulation includes a list of relevant conventions[157] and must source data on compliance of ILO Conventions and MEAs when searching for representative countries.[158] Also note that the text of the provision states "may use" and "where appropriate", thus securing discretionary power for the Commission, limiting such a challenge.

The Commission practice on this secondary criterion has been limited.[159] Thus far, only in this one instance, by the time the various steps were considered, the EU applied the social and environmental standard test to eliminate Malaysia in favour

---

[149] Trapp (2021), pp. 198–199.

[150] European Commission, Commission Working Staff Document on Significant Distortions in the Economy of the People's Republic of China for the Purposes of Trade Defence Investigations, SWD(2017) 483 final/2, 20 December 2017.

[151] European Commission, Commission Working Staff Document on Significant Distortions in the Economy of the Russian Federation for the Purposes of Trade Defence Investigations, SWD(2020) 242 final, 20 October 2020.

[152] Natens (2020), p. 110.

[153] See Sect. 3.3.2 above.

[154] See Commission Implementing Regulation (EU) 2019/1198, para. 145.

[155] Vermulst and Sud (2018), pp. 63–87.

[156] General Court, *Shanxi Taigang Stainless Steel Co Ltd v European Commission*, case C-436/18 P, judgment of 29 July 2019, ECLI:EU:C:2019:643, para. 61.

[157] Annex Ia to Regulation (EU) 2018/825.

[158] Recital 6 to Regulation 2017/2321.

[159] See Reinhold and Van Vaerenbergh (2021), p. 198.

of Mexico.[160] The non-enforcement of environmental standards, as documented by the OECD in 2006,[161] was brought forward by the applicants.[162] The applicant contrasts this with strict environmental standards, for instance as set out in the REACH Regulation.[163] In all other instances, there was no choice left after application of the three primary criteria, and therefore environmental considerations did not influence the choice of analogue country. The Commission selected Turkey, Mexico, Thailand, and Serbia as countries to compare prices.[164] Following the determination of the third country, the Commission continues to establish the constructed normal value.

In sum, it is considered that it shall have a rather symbolic influence, rather than actual monetary impact on the values.[165] In the EU, this has been taken up as a stance for green governance, but given the secondary nature of the criterion, it becomes a meaningless criterion with not much more than a symbolic value.

---

[160] See Commission Implementing Regulation (EU) 2019/687 of 2 May 2019 imposing a definitive anti-dumping duty on imports of certain organic coated steel products originating in the People's Republic of China following an expiry review pursuant to Article 11(2) of Regulation (EU) 2016/1036 of the European Parliament and of the Council, OJ 2019 L 116/5, rec. 110–112.

[161] OECD, Environmental Compliance and Enforcement in China, An Assessment of Current Practices and Ways Forward, OECD Study 2006.

[162] Commission Implementing Regulation (EU) 2019/687 of 2 May 2019 imposing a definitive anti-dumping duty on imports of certain organic coated steel products originating in the People's Republic of China following an expiry review pursuant to Article 11(2) of Regulation (EU) 2016/1036 of the European Parliament and of the Council, OJ 2019 L 116/5, rec. 52.

[163] *Ibid.*

[164] Commission Implementing Regulation (EU) 2019/915 of 4 June 2019 imposing a definitive anti-dumping duty on imports of certain aluminium foil in rolls originating in the People's Republic of China following an expiry review under Article 11(2) of Regulation (EU) 2016/1036 of the European Parliament and of the Council, OJ 2019 L 146/63, rec. 123; Commission Implementing Regulation (EU) 2019/1198 of 12 July 2019 imposing a definitive anti-dumping duty on imports of ceramic tableware and kitchenware originating in the People's Republic of China following an expiry review pursuant to Article 11(2) of Regulation (EU) No 2016/1036, OJ 2019 L 189/8, rec. 153; Commission Implementing Regulation (EU) 2019/687 of 2 May 2019 imposing a definitive anti-dumping duty on imports of certain organic coated steel products originating in the People's Republic of China following an expiry review pursuant to Article 11(2) of Regulation (EU) 2016/1036 of the European Parliament and of the Council, OJ 2019 L 116/5, rec. 113; Commission Implementing Regulation (EU) 2019/1259 of 24 July 2019 imposing a definitive anti-dumping duty on imports of threaded tube or pipe cast fittings, of malleable cast iron and spheroidal graphite cast iron, originating in the People's Republic of China and Thailand, following an expiry review pursuant to Article 11(2) of Regulation (EU) 2016/1036 of the European Parliament and of the Council, OJ 2019 L 197/2, rec. 121; Commission Implementing Regulation (EU) 2019/1267 of 26 July 2019 imposing a definitive anti-dumping duty on imports of tungsten electrodes originating in the People's Republic of China following an expiry review under Article 11(2) of Regulation (EU) 2016/1036, OJ 2019 L 200/4, rec. 108; Commission Implementing Regulation (EU) 2019/1379 of 28 August 2019 imposing a definitive anti-dumping duty on imports of bicycles originating in the People's Republic of China as extended to imports of bicycles consigned from Indonesia, Malaysia, Sri Lanka, Tunisia, Cambodia, Pakistan and the Philippines, whether declared as originating in these countries or not, following an expiry review pursuant to Article 11(2) of Regulation (EU) No 2016/1036, OJ 2019 L 225/1, rec. 146.

[165] Gustafsson and Crochet (2020), pp. 187–206.

Arguably, it would make more sense to use social and environmental protection standards in the determination whether a third country is at a similar level of economic development, also from the point of view of a WTO challenge.[166]

The EU's new methodology, which captures both NME-like situations as well as input dumping situations, was challenged by China. In the challenge of the EU anti-dumping methodology post-December 2016, China had expanded its panel request in *EU – Price Comparison Methodologies* to be expanded to "any modification, replacement or amendment to the [NME] measures [...]. and any closely connected, subsequent measures."[167] As the Panel's authority lapsed, the Panel report was never published nor adopted.

6.3.3.3.2 US TPEA Amendment

USDOC maintains a different methodology for dealing with dumped Chinese imports based on distorted prices. The US opted to construct the normal value by using surrogate values on a factor-by-factor basis for each material input which then totalled a constructed analogue cost of manufacture plus SG&A costs were constructed using ratios of these elements in an economically comparable third country.[168] Only when this method is not available in an individual investigation, USDOC will resort to using direct prices or costs in third countries.[169] In other words, it does not compare Chinese sales prices or costs with sales prices or costs of the like product in a third country as the EU, but rather to a constructed price in a surrogate country based on the factors of production methodology.[170] This essentially amounts to a surrogate constructed value.[171] Only in cases this is not possible, the US Department of Commerce will use prices or costs in third countries directly.[172]

In the advent towards the lapse of the CAP-mandated NME methodology for imports from China, *Watson* has considered the various options for the US trade policy in anti-dumping cases towards China after 2016, and discussed various options including the application of a PMS, development of an OCT-argument, a shift in the burden of proof, or abolishing the NME-concept as a whole.[173] Nonetheless, the US practice towards NMEs exists in constructing normal value based on surrogate factors of production, rather than domestic prices or export prices of the country under investigation towards third countries. This methodology

---

[166] Lester (2017).

[167] Request for the Establishment of a Panel by China, *European Union – Measures Related to Price Comparison Methodologies*, WT/DS516/9, 7 March 2017.

[168] Sect. 773(c) Tariff Act of 1930, 19 USC §1677b(c) and US Department of Commerce Anti-Dumping Regulations, 19 C.F.R. §351.408 (2005).

[169] Sect. 773(c)(2) Tariff Act of 1930, 19 U.S.C. § 1677b(c)(2).

[170] Vermulst and Meng (2017), p. 337.

[171] Stewart and Mueller (2008), Art. 2 ADA, para. 124.

[172] Sect. 773(c)(2) Tariff Act of 1930, 19 U.S.C §1677b(c)(2).

[173] Watson (2014), pp. 11–13.

was vested on the expired Sect. 15 of the CAP and has been replaced by a new methodology in 2015. As discussed above, the choice was made to shift towards a broadened approach under the concepts of OCT and PMS instead: the scope of the OCT has been radically expanded to include PMS situations—and at the same time the concept of PMS is expanded to situations where cost of raw materials does not accurately reflect the cost of production in the OCT. This essentially merged both concepts, thereby elevating the PMS concept as both a means to resort to the CNV method as well as the basis to ignore the producers' records in the calculation of the CNV.[174]

6.4   Fair Comparison and Environmentally Motivated Adjustments to the Dumping Margin

After establishing the export price and normal value of the products under investigation, the investigating authority carries an obligation to make a 'fair comparison' between those two values. To facilitate a fair comparison, investigating authorities may make adjustments to the export price and normal value. It could be considered whether adjustments for environmental costs, e.g. to reflect GHG emissions, could be made in application of the fair comparison requirement. Accordingly, this section deals with price comparability, fair comparison and adjustments (Sect. 6.4.1) to investigate whether environmentally motivated adjustments to the dumping margin are possible (Sect. 6.4.2).

6.4.1   Price Comparability, Fair Comparison, and Adjustments (Art. VI:1 GATT and Art. 2.4 ADA)

In line with the polluter-pays principle, environmentally motivated adjustments to the dumping margin could be considered to reflect the true cost of the environment in the price of the products under investigation. Some commentators have suggested that an argument against eco-dumping could be made under this provision.[175] In the same vein, it has been argued that the value of environmental resources used in production, the cost of damage caused to the environment (measured as clean-up cost) should be permissible adjustments to the export price under Art. VI GATT.[176] The Australian Dumping Authority, for instance, suggested environmental regulation could affect price comparability—*albeit* in the verge of a proper comparison

---

[174] Nicely and Gatta (2016), p. 239.

[175] Sands and Peel (2018), p. 899.

[176] Patterson (1992), p. 104.

investigation at the level of PMS.[177] Also, the Australian Trade Measures Review Officer noted government environmental measures as an illustration that domestic prices are not suitable for comparison with export prices would be affected only if it has affected the two prices to a different degree.[178]

Art. VI:1 GATT foresees that due allowance should be given to factors affecting price comparability: "Due allowance shall be made in each case for differences in conditions and terms of sale, for differences in taxation, and for other differences affecting price comparability."[179] Listed in the provision are differences in conditions and terms of sale and differences in taxation.[180] However, since the formulation of Art. VI:1 GATT is open-ended ("other differences affecting price comparability"), it leaves investigating authorities with freedom to consider any relevant factor in a given investigation. In 1961, the Report of the Group of Experts on "Anti-Dumping and Countervailing Duties" confirmed this open nature of the provision and left the exact contours of "other" unattended.[181]

Art. 2.4 ADA also contains provisions on the price comparison and elaborates on the relevant circumstances that may affect price comparability.[182] The provision is equally open-ended, referring to "any other differences demonstrated to affect price comparability".[183] In this case, however, the Uruguay Round text added a requirement "also demonstrated" to modify "other differences".[184] The burden is on the investigating authorities and not on the exporters to compare normal value and

---

[177] Decision of the Trade Measures Review Officer, Hollow Structural Sections, Review of Decisions to Publish A Dumping Duty Notice and A Countervailing Notice, 14 December 2012. This decision was not followed by the Anti-Dumping Review Panel (ADRP). See for instance, Decision of the Anti-Dumping Review Panel, Review of Decisions Regarding Dumping Duties and Countervailing Duties for Zinc Coated (Galvanized) Steel and Aluminium Zinc Coated Steel Exported from the People's Republic of China, 15 November 2013, para 56. See Zhou and Percival (2016), p. 881.

[178] *Ibid.*

[179] Art. VI:1 GATT.

[180] See also the second *Ad* Note to Art. VI:1 GATT, noting that difficulties with price comparability may arise in deals situations of trade between associated houses and products from countries with a government monopoly.

[181] Report of group of experts on anti-dumping and countervailing duties, 1961. See GATT Analytical index (pre-WTO), p. 230.

[182] The provision illustrates aspects that may affect price comparability "including differences in conditions and terms of sale, taxation, levels of trade, quantities, physical characteristics, and any other differences which are also demonstrated to affect price comparability." See Art. 2.4, third sentence ADA. The footnote to the provision explains that "[i]t is understood that some of the above factors may overlap, and authorities shall ensure that they do not duplicate adjustments that have been already made under this provision."

[183] Panel report, *Argentina – Definitive Anti-Dumping Measures on Carton-Board Imports from Germany and Definitive Anti-Dumping Measures on Imports of Ceramic Tiles from Italy*, WT/DS189/R, adopted 5 November 2001, para. 6.113.

[184] Stewart and Mueller (2008), Art. 2 ADA, para. 89.

export price in a fair manner.[185] As such, it is required to positively establish that the differences have affected price comparability.[186]

Also the Appellate Body underlined the importance of considering any possible factor impacting price comparability. It stated that there are no differences that are *a priori* precluded from being the object of an allowance.[187] Considering environmental regulation as a factor that impedes price comparability is therefore not excluded. However, only those differences that affect the price comparability shall be adjusted; *a contrario*, differences that do not affect shall not be adjusted.[188] Against that background, the Panel in *US – Softwood Lumber V* underlined that a case-by-case analysis is essential.[189] Many investigating authorities would not take into account indirect expenses that cannot be assigned to a particular sale—such as general environmental cost in the production process—due to the heavy burden of complexity in calculations.[190]

Some domestic legal frameworks have detailed out the relevant considerations affecting comparison. Under EU law, for instance, Art. 2(10) BADR implements this provision by listing possible adjustments to be made to export price and/or normal value to establish the dumping margin. None of the circumstances can be used directly for adjustments for differences in environmental standards. Art. 2(10)(k) BADR, however, includes a residual category of adjustments, which may make an argument for adjustment for environmental reasons possible. In addition, international prices have been used as information from representative markets for Russian gas prices adjustment under Art. 2(5) BADR.[191]

In sum, the open-ended formulation of both Art. VI:1 and Art. 2.4 ADA allow investigating authorities to consider any factor which impacts price comparability. If the effects of environmental legislation would be considered under this flexibility, the burden lies with investigating authorities to demonstrate the impact the differences in environmental protection on price comparability. Investigating authorities have no specific guidance in the text as to how to investigate price comparability,[192] leaving some discretionary powers to create procedures and methodologies.

---

[185] Appellate Body report, *United States – Anti-Dumping Measures on Certain Hot-Rolled Steel Products from Japan*, WT/DS184/AB/R, adopted 23 August 2001, para. 177–180.

[186] *Ibid.*

[187] Appellate Body report, *United States – Anti-Dumping Measures on Certain Hot-Rolled Steel Products from Japan*, WT/DS184/AB/R, adopted 23 August 2001, para. 177.

[188] Appellate Body report, *United States – Laws, Regulations and Methodology for Calculating Dumping Margins (Zeroing)*, WT/DS294/AB/R, adopted 9 May 2006, para. 156.

[189] Panel report, *United States – Final Dumping Determination on Softwood Lumber from Canada – Recourse to Article 21.5 of the DSU by Canada*, WT/DS264/RW, adopted 1 September 2006, para. 7.357.

[190] See Stewart and Mueller (2008), Art. 2 ADA, para. 95.

[191] General Court, *Acron OAO and Dorogobuzh OAO v Council of the European Union*, case T-2335/08, judgment of 26 September 2013, ECLI:EU:C:2013:65, para. 19.

[192] Panel report, *European Communities – Definitive Anti-Dumping Measures on Certain Iron or Steel Fasteners from China*, WT/DS397/R, adopted 28 July 2011, para. 7.297.

6.4.2 Environmentally Motivated Adjustments to the Dumping Margin

A fair comparison may be ensured out through carrying out adjustments, as appropriate, to the export price and/or normal value.[193] Regarding adjustments, the central question is whether government distortions of market prices due to insufficient environmental protection affect the normal value and the export price *to a different extent*. To explore these questions, a differentiation must be made between the different methodologies of determining normal value for market economies (Sect. 6.4.2.1) and non-market economies (Sect. 6.4.2.2).

6.4.2.1 Imports from Market Economies

6.4.2.1.1 Application of the Standard Methodology

The default situation is the one where domestic price on the market in the country of exportation are compared with the export price. It is unlikely that investigating authorities would find that insufficient levels of environmental regulation would affect prices of goods on domestic markets and export markets to a different extent.

6.4.2.1.2 Application of Alternative Methodologies Based on a Finding that a PMS Does Not Permit a Proper Comparison

If the anti-dumping investigation was carried out according to an alternative methodology because a PMS was found to affect price comparability, the situation becomes more complex. Art. 2.2 ADA embeds a requirement of price comparability as an additional prerequisite for a PMS to be a ground to disregard domestic prices.[194] The same question arises again at the level of the fair comparison. The question arises whether differences in price levels due to insufficient environmental regulation must be considered at the level of the PMS (within the normal value) or the fair comparison (between export price and normal value).

Jurisprudence of the Appellate Body dealt with that question in relation to government-distorted costs and prices. In the seminal *EU – Biodiesel* case, the

---

[193] See Panel report, *Egypt – Definitive Anti-Dumping Measures on Steel Rebar from Turkey*, WT/DS211/R, adopted 1 October 2001, para. 7.333–7.335; Panel report, *Argentina – Definitive Anti-Dumping Duties on Poultry from Brazil*, WT/DS241/R, adopted 19 May 2003, para. 7.265; Panel report, *United States – Laws, Regulations and Methodology for Calculating Dumping Margins (Zeroing)*, WT/DS294/R, adopted 6 May 2006, para. 7.252–7.275. See, generally, De Baere et al. (2021), para. 314.

[194] See Sect. 6.3.2.2.1.2 above.

Appellate Body refrained from assessing price comparability under Art. 2.4 ADA.[195] It did express doubts about the Panel's finding that price differences arising from the methodology of determining the normal value could not be challenged under Art. 2.4 ADA as differences affecting price comparability.[196] The Appellate Body particularly pointed to the difference in *EC – Fasteners (China) (Article 21.5 – China)* where Art. 2.4 ADA was read in the context of the second *Ad* Note to Art. VI:1 GATT and Sect. 15(a) CAP, which are not relevant in cases where market economy methodologies—such as the PMS methodology and alternative normal value methodologies—are used.[197] Nonetheless, the question may be posited whether the EU did not violate the fair comparison requirement by comparing CNV values that neglect actual input costs with export prices that do reflect those actual costs.[198] Based on *EU – Biodiesel*, *Zhou/Percival* opine that the consideration must be made at the level of PMS and that it is uncertain whether this parallel adjustment could be carried out by the fair comparison requirement.[199] Therefore, if the adjustments are not made under the finding of a PMS, then the different cost bases (*i.e.* undistorted vs. distorted prices) should be adjusted under Art. 2.4 ADA to ensure a fair comparison between the two prices.[200]

The Panel in *Australia – A4 Copy Paper* has shed light on the relationship between the fair comparison under Art. 2.4 ADA and the proper comparison requirement at the level of the PMS which affects price comparability. In the same vein, the Panel effectively posits the issue of input dumping under the "proper comparison" aspect of the PMS methodology in Art. 2.4 ADA.[201] The Panel clarified that artificially lowered input costs can affect domestic and export prices in varying degrees, and that this must be considered by investigating authorities.[202] Relevant factors include prevailing competitive factors on each market, existing relationships between price and cost, and private commercial decisions of producers and exporters.[203] *Zhou/Peng* have found confirmation for the even-handedness test at the level of the PMS.[204] This does not mean that there may not be more or other elements that need adjustment at the later stage under Art. 2.4 ADA.

Thus, differences in impact of environmental regulation are to be dealt with under Art. 2.4 ADA rather than on the comparison obligation of the PMS. Nonetheless, practice in the US and Australia shows that investigating

---

[195] Appellate Body report, *European Union – Anti-Dumping Measures on Biodiesel from Argentina*, WT/DS473/AB/R, adopted 26 October 2016, para. 6.87.

[196] *Ibid.*

[197] *Ibid.* See in detail Sect. 6.3.2.2 above.

[198] Shadikhodjaev (2019), p. 98.

[199] Zhou and Percival (2016), pp. 883–885.

[200] Zhou (2018), p. 632.

[201] See Sect. 6.3.2.2.1 above.

[202] Panel report, *Australia – Anti-Dumping Measures on A4 Copy Paper*, WT/DS529/R, adopted 4 December 2019, para. 7.76 and 7.80.

[203] *Ibid.*

[204] Zhou and Peng (2021), p. 99.

authorities often take a shortcut and fail to address government intervention under the fair comparison requirement.[205]

6.4.2.1.3 Application of Alternative Methodologies Based on a Finding of Sales Outside OCT

The situation is different if the application of the alternative methodology under Art. 2.2 ADA is based on a finding that there are no sales in the OCT. This ground is not linked in the text to a finding that a proper comparison is affected in the text of Art.2 .2 ADA. Therefore, the OCT aspect would not affect the debate at which level adjustments could be made since it is not linked to the notion of affecting price comparability at the level of the ground for disregarding domestic prices. In that case, the debate shifts back to the Art. 2.4 ADA adjustments. The same considerations as in case of the standard methodology apply.[206]

6.4.2.2 Imports from Non-Market Economies

When investigating authorities rely on NME surrogate costs or prices methodologies, this may affect the adjustments at the level of fair comparison. It should be recalled that the second *Ad* Note to Art. VI:1 GATT explicitly considers the existence of a state monopoly as a reason that will affect the price comparability. Accordingly, the provision allows a different benchmark reference point that is based on price in third market economy countries instead of the domestic market of the state monopolistic country. In such cases, if investigating authorities are required to carry out adjustments to the costs and prices, that would then equal out price differences. In *EC – Fasteners (Art. 21.5 – China)*, therefore, the Appellate Body seems to have allowed adjustments *within* the normal value—not *between* the normal value and export price. It noted that adjustments are not required in such cases, when it "would lead the investigating authority to adjust back to the costs in the [*in casu* Chinese] industry that were find to be distorted".[207] This would undermine an investigating authority's right to resort to the analogue country method.[208] Through this reasoning, the Appellate Body was concerned that adjustments would reintroduce distorted elements into the price.[209] The reasoning seems to connect to a defining feature of the NME methodology, which accepts that domestic prices are unfit for comparison.

---

[205] Lesmana and Koesnaidi (2019), p. 418.

[206] See Sect. 6.4.2.1 above.

[207] Appellate Body Report, *European Communities – Definitive Anti-Dumping Measures on Certain Iron or Steel Fasteners from China (Recourse to Article 21.5 of the DSU by China)*, WT/DS397/AB/RW, adopted 12 February 2016, para. 5.207 and 5.231.

[208] *Ibid*, para. 5.125.

[209] Zhou and Percival (2016), p. 884.

In essence, the Appellate Body defends a middle ground between market economies and NMEs, where NME prices can be used if they are untainted and substituted when they are tainted.[210] The Appellate Body's position suggests that it would allow adjustment of a single cost in the calculation of the normal value using the analogue country method.[211] If certain costs are found to be distorted in NMEs due to insufficient environmental regulation, the investigating authorities could therefore replace just that cost, while relying on domestic costs for other aspects. This would present a more flexible way of dealing with certain distorted costs instead of the binary rejection of all costs in the NME surrogate cost methodology when determining the normal value. The approach stands in contrast with for instance the Panel in *EU – Biodiesel* which held that differences arising from the normal value methodology cannot in principle be challenged under Art. 2.4 ADA.[212]

Whether this jurisprudence can be replicated in other NME- or NME-like situations remains to be seen. The Appellate Body's interpretation remained vague and limited to suggestions. It linked its interpretation to the analogue country under the second *Ad* Note to Art. VI:1 GATT and Sect. 15 CAP, therefore making the practical application moot post-2016.[213] Moreover, it is questionable whether such complex differentiation is workable for investigating authorities around the world, and it would be a stretch of Art. 2.4 and the interplay between Art. 2.2 and 2.4 ADA.[214] Nonetheless, the question arises whether it could be the basis for an argument relating to the PMS methodology which, as noted above, aims at reconstructing the prices in the country of production.

6.5   Reform of the Anti-Dumping Regime

The current anti-dumping rules display several shortcomings to deal with price distortions stemming from environmental regulation. Several recent developments have highlighted the need for reform of the anti-dumping regime to provide tools to challenge NME-like situations or use existing the anti-dumping concepts and procedures for new tools. This chapter revises the possibility of multilateral negotiations on the concept of dumping (Sect. 6.5.1) and the potential role of the WTO dispute settlement and other bodies in the WTO to interpret the existing provisions of the ADA (Sect. 6.5.2).

---

[210] Espa and Levy (2018), pp. 321–322.

[211] *Ibid*, p. 318.

[212] Panel report, *European Union – Anti-Dumping Measures on Biodiesel from Argentina*, WT/DS473/R, adopted 26 October 2016, para. 7.304.

[213] Appellate Body report, *European Union – Anti-Dumping Measures on Biodiesel from Argentina*, WT/DS473/AB/R, adopted 26 October 2016, para. 5.205.

[214] Espa and Levy (2018), p. 323.

6.5.1   *Expanding the Concept of 'Dumping'*

The ADA could be reformed to deal specifically with the underlying issues of eco-dumping. Should amending the basic agreements be a realistic possibility, one far-going option could be to include policy considerations in ADA. An objective to repurpose the notion of dumping could achieve a better alignment with normal competition or antitrust rules. This would involve, *inter alia*, revision of the definition of abuse of dominant position and of dumping so that the rules specifically target anti-competitive behaviour (rather than international price discrimination).[215] This may then include aspects of unfair competitive and/or trade practices on account of insufficient environmental standards. Accordingly, the definition of dumping could then include anti-competitive strategies disregarding environmental standards or social standards.

The ADA could also deal explicitly with input dumping schemes, which would consequently also remedy their negative environmental impacts. Input dumping was discussed by WTO Members in the advent of the Uruguay Round of negotiations. The Anti-Dumping Committee and the *Ad Hoc* Group on the Implementation of the Anti-Dumping Code circulated a Draft Recommendation concerning the treatment of input dumping.[216] The WTO Members recognised that neither the GATT nor the ADA contained explicit provisions dealing with the trade practice.[217] Furthermore, it considered that, besides the situation of input dumping where the producer of the input and the manufacturer of the end-product are related, investigating authorities may face practical difficulties in obtaining and verifying costs and prices from unrelated suppliers of inputs.[218] As such, the document concludes, "any anti-dumping measures applied following investigations of this kind would be contrary to the spirit and provision of the General Agreement and the Anti-Dumping Code."[219] Accordingly, the issue of input dumping was not included in the final draft of the ADA in the Uruguay Round.[220]

Nonetheless, if WTO Members want to regulate input dumping explicitly in the ADA, they may want to allow action against raw material distortions explicitly, per analogy to the non-market economy analogue or surrogate country method.[221] This would align the anti-dumping rules with comparable legal regimes addressing similar market distortions that do allow for adjustments to be made under the WTO disciplines: NME methodologies under Art. 2.7 ADA and the second *Ad* Note to

---

[215] Meléndez-Ortiz (2016), p. 11.

[216] Committee on Anti-Dumping Practices and Ad-Hoc Group on the Implementation of the Anti-Dumping Code, Draft Recommendation Concerning the Treatment of the Practice Known as Input Dumping, ADP/W/83/Rev.2, 19 December 1984.

[217] *Ibid*, para. 2.

[218] *Ibid*, para. 6.

[219] *Ibid*, para. 6.

[220] Shadikhodjaev (2019), p. 96.

[221] *Ibid*, p. 103.

Art. VI:1 GATT as well as CVD rules under the pass-through test and the explicit allowance to use out-of-country proxies.[222] A reform of the ADA could therefore allow investigating authorities to use undistorted surrogate costs for establishing normal value of distorted inputs, as long as the actual export prices are also adjusted, or prove that export prices were not affected.[223]

A vital prerequisite for the inclusion of new provisions in the ADA dealing with input dumping is that a parallel adjustment of the export prices is also carried out. A parallel adjustment of export prices is the only remaining possibility for investigating authorities to carry out trade policy preferences,[224] including when it comes to costs to adhere to environmental regulation. Calculating environmental costs into the dumping margin may only stand the test of the comparison inherent to the ADA if a parallel adaptation of the export price for environmental costs will be carried out as well. Also *Patterson* has argued in favour of including environmental resources cost in the production and clean-up costs for damage to the environment as adjustments to the export price.[225] An adequate calculation of equivalent carbon costs on the export price and the normal value equally will lower the impact of calculating environmental costs on the dumping margin, since the difference between export price and normal value will not be reduced. It is up to the investigating authorities to prove then that the environmental costs have impacted the prices on the domestic market and on the export market differently—a hard, if not impossible, task.

In the verge of this discussion, it has been argued that a better multilateral solution would be to resort to diplomatic channels to bring energy price levels to competitive levels instead of relying on anti-dumping rules, for instance through initiatives to integrate former CIS countries in the Energy Community Treaty or accession negotiations to the WTO.[226] This does not remedy the situation short-term for WTO Members. Negotiations on dual pricing are also topics of negotiations in the framework of the ADA. In addition, WTO Members have raised the concern that dual pricing schedules result in sales below normal value and could therefore be challenged by imposition of anti-dumping duties in export markets during negotiations with Russia during its accession to the WTO.[227]

---

[222] *Ibid*, pp. 102–103.

[223] *Ibid*, p. 104.

[224] *Ibid*, pp. 104–106.

[225] Patterson (1992), p. 104.

[226] Pogoretskyy (2011), pp. 221–222.

[227] Report of the Working Party on the Accession of the Russian Federation to the World Trade Organization, WT/ACC/RUS/70, 17 November 2011, para. 90 and 120.

6.5.2   Interpreting the Existing ADA Rules

One option to clarify the position of the ADA on including environmental costs is to await clarification by the WTO's judicial arm on treatment of government distortions under the anti-dumping rules. Art. 2.2, 2.2.1.1 and 2.4 ADA are at the centre stage of the discussion. The WTO DSB has a high influence in further developing the interpretation of these provisions. However, most of the cases regarding cost adjustment methodologies surrounding the methodology of the EU have been resolved. The EU has even blocked the adoption of the latest report by resorting to an appeal into the void, which it sought to prevent itself by establishing the Multi-Party Interim Appeal Arbitration Arrangement (MPIA).[228] In *EU – Cold-Rolled Steel (Russia)*, the Panel has been established in July 2020.[229] In the current state of things, the Appellate Body remains inoperable. The prospects of new Director-General *Okonjo-Iweala* are to resolve the deadlock as one of the priorities for the WTO. The danger of inflated dumping margins and an overly activist approach by the Appellate Body on interpreting the ADA provisions will have to be considered carefully to be acceptable for the US, given that their opposition to the findings of the DSB on the issue of zeroing underlie the reasons for blocking the appointments of Appellate Body Members rendering the body inoperative.[230]

Nonetheless, the DSB can take an activist approach and interpret treaty provisions dynamically in light of the changed circumstances and the central objectives of the WTO Agreements.[231] In addition, making a differentiation based on policy considerations would be necessary to have an impact, as the Appellate Body did with regard to renewable energy subsidies.[232] To some extent, this is already happening with regard to the permissibility of assessing reasonableness of costs as reflected in the producers' records under Art. 2.2.1.1 ADA. The line of case law is currently open at the point where it is not excluded that a reasonableness test is included in the word "normally". As such, it could be argued that environmental costs are normal to be included in the costs of production, even in countries that do not adhere to high standards of environmental protection. Remaining discussions

---

[228] Notification of an Appeal by the European Union Under Article 16.4 and Article 17.1 of the Understanding on Rules and Procedures Governing the Settlement of Disputes (DSU), and Under Rule 20(1) of the Working Procedures for Appellate Review, *European Union – Cost Adjustment Methodologies and Certain Anti-Dumping Measures on Imports from Russia – (Second Complaint)*, WT/DS497/7, 1 September 2020. The Russian Federation also appealed, see WT/DS497/8.

[229] Constitution of the Panel Established at the Request of the Russian Federation, *European Union – Anti-Dumping Measures on Certain Cold-Rolled Flat Steel Products from Russia*, WT/DS521, 17 March 2020.

[230] See United States Trade Representative Ambassador Robert E. Lightizer, Report on the Appellate Body of the World Trade Organization, February 2020, pp. 95 ff.

[231] See Sect. 2.2.2 above.

[232] See Appellate Body report, *Canada – Certain Measures Affecting the Renewable Energy Generation Sector*, WT/DS412/AB/R, adopted 24 May 2013; Appellate Body report, *Canada – Measures Relating to Feed-In Tariff Program*, WT/DS426/AB/R, adopted 24 May 2013.

are possible to interpret prices not internalising environmental costs as "sales outside the OCT".

A binding interpretation as an option to interpret one of the provisions of the ADA is also possible (Art. 2.2, 2.2.1.1, 2.4 ADA). For instance, an interpretative understanding of the fair comparison requirement within the meaning of Art. 2.4 ADA could take into account distortions in domestic and global energy markets that make it difficult or impossible to properly compare prices using any of the methodologies prescribed in the ADA.[233] Art. IX:2 WTO Agreement mandates the Ministerial Conference and the General Council to adopt interpretations of the WTO Agreements on the basis of a recommendation by the Council overseeing the agreement—*in casu*, the Anti-Dumping Committee. Authoritative interpretations, however, cannot add obligations, or modify their content, but rather clarify the meaning of the existing obligations.[234] It seems unlikely that this is a valid avenue. Rather, new rulemaking is only possible though an amendment or a waiver to incorporate new rights and obligations to the ADA.[235]

Also in relation to dual pricing schemes, the definition of the 'like product' for input dumping or input subsidy investigation procedures may be relevant. In principle, the anti-dumping rules would prevent the imposition of ADDs on the input because it is not sold on the export market as well as on the final product because that product is not dumped. Accordingly, downstream dumping would fall through the mazes of the anti-dumping disciplines, which the Anti-Dumping Committee may want to address.[236] Nonetheless, issues with input dumping have been considered by investigating authorities and the Appellate Body in various cases.

6.6 Chapter Summary

The maintenance of low environmental standards or the lax enforcement thereof may lead exporting companies to put goods on the international market at less than their normal value. This phenomenon has popularly been considered as "eco-dumping" and refers to situations where the price of goods does not fully internalise environmental costs. However, the ADA disciplines on dumping aim to counter price dumping and excludes other forms of dumping such as eco-dumping from its scope of application.

Investigating authorities have nonetheless dealt with government-distorted costs and prices in the calculation of ADD levels. Investigating authorities can influence the benchmark price to include government-distorted costs both at the stage of determining the normal value as well as at the stage of price comparability.

---

[233] Howse (2013), p. 51.
[234] Van Damme (2010), p. 612.
[235] Art. X WTO Agreement; Art. XI:3 and 4 WTO Agreement.
[236] Matsushita et al. (2015), pp. 384–385.

First, the normal value calculation rules focus in principle on the market conditions in the country of production and therefore include the government distortions. Low environmental standards may play a role in arguing that the actual prices must be disregarded. The interpretations by the DSB of Art. 2.2 ADA reveal significant hurdles. Regardless of whether the government intervention distorts the domestic prices or the input prices, there is a possible case to make, and irrespective whether such distortions affect only domestic sales or also export sales prices. Once investigating authorities rely on alternative methodologies, environmental costs could be included in the benchmark normal value—although the aim shall be for investigating authorities to recreate the conditions of the country of production. NME methodologies are in essence used to address general distortions in the market, not environmental regulation as a stand-alone government policy.

Second, price comparability and adjustment arguments motivated by differences in the environmental cost or carbon content of goods will only be successful if they are demonstrated to affect price comparability. In case of differences in environmental protection standards, this shall generally not be the case. In the case of input dumping, the case may be different, and arguments could be sustained.

It is therefore hard to sustain an argument based on the current rules of the WTO trade remedy rules and jurisprudence to calculate environmental costs in the level of duty. Legislative amendments to the basic trade remedy rules would be required. Although such amendments are politically unlikely to be successful, investigating authorities continue exploring how to deal with government-distorted costs and prices and the inclusion of environmental costs of production in the calculation of ADDs.

References

Antonini R (2018) A 'MES' to be adjusted: past and future treatment of Chinese imports in EU anti-dumping investigations. Global Trade Cust J 13(3):79–94

Charnovitz S (1993) A taxonomy of environmental trade measures. Georgetown Int Environ Law Rev 6(1):1–46

Choi H, Lee SH (2017) Using modified anti-dumping mechanisms for sustainable development: the case of the Chinese Iron and Steel Industry. ASAN Report

Crowley MA, Hillman JA (2018) Slamming the door on trade policy discretion? The WTO Appellate Body's ruling on market distortions and production costs in *EU-Biodiesel (Argentina)*. World Trade Rev 17(2):195–213

De Baere P (2021) The EU's amended basic anti-dumping regulation – a practitioner's view. In: Hahn M, Van der Loo G (eds) Law and practice of the common commercial policy: the first 10 years after the Treaty of Lisbon. Brill/Nijhoff, Leiden/Boston, pp 356–379

De Baere P, du Parc C, Van Damme I (2021) The WTO Anti-Dumping Agreement. A detailed commentary. Cambridge University Press, Cambridge

Eliason A, Fiorini M (2020) Australia – anti-dumping measures on A4 copy paper: opening a door to more anti-dumping investigations. EUI Working Paper RSCAS 2020/87

Espa I, Levy PI (2018) The analogue method comes unfastened – the awkward space between market and non-market economies in EC–Fasteners (Article 21.5). World Trade Rev 17(2):313–334

Esty DC (1994) Greening the GATT. Trade, environment, and the future. Institute for International Economics, Washington

Furculiță C (2017) Cost of production calculation in EU anti-dumping law: WTO consistent 'as such' after EU – Biodiesel. Global Trade Cust J 12(9):360–366

Geraets D (2018) The continued quest for a single set of rules for two economic systems: addressing 'significant distortions' arising from state influence. Global Trade Cust J 13(11):491–495

Gustafsson M, Crochet V (2020) At the crossroads of trade and environment. The growing influence of environmental policy on EU trade law. In: Orsini A, Kavvatha E (eds) EU environmental governance. Current and future challenges. Taylor & Francis, London, pp 187–206

Hoffmeister F (2021) The devil is in the detail – a first guide on the EU's new trade defence rules. In: Hahn M, Van der Loo G (eds) Law and practice of the common commercial policy. The first 10 years after the Treaty of Lisbon. Brill/Nijhoff, Leiden/Boston, pp 335–354

Horlick G (2013) Trade remedies and development of renewable energy. In: E15 Expert Group on Clean Energy Technologies and the Trade System (ed) Clean energy and the trade system: proposals and analysis. ICTSD/WEF, Geneva, pp 69–73

Howse R (2013) Securing policy space for clean energy under the SCM Agreement: alternative approaches. In: E15 Expert Group on Clean Energy Technologies and the Trade System (ed) Clean energy and the trade system: proposals and analysis. ICTSD/WEF, Geneva, pp 47–51

Kampel K (2017) Options for disciplining the use of trade remedies in clean energy technologies. ICTSD Issue Paper

Kim SM, Bohanes J (2020) Case summary: Australia – anti-dumping measures on A4 Copy Paper, DS529. World Trade Rev 19(3):480–484

Lesmana YY, Koesnaidi JW (2019) Particular market situation: a newly arising problem or a new stage in the anti-dumping investigation? Asian J WTO Int Health Law Policy 14(2):405–422

Lester S (2017) Social and environmental protection in EU anti-dumping calculations. IELP Blog. https://ielp.worldtradelaw.net/2017/11/social-and-environmental-protection-in-eu-anti-dumping-calculations.html. Accessed 23 June 2023

Lothe S (2001) Contradictions between WTO and sustainable development? The case of environmental dumping. Sustain Dev 9:197–203

Matsushita M, Schoenbaum T, Mavroidis P, Hahn M (2015) The World Trade Organization, law, practice, and policy, 3rd edn. Oxford University Press, Oxford

Meléndez-Ortiz R (2016) Enabling the energy transition and scale-up of clean energy technologies: options for the global trade system. E15 Expert Group on Clean Energy Technologies and the Trade System, Policy Options Paper

Müller S (2018) The use of alternative benchmarks in anti-subsidy law. A study on the WTO, the EU and China. Springer, Cham

Müller-Ibold T (2020) Der Einfluss Chinas auf die Wirtschaft – Konsequenzen für die Europäische Wettbewerbs- und Außenhandelspolitik. Zeitschrift für Europarechtliche Studien 23(2):239–265

Natens B (2020) Belangrijkste wijzigingen aan de Europese antidumpingregelgeving: Het pad naar (nog) meer onzekerheid. Tijdschrift voor Europees en economisch recht 20(3):106–115

Nicely MR, Gatta B (2016) U.S. Trade Preferences Extension Act (TPEA) of 2015 could lead to increased use of "particular market situation" in calculating normal value in anti-dumping cases. Global Trade Cust J 11(5):238–243

Noël S (2016) Why the European Union must dump so-called "non-market economy" methodologies and adjustments in its anti-dumping investigations. Global Trade Cust J 11(7/8):296–305

Noël S, Zhou W (2016) Replacing the non-market economy methodology: is the European Union's alternative approach justified under the World Trade Organization Anti-Dumping Agreement? Global Trade Cust J 11(11/12):559–567

Palmeter D (1998) The WTO antidumping agreement and the economies in transition. In: Cottier T, Mavroidis P (eds) State trading in the twenty-first century: world trade forum, vol 1. University of Michigan Press, Michigan, pp 115–119

Patterson E (1992) GATT and the environment. Rules challenges to minimize adverse trade and environmental effects. J World Trade 26(3):99–109

Pauwelyn J (2013) Carbon leakage measures and border tax adjustments under WTO law. In: Prévost D, Van Calster G (eds) Research handbook on environment, health and the WTO. Edward Elgar Publishing, Cheltenham/Northampton, pp 448–506

Pogoretskyy V (2011) Energy dual pricing in international trade: subsidies and anti-dumping perspectives. In: Selivanova Y (ed) Regulation of energy in international trade law: WTO, NAFTA and Energy Charter. Kluwer Law International, Alphen aan den Rijn, pp 181–228

Polouektov A (2002) Non-market economy issues in the WTO anti-dumping law and accession negotiations. Revival of a two-tier membership? J World Trade 36(1):1–37

Rauscher M (1994) On ecological dumping. Oxf Econ Pap 46(Suppl 1):822–840

Reinhold P, Van Vaerenbergh P (2021) Significant distortions under Art. 2(6a) BADR: three years of commission practice. Global Trade Cust J 16(5):193–202

Ruessmann L, Beck J (2014) 2016 and the application of an NME methodology to Chinese producers in anti-dumping investigations. Global Trade Cust J 9(10):457–463

Sands P, Peel J (2018) Principles of international environmental law, 4th edn. Cambridge University Press, Cambridge

Selivanova Y (2008) Energy dual pricing in the WTO: analysis and prospects in the context of Russia's Accession to the World Trade Organization. Cameron May, London

Shadikhodjaev S (2019) Input cost adjustments and WTO anti-dumping law: a closer look at the EU practice. World Trade Rev 18(1):81–107

Stewart TP, Mueller DP (2008) Art. 2 ADA. In: Wolfrum R, Stoll PT, Koebele M (eds) Max Planck commentaries on trade law – trade remedies. Brill, Leiden

Tereposky & Derose LLP (2019) Canada implements new anti-dumping rules targeting related-company input dumping and "particular market situation" input distortions. Trade & ISDS News. https://tradeisds.com/canada-implements-new-anti-dumpingrules-re-input-cost-distortions/. Accessed 23 June 2023

Tietje C, Sacher V (2018) The new anti-dumping methodology of the European Union: a breach of WTO law? In: Bungenberg M, Hahn M, Herrmann C, Müller-Ibold T (eds) The future of trade defence instruments. Global policy trends and legal challenges. Springer, Cham, pp 89–105

Tietje C, Kluttig B, Franke M (2011) Cost of production adjustments in anti-dumping proceedings: challenging raw material inputs dual pricing systems in EU anti-dumping law and practice. J World Trade 45(5):1071–1102

Trapp P (2021) "Global Green Governance" oder "Veiled Protectionism"? Die Berücksichtigung sozial- und umweltpolitischer Belange in den reformierten Grundverordnungen der EU zur Verhängung von Anti-Dumping- und Ausgleichsmaßnahmen. Nachhaltigkeitsrecht 1(2):195–204

Van Bael & Bellis (2019) EU anti-dumping and other trade defence instruments, 6th edn. Wolters Kluwer, Alphen aan den Rijn

Van Damme I (2010) Treaty interpretation by the WTO Appellate Body. Eur J Int Law 21(3):605–648

Vermulst E (2005) The WTO Anti-Dumping Agreement. Oxford University Press, Oxford

Vermulst E, Meng M (2017) Dumping and subsidy issues in the renewable energy sector. In: Cottier T, Espa I (eds) International trade in sustainable electricity regulatory challenges in international economic law. Cambridge University Press, Cambridge, pp 336–355

Vermulst E, Sud JD (2018) The new rules adopted by the European Union to address "significant distortions" in the anti-dumping context. In: Bungenberg M, Hahn M, Herrmann C, Müller-Ibold T (eds) The future of trade defence instruments. Global policy trends and legal challenges. Springer, Cham, pp 63–87

Watson KW (2014) Will nonmarket economy methodology go quietly into the night? CATO Institute Policy Analysis No. 763

Yamaoka T (2013) Analysis of China's accession commitments in the WTO: new taxonomy of more and less stringent commitments, and the struggle for mitigation by China. J World Trade 47(1):105–157

Yun M (2017) The use of "Particular Market Situation" provision and its implications for regulation of antidumping. East Asian Econ Rev 21(3):231–257

Zhang MQ (2011) *EC – Fasteners*: opening the Pandora's box of non-market economy treatment. J Int Econ Law 14(4):869–892

Zhou W (2018) Appellate Body Report on EU – Biodiesel: the future of China's state capitalism under the WTO Anti-Dumping Agreement. World Trade Rev 17(4):609–633

Zhou W, Peng D (2021) Australia – anti-dumping measures on A4 Copy Paper, WT/DS529/R. Am J Int Law 115(1):94–101

Zhou W, Percival A (2016) Panel Report on EU – Biodiesel: a glass half full? – Implications for the rising issue of "particular market situation". Chin J Global Gov 2(2):142–163

Chapter 7
Low Environmental Standards and the SGA Rules

7.1 Introduction

The scope of safeguard measures could be expanded to remedy foreign policies on environmental protection and climate change. It has been argued that instead of attempting to broaden the scope of applicability of trade remedies, safeguards measures could be a tool to remedy surges of imports that can be allocated to non-trade concerns such as environmental protection.[1] Environmental considerations in the SGA could mean allowing safeguards measures against a surge of low-priced imports from countries that do not adhere to environmental standards. This requires an investigation of the prerequisites for the imposition of a safeguard measure, namely an unforeseen development and an increase of imports.

7.2 Environmental Considerations in Safeguards Investigations

The SGA details out substantive requirements that may trigger the imposition of safeguard measures: "A Member may apply a safeguard measure to a product only if [...] such product is being imported into its territory in such increased quantities [...] as to cause or threaten to cause serious injury to the domestic industry that produces like or directly competitive products."[2]

The substantive requirements to be investigated include an increase in imports, due to unforeseen developments, causing serious injury. First, safeguard measures

---

[1] Barceló (1994), pp. 16–17.

[2] Art. 2.1 SGA.

© The Author(s), under exclusive license to Springer Nature Switzerland AG 2023
P. Van Vaerenbergh, *Greening Trade Remedies*, EYIEL Monographs - Studies in European and International Economic Law 31,
https://doi.org/10.1007/978-3-031-38172-0_7

would only be mandated as a reaction on a steep increase in imports of a certain product. The Appellate Body clarified, in *Argentina – Footwear*, that the investigating authority must find an increase in important that has been "recent enough, sudden enough, sharp enough and significant enough, both quantitatively and qualitatively."[3] An investigation of the trend of imports during the period of investigation is necessary, not an end-to-end comparison which is not sufficient in the eyes of the Appellate Body.[4] Second, the increased import levels must be the consequence of unforeseen developments. The moment in time to judge the unforeseeable nature of the developments is the time of the last tariff negotiation that was concluded, *i.e.* the conclusion of the Uruguay Round negotiation.[5] Third, the sudden increase of imports must cause or threaten to cause serious injury to domestic industries to justify the imposition of safeguard measures. The Appellate Body confirmed that standard of "serious injury" in the SGA embodies a significantly higher standard than the "material injury" standard in anti-dumping and anti-subsidy investigations.[6] These material requirements may be used to consider the impact of environmental regulation on trade flows through the safeguards mechanism.

A finding that "unforeseen developments" cause a surge of imports of a certain good is one of the requirements to impose a safeguard measure.[7] Environmental policies have been considered as an unforeseen development, which mandates the imposition of safeguards measures in the sense of Art. 4 SGA. For instance, in the 2020 safeguards investigation on lubricant oils, the National Trade Remedies Authority in Madagascar (ANMCC) linked environmental policies abroad to unforeseen developments mandating safeguards.[8] It established a sudden, recent, significant and sharp increase in imports of lubricant oils due to unforeseen developments, in particular the energy transition of developed countries, including some countries or economic unions that have adopted energy transition policies and strategies since 2015. As a result, so argued the ANMCC, developing countries became the main destination of mineral oil lubricants, in the absence of similar energy transition policies. The ANMCC is yet to propose a measure to follow up on the finding of serious injury. Nevertheless, high standard environmental policies in developing

---

[3] Appellate Body report, *Argentina – Safeguard Measures on Imports of Footwear*, WT/DS121/AB/R, adopted 12 January 2000, para. 131.

[4] Appellate Body report, *United States – Definitive Safeguard Measures on Imports of Certain Steel Products*, WT/DS248, 249, 253, 258/AB/R, adopted 10 December 2003, para. 353–356.

[5] Panel report, *Argentina – Definitive Safeguard Measure on Imports of Preserved Peaches*, WT/DS238/R, adopted 15 April 2003, para. 7.35; Panel Report, *Dominican Republic – Safeguard Measures on Imports of Polypropylene Bags and Tubular Fabric*, WT/DS417/R, adopted 22 February 2012, para. 128–129.

[6] Appellate Body, *United States – Safeguard Measures on Imports of Fresh, Chilled or Frozen Lamb from New Zealand*, WT/DS177/AB/R, adopted 16 May 2001, para. 124 and 126.

[7] See Sect. 3.2.3.2.3 above.

[8] See Committee on Safeguards, Notification Under Article 12.1(b) of the Agreement on Safeguards of a Finding of Serious Injury or Threat Thereof Caused by Increased Imports, Madagascar, Lubricating oils, G/SG/N/8/MDG/7, 20 July 2020.

countries were argued to create unforeseen developments in a safeguard investigation in a developing country.

Similarly, the DSB has considered the domestic policies in low-standard countries under the notion of unforeseen developments. Most recently, the Panel in *US – Solar Safeguard* also considered the domestic policies in China as an unforeseen development.[9] The Panel noted that "China's industrial policies, five-year plans and other government support programs" were a development that could not have been foreseen by US negotiators.[10]

Not only foreign policies, but also domestic environmental targets have played a role in the imposition of safeguard measures. India's Director General of Trade Remedies (DGTR) has recommended to impose safeguard duty on solar cells whether or not assembled in modules or panels.[11] As an unforeseen development, the investigation noted the confluence of simultaneous imposition of trade remedy measures in the US and the EU leading to a rerouting of Chinese solar panels into the Indian market, in combination with the commitment undertaken by India under the Paris Agreement, according to which it aims to reduce CO_2 emissions by 33–35% from 2005 levels by achieving 100 GW of Solar power generation by the year 2022.

Furthermore, adherence to appropriate environmental standards has also been considered when investigating whether the unforeseen development caused the material injury in the market. As part of their investigation, domestic authorities must examine whether an increase in imports is solely to be attributed to the unforeseen development.[12] The Indonesian investigating authority, for instance, in an investigation on coated paper and paperboard, cited adherence of the product to all international standard, including the highest environmental standards, as sufficient ground to conclude that the quality of the product could not be seen as the driver of increased imports.[13]

Yet another instance where environmental efforts are recognised in safeguards measures is when evaluating adjustment plans. According to Art. 5 SGA, Members shall facilitate adjustments to the safeguard measures. Although this does not imply

---

[9] Panel report, *United States – Safeguard Measure on Imports of Crystalline Silicon Photovoltaic Products*, WT/DS562/R, circulated 2 September 2021, para. 7.26.

[10] *Ibid.*

[11] Committee on Safeguards, Notification Under Article 12.1(b) of the Agreement on Safeguards on Finding a Serious Injury or Threat Thereof Caused by Increased Imports, Notification of a Proposal to Impose a Measure, Notification Pursuant to Article 9, Footnote 2, of the Agreement on Safeguards, India, Solar Cells Whether or not assembled in modules or panels, G/SG/N/8/IND/31/SUPPL.1, 2 August 2018.

[12] Art. 2.1 SGA.

[13] See Committee on Safeguards, Notification under Article 12.4 of the Agreement on Safeguards Before Taking a Provisional Safeguard Measure Referred to in Article 6, Notification under Article 12.1(b) of the Agreement on Safeguards on Finding a Serious Injury or Threat Thereof Caused by Increased Imports, Notification Pursuant to Article 9, Footnote 2 of the Agreement on Safeguards, India, Sodium Hydroxide, also known as Caustic Soda, G/SG/N/8/IDN/19; G/SG/N/10/IDN/19, 23 November 2009.

an obligation to consider adjustment plans,[14] such plans are a frequent practice among WTO Members. The Egyptian investigating authority accepted a viable adjustment plan from the domestic industry, which focused *inter alia* on improving quality infrastructure to match the environmental requirements.[15] Also the Indonesian authority noted restructuring efforts made by the domestic industry with a view to improve safety, health and environmental protection by complying with (environmental) certification obligations and investing in and researching about environmentally friendly production facilities.[16] Similarly, in another case it accepted adjustment of the domestic industry through modernisation of machinery with the aim of increasing efficiency in energy use by using alternative energy other than electricity, such as gas or coal.[17]

In sum, although environmental regulations have been considered in the framework of safeguards investigations, examples of investigating authorities relying on environmental standards are scarce. The scope of the SGA notion of unforeseen developments remains therefore largely untested.

7.3 Expanding the Scope of Safeguards Measures

Besides limited examples of safeguard investigations in practice, discussions exist on the expansion of the notion of safeguards to address other injury than competitive injury on the domestic market. *Trebilcock/Trachtman* have noted that existing reform proposals for the safeguards regime include a reconceptualisation of the material injury to entail impacts on disadvantaged workers and communities in the country of importation instead of competitive impacts on the domestic industry.[18] This would align with the original purpose of safeguard measures, namely the protection of domestic businesses and workers that suffer trade-related injury linked to

---

[14] Panel report, *Korea – Definitive Safeguard Measure on Imports of Certain Dairy Products*, WT/DS98/R, adopted 12 January 2000, para. 7.108.

[15] See Committee on Safeguards, Notification under Article 12.1(b) of the Agreement on Safeguards on Finding a Serious Injury or Threat Thereof Caused by Increased Imports, Notification under Article 12.1(c) of the Agreement on Safeguards on Taking a Decision to Apply a Safeguard Measure, Notification Pursuant to Article 9, Footnote 2, of the Agreement on Safeguards, Egypt, Automotive Batteries, G/SG/N/8/EGY/8; G/SG/N/10/EGY/8; G/SG/N/11/EGY/10, 26 October 2015.

[16] See Committee on Safeguards, Notification under Article 12.5 of the Agreement on Safeguards of the Results of a Mid-Term Review Referred to in Article 7.4, Indonesia, Seamless pipe casing and tubing, G/L/1120; G/SG/N/13/IDN/2, 8 September 2015.

[17] See Committee on Safeguards, Notification Under Article 12.1(b) of the Agreement on Safeguard on Finding a Serious Injury or Threat Thereof Caused by Increased Imports, Notification of a Proposal to Extend a Measure, Indonesia, I and H Sections of Other Alloy Steel, G/SG/N/8/IDN/4/SUPPL.3; G/SG/N/10/IDN/4/SUPPL.3, 13 May 2022.

[18] Trebilcock and Trachtman (2020), pp. 112–113.

an unforeseen surge in imports.[19] *Patterson*, for instance, proposed to design an emergency clause which allows importing countries to impose measures against sudden peaks in import of goods that would cause environmental harm in the country of importation.[20] With such an emergency clause, the GATT would be equipped with a mechanism to respond to unexpected changes in the recognised environmental impact of a product, due to disaster, changes in the production process, or environmental vulnerability of the importing country.[21] The investigating authority would have to show that this causes environmental harm in the importing country and that this harm is new and unexpected.[22] The injury orientation should therefore be shifted towards environmental injury in the country of importation.

Another proposal is to expand the scope of the safeguards mechanism motivated by non-economic considerations. According to *Rodrik*, countries may legitimately wish to restrict trade for policy reasons going beyond competitive threats to their domestic industries.[23] One reason to expand the scope of the safeguards regime, he argues, may be "distributional conflicts with domestic normal or social arrangements".[24] In such broadened conception of safeguard measures, an evaluation of distributional considerations, conflict with domestic social balance, or erosion of domestic regulations including environmental standards would be a ground to apply safeguard measures.[25] A broadened scope of the Safeguards Agreement would not only consider protection of domestic but also of foreign workers. Such an expanded safeguard mechanism can be a safety-valve that allows principled objections to free trade, which would make it easier to respond to the protectionist objections.[26]

7.4   Chapter Summary

Environmental policies and environmental measures have been considered in the framework of safeguard investigations as unforeseen developments. Notably, both foreign policies as well as domestic policies have been referenced by investigating authorities. In some instances, countries directly referred to foreign policies causing an increase in imports mandating protective measures because they caused serious injury on the domestic market. Notably, most examples discussed involved safeguards measures from developing countries and LDCs.

---

[19] See Sect. 3.2.2.3 above.

[20] Patterson (1992), pp. 103–104.

[21] *Ibid.*

[22] *Ibid.*

[23] Rodrik (2018), p. 4.

[24] *Ibid*, p. 5.

[25] Rodrik (2011), pp. 252–259.

[26] Rodrik (2018), p. 5.

Besides this limited practice, proposals to expand the scope of the SGA to include environmental harm both on the territory of the importing country as well as on the territory of the exporting country have been advanced. Especially the latter is controversial and would necessitate procedural and substantive assurances if developed into a trade tool.

References

Barceló JJ III (1994) Countervailing against environmental subsidies. Can Bus Law J 23(1):3–22

Patterson E (1992) GATT and the environment. Rules challenges to minimize adverse trade and environmental effects. J World Trade 26(3):99–109

Rodrik D (2011) The globalization paradox: democracy and the future of the world economy. W.W. Norton & Co., New York

Rodrik D (2018) Towards a More Inclusive Globalization: An Anti-Social Dumping Scheme. ECONFIP Research Brief

Trebilcock MJ, Trachtman J (2020) Advanced introduction to international trade law, 2nd edn. Edward Elgar, Cheltenham/Northampton

Chapter 8
Environmental Injury and Trade Remedy Rules

8.1 Introduction

The imposition of trade remedy duties and measures is conditioned on a finding that the imports cause injury to the domestic industry, and does not consider harm or injury to the environment or global commons. Challenging this basic principle in the WTO trade remedy agreements, *Choi/Lee* argue that environmental injury merits more attention in the context of international trade rules.[1] Factoring in environmental aspects in the investigatory step on injury could include considering environmental harm next to and/or in addition to economic harm—be it environmental harm in the market of the importing country, or environmental injury caused to the global commons and the country of production.

Examining injury can be done jointly for all three types of trade remedies. The standards for injury and causation are nearly identical for the ADA and ASCM.[2] The DSB has cross-referenced between both agreements, for instance on causation and non-attribution,[3] and WTO Members have called for a consistent resolution of disputes arising from anti-dumping and anti-subsidy measures.[4] Although ADDs are a reaction to exporters positioning products on foreign markets at less than their normal value and CVDs to government-subsidised goods, in both cases, the aim is to remedy the injurious effects of these imports on the market of the importing

---

[1] Choi and Lee (2017).

[2] Barceló (1980), p. 285.

[3] See, for instance, Panel report, *European Communities – Countervailing Measures on Dynamic Random Access Memory Chips from Korea*, WT/DS299/R, adopted 3 August 2005, para. 7.404.

[4] See Declaration on Dispute Settlement Pursuant to the Agreement on Implementation of Article VI of the General Agreement on Tariffs and Trade 1994 or Part V of the Agreement on Subsidies and Countervailing Measures, 15 December 1993.

© The Author(s), under exclusive license to Springer Nature Switzerland AG 2023
P. Van Vaerenbergh, *Greening Trade Remedies*, EYIEL Monographs - Studies in European and International Economic Law 31,
https://doi.org/10.1007/978-3-031-38172-0_8

Member.[5] Although the SGA sets out a higher standard of 'serious injury' as compared to 'material injury',[6] the injury requirement as such equally refers to economic harm on the domestic market of the importing Member.

In its current conception, environmental injury does not play a role in assessing material or serious injury in the context of trade remedy investigations. First, this chapter outlines the role of environmental harm under the injury rules (Sect. 8.2). Nonetheless, the scope of trade remedies could be expanded motivated by environmental considerations through the creation of novel trade instruments, in line with current legislative developments (Sect. 8.3, 8.4). This section concludes that although reconceptualising the injury notion in terms of environmental harm would be controversial and complex to implement within the current framework, the creation of a trade remedy-like instrument could address environmental injury (Sect. 8.5).

8.2   Environmental Harm and the Injury Rules: State of Play

8.2.1   Environmental Harm in Trade Remedy Injury Determinations

Under the current trade remedy provisions on injury, environmental harm is in principle not considered, unless it leads to economic harm to the domestic industry. Injury determination in case of dumped or subsidised imports consists of four interrelated steps: (1) the definition of the like product, (2) the definition of the domestic industry, (3) the determination of material or serious injury, and (4) the establishment of a causal link. Similarly, the SGA requires a definition of the domestic industry and consideration of all relevant (economic) factors having a bearing on the state of the industry.[7] Environmental harm can therefore only be considered in the injury determination when resulting in economic losses for the domestic industry.

The ADA and ASCM provisions foresee that injury is to be determined on the basis of a positive evidence and objective examination of (a) the volume of the dumped imports and the effect on prices, and (b) the consequent impact of these imports on the domestic producers.[8] If low-priced goods not internalising environmental costs cause harm to the domestic industry, this could be regarded an effect on prices, evidenced by price undercutting of the dumped/subsidised imports as compared to the prices of the like products of the importing country. Moreover, Art.

[5] Nedumpara (2016), p. 54.

[6] Appellate Body report, *United States – Safeguard Measure on Imports of Fresh, Chilled or Frozen Lamb from New Zealand*, WT/DS177/AB/R, adopted 16 May 2001, para. 124; Appellate Body report, *United States – Definitive Safeguard Measures on Imports of Wheat Gluten from the European Communities*, WT/DS166/AB/R, adopted 19 January 2001, para. 149; Appellate Body report, *Argentina – Safeguard Measures on Imports of Footwear*, WT/DS122/AB/R, adopted 10 January 2000, para. 94. See also Nedumpara (2016), p. 61.

[7] Art. 4 SGA.

[8] Art. 3 ADA; Art. 15 ASCM.

3.4 ADA and Art. 15.4 ASCM foresee that all relevant economic factors and indices having a bearing on the state of the industry shall be considered.[9] The impact of low-priced environmentally harmful goods must be connected to one of these factors to be considered.

One example where environmental costs can be considered is situations where environmental costs are higher in the domestic industry as compared to the foreign industry. In *Tungstic Oxide and Tungstic Acid*, for instance, the European Commission considered the impact of Chinese products on the Union industry in the injury analysis, pointing out that environmental costs render the transformation from APT to oxide/acid higher in the EU than in China—although not significantly in that case.[10]

The injury threshold is higher in case of safeguard measures. Art. 4 SGA requires "serious injury" to be established before safeguard measures may be mandated. Serious injury is defined as a significant overall impairment in the position of a domestic industry.[11] The term "serious" injury implies a very high standard of injury—which can be allocated to the fact that the SGA does not react to unfair trade.[12] The analysis to be carried out by the investigating authority is an evaluation of trends in the volume or market share of imports on the basis of the factors listed,[13] including rate and amount of the increase in imports, share of the domestic market of the increased imports, changes in level of sales, production, productivity, capacity utilisation, profits and losses, and employment.[14] Again, only insofar as differences in environmental costs affect the position of the domestic industry, it may have a bearing on the injury determination.

8.2.2   *Environmental Costs in the Calculation of the Injury Margin*

Environmental harm to the domestic industry may be relevant when calculating the injury margin. Investigating authorities calculate the injury margin upon the application of the LDR.[15] Art. 9.1 ADA and Art. 19.2 ASCM prescribe a non-mandatory

---

[9] See, for dumping, De Baere et al. (2021), para. 458–461.

[10] Commission Decision of 20 March 1998 terminating the anti-dumping proceeding concerning imports of tungstic oxide and tungstic acid originating in the People's Republic of China, OJ 1998 L 87/24, rec. 48.

[11] Art. 4.1(a) SGA.

[12] See Appellate Body report, *United States – Safeguard Measure on Imports of Fresh, Chilled or Frozen Lamb from New Zealand and Australia*, WT/DS177/AB/R, WT/DS178/AB/R, adopted 16 May 2001, para. 124; Appellate Body report, *Argentina – Safeguard Measures on Imports of Footwear*, WT/DS121/AB/R, adopted 12 January 2000, para. 94.

[13] Prost and Berthelot (2008), Art. 4 SGA, para. 8–9.

[14] Art. 4.2(a) SGA.

[15] See Sect. 3.2.3.3 above.

LDR[16] by holding that "it is desirable that [...] the duty be less than the margin if such lesser duty would be adequate to remove the injury to the domestic industry." The LDR is a beneficial measure which investigating authorities may apply, resulting in lower duty levels of ADDs or CVDs.[17] The LDR is applied in case investigating authorities find that a duty at the level of the injury margin would suffice to protect the domestic industry, rather than the full margin of dumping or amount of subsidy respectively. Under WTO rules, it is a voluntary measure for Members to apply, leading to lower ADDs or CVD duty levels. The injury margin level calculates the level of duty necessary to alleviate the harm in the domestic industry. Accordingly, it quantifies the price undercutting level in the domestic industry. The consideration of environmental costs borne by the domestic industry, for instance in the form of extra costs for compliance with stringent environmental legislation, into the injury margin level would lift the trade remedy burden again.

The EU has been the first jurisdiction in the world to include environmental costs in the calculation of the injury margin. Since the 2018 legislative reform, the EU calculates actual and future environmental costs in the injury margin. Art. 7(2a) BADR foresees that raw material distortions with regard to the product concerned shall be considered in the calculation of the injury margin. When the injury margin is calculated on the basis of a target price, the target price to be used shall include the actual cost of production of the EU industry resulting from inter alia MEAs and protocols thereunder.[18] As illustrated by Fig. 8.1, this EU 'target price' exists of the product costs plus a reasonable profit margin of at least 6% and will be used as benchmark for comparison with exporting producers' price on the EU market. The injury margin calculation has been criticised as one of the most problematic areas of confidential information, which allows too much administrative discretion by the investigating authorities.[19] The new rules will not alleviate such criticism, but only strengthen it.

The new EU methodology does not only include actual environmental compliance costs, but also future costs.[20] This aspect is a single prospective element in an otherwise completely retrospective investigation, which is not taken into account on the side of the exporting producer.[21] In *Urea and Ammonium Nitrate from China*, the Commission included costs relating to the Emissions Trading Scheme (ETS) as future costs.[22] It calculated the future costs of the industry for complying with the EU's emissions trading system into account when determining the minimum level of duty required to offset the injury to the EU industry. Consequently, the

---

[16] De Baere et al. (2021), para. 924.

[17] *Ibid.*

[18] Art. 7(2c) BADR, first sentence.

[19] Vermulst and Sud (2018), pp. 70–71.

[20] Art. 7(2c) BADR, second sentence.

[21] Natens (2020), p. 115.

[22] Commission Implementing Regulation (EU) 2019/576 of 10 April 2019 imposing a provisional anti-dumping duty on imports of mixtures of urea and ammonium nitrate originating in Russia, Trinidad and Tobago and the United States of America, OJ 2019 L 100/7, rec. 202.

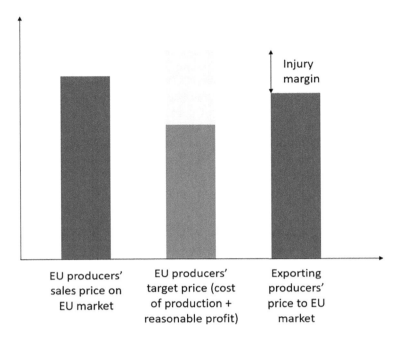

Fig. 8.1   Target price determination in the EU. Source: Author's own creation

non-injurious price was elevated with 3.8%, the underselling margin was higher, and the duty level was higher. It can be expected that more such examples will follow. However, the ETS does not apply to all sectors of EU industry, it applies to only two (major) sources of GHG emissions, namely heavy energy-using installations (power stations and industrial plants) and airlines. In the new industrial policy and the European Green Deal, the Commission is examining the possibility to extend the ETS scheme to other sectors, which would consequently also be covered by this new mechanism in anti-dumping procedures. It is unclear whether other types of future environmental costs may be considered too. It has been held that it is problematic that similar future costs for adherence to MEAs are not calculated for the exporting producer, which may raise concerns about discriminatory treatment.[23]

Given the LDR's voluntary nature and the wide discretion of investigating authorities,[24] these environmentally motivated modifications to the LDR in the EU legal framework will be hard to challenge. LDR applications have not been challenged yet in DSB jurisprudence but could theoretically face litigation under the standard of Art. 17.6(i) ADA where the investigating authorities' establishment of

---

[23] Natens (2020), p. 115.

[24] Panel report, *European Union – Anti-Dumping Measures on Certain Footwear from China*, WT/DS405/R, adopted 28 October 2011, para. VII.920–VII.935.

the facts was improper or the evaluation thereof biased/not objective.[25] Nonetheless, it has been argued that the combination of the removal of the LDR and the application of the new significant distortions methodology may give rise to WTO compatibility issues on account of "double counting".[26] The problem of double remedies arises when the simultaneous application of ADDs and CVDs on the same imported products results, at least to some extent, in offsetting the same subsidisation twice.[27] Under the new EU rules, the danger of double remedies arises where subsidies would be counted as a key element in assessing significant distortions and then consequently the LDR would not be applied in the anti-dumping and/or anti-subsidy investigation.[28] For the LDR in ADDs, this depends on whether the structural raw material distortions threshold is met.

8.3 Expanding the Scope of Trade Remedies: Recent Developments and Legislative Proposals

Novel approaches in rulemaking increasingly deal with environmental considerations in trade remedy injury determinations rather than competitive harm. Discussions are not only pinned on a concern about environmental damage and injury, but also how to curb this damage through imposition of duties which are either trade remedy duties or measures modelled after trade remedy duties. Accordingly, this section reviews developments and proposals where the injury investigation is approached as including harm to the environment, as well as competitors—to include possible harm caused by local producers. It considers the proposed expansion of the scope of the CVDs to counter low environmental standards (Sect. 8.3.1), disciplines for subsidies with environmentally harmful effects (Sect. 8.3.2), new instruments allowing duties for environmental protection in the EU-UK TCA (Sect. 8.3.3), and a proposed expansion of the scope of safeguard measures (Sect. 8.3.4).

---

[25] Vermulst (2005), p. 173.

[26] Vermulst and Sud (2018), pp. 83 ff.

[27] Appellate Body report, *United States – Definitive Anti-Dumping Duties and Countervailing Duties on Certain Products from China*, WT/DS379/AB/R, adopted 11 March 2011, para. 541.

[28] Vermulst and Sud (2018), p. 85.

8.3.1   US Environmental CVD Proposal

In December 2020, the US presented a proposal to the WTO General Council about advancing sustainable development goals through trade rules to level the playing field.[29] The US proposed a ministerial decision that accepts the "failure of a government to adopt, maintain, implement and effectively enforce laws and regulations that ensure environmental protections" as an actionable subsidy under the ASCM, allowing Members to impose duties to offset the benefits received by the subsidised industry.[30] Moreover, countervailing duties would also be allowed if one industry disproportionately benefits from sub-standard pollution controls or other environmental measures.[31]

The proposal's consistency with the ASCM definition of a subsidy has been discussed above.[32] By tabling this proposal, the US re-opened the debate as to the qualification of low environmental standards as subsidies under the ASCM.[33] This US proposal is in line with the long-standing concerns of the US regarding differential standards of environmental protection. In the past, voices have been raised to design a GATT Environment Agreement, which would have used international environmental agreements as standards against which trade sanctions can be imposed, as well as Green 301 amendments allowing for retaliation against MEA-unworthy behaviour.[34] *Schoenbaum*, for instance, argued that an environmental code under that GATT is necessary to tackle differences in environmental protection standards, violations of which are to be regarded as subsidies sanctioned with CVD.[35]

8.3.2   Regulating Environmentally Harmful Subsidies

Subsidies that do not cause trade injury, but which harm the global commons are not disciplined under the current subsidy rules, due to the narrow definition of a subsidy in the ASCM, although environmental standards may be a constraint on their use.[36] If it is accepted that certain subsidies create negative externalities—such as damaging the environment—disciplines may be warranted. Prominent examples include fossil fuel subsidies, which encourage exploration, production and use of fossil fuels leading to a rapid depletion of non-renewable natural resources and the

---

[29] General Council, Draft Ministerial Decision, Advancing Sustainable Development Goals Through Trade Rules to Level the Playing Field, WT/GC/W/814, 17 December 2020.

[30] *Ibid.*

[31] *Ibid.*

[32] See Sect. 5.2 above.

[33] Cima and Mbengue (2021), p. 1.

[34] Fletcher (1996), p. 362.

[35] Schoenbaum (1992), p. 723; see also Komoroski (1988), pp. 203 ff.

[36] Horlick and Clarke (2017), p. 694. See also Sect. 3.2.2.2 above.

creation of GHG emissions, as well as fisheries subsidies promoting illegal, unreported, and unregulated fishing (IUU fishing), fishing overfished stocks and fishing adding to overcapacity. The argument can be expanded to any resource-depleting subsidies affecting global commons including forests, air, water, and biological diversity.[37]

Discussions on disciplining these types of subsidies start from a concern about environmental harm rather than economic harm. This has ramifications on the remedies, including potentially unilateral remedies in the form of trade remedy duties or trade remedy-like duties. This section reviews fisheries subsidies (Sect. 8.3.2.1), fossil fuel subsidies (Sect. 8.3.2.2) and agricultural subsidies (Sect. 8.3.2.3).

8.3.2.1   Fisheries Subsidies

Current negotiations on fisheries subsidies are motivated by a consideration of environmental harm rather than harm to the domestic industry. Negotiations are based on the DDA and Hong Kong Ministerial mandate to "strengthen disciplines on subsidies in the fisheries sector, including through the prohibition of certain forms of fisheries subsidies that contribute to overcapacity and over-fishing", and was strengthened by the SDG 14.6, which explicitly called on the WTO for a prohibition on harmful fisheries subsidies.[38]

On account of remedies, currently, the ASCM includes two remedies: a multilateral and unilateral track. On the multilateral level, Art. 4 ASCM foresees multilateral dispute settlement procedures aiming at the withdrawal of the WTO-inconsistent subsidy and ultimately appropriate countermeasures. Art. 22 DSU sets the level of retaliation in monetary terms, which does not provide remedy for environmental harm. This remedy does not consider the environmental objective of the Fisheries Subsidies negotiations. It is therefore contemplated whether a special consultation procedure should be envisaged to duly consider the environmental nature of the disciplines.[39] This would offer WTO Members a forum to exchange information and discuss the environmentally harmful effect of the subsidies, provide a possibility to voluntarily rectify the injurious effects, and ultimately minimise the reliance on litigation.[40]

---

[37] *Ibid. p.* 684.

[38] Doha Development Agenda, para. 28; in 2005, at the Hong Kong Ministerial Conference, ministers elaborated on the mandate; in 2017, the MC in Buenos Aires, ministers decided on a work programme to conclude the negotiations. See also SDG 14.6: "by 2020, prohibit certain forms of fisheries subsidies which contribute to overcapacity and overfishing, and eliminate subsidies that contribute to IUU fishing, and refrain from introducing new such subsidies, recognizing that appropriate and effective special and differential treatment for developing and least developed countries should be an integral part of the WTO fisheries subsidies negotiation."

[39] Tipping and Irschlinger (2020), pp. 19–20.

[40] *Ibid.*

On the unilateral level, the ASCM foresees the possibility to apply CVDs. Whether the remedy of CVDs will become a possibility in the final draft of the Fisheries Subsidies text is unclear. It would need a reconceptualisation of the material injury standard that considers the environmental harm which deviates from the ASCM rules that look at competitive harm of the domestic industry. Alternatively, if the Fisheries Subsidies Agreement allows unilateral remedies, a different type of countervailing measure that offsets a subsidy's impact on fish stocks could be envisaged.[41] If the negotiations on fisheries subsidies are concluded successfully, they may open a gateway to disciplining other forms of environmentally harmful subsidies—most notably fossil fuel subsidies, but also by extension any subsidy that has adverse effects to the environment.[42] Some have observed that allowing unilateral measures against environmentally harmful subsidies may be too sensitive and not fitting as a remedy.[43] Nonetheless, historically, the unilateral track of CVDs has been used against fisheries subsidies.[44]

In May 2021, the Chair of the Negotiating Group on Rules, Ambassador *Wills*, circulated a draft negotiating text on the new fisheries subsidies disciplines.[45] Dispute resolution will be based on the existing DSU rules and the remedies against prohibited subsidies in Art. 4 ASCM.[46] Some Members expressed interest to design fisheries subsidies-specific remedies and/or countermeasures.[47] Countermeasures have been found to be appropriate when corresponding to the total amount of the subsidy[48] or in one case even 20% above that amount, which the arbitrator noted was to "induce compliance" by Canada.[49] There is no mention of the applicability of unilateral measures in the sense of Art. 10 ASCM.

An example of successfully concluded negotiations on subsidies disciplines may be found on the bilateral level. The CPTPP formed the framework for multilateral negotiations on Fisheries. The CPTPP Contracting Parties recognise that proper fisheries management may have to include control, reduction and eventual

---

[41] *Ibid.*

[42] Generally, see Bigdeli (2008).

[43] See, for instance, Cho (2015), pp. 13–14.

[44] See, for instance, Final Affirmative Countervailing Duty Determination, Certain Fresh Atlantic Groundfish from Canada, 51 Fed. Reg. 10041-10042 (1986); GATT Panel report, *United States – Imposition of Countervailing Duties on Imports of Chilled Atlantic Salmon from Norway*, GATT Doc. SCM/153, adopted 4 December 1992.

[45] Negotiating Group on Rules, Fisheries Subsidies, Draft Consolidated Chair Text, Communication from the Chair, TN/RL/W/276, 11 May 2021.

[46] Negotiating Group on Rules, Fisheries Subsidies, Draft Consolidated Chair Text, Chair's Explanatory Note Accompanying TN/RL/W/276, TN/RL/W/276/Add.1, 11 May 2021, para. 131.

[47] *Ibid*, para. 132.

[48] Decision by the Arbitrators, *Brazil – Export Financing Programme for Aircraft*, Recourse to Arbitration by Brazil under Article 22.6 of the DSU and Article 4.11 of the SCM Agreement, WT/DS46/ARB, circulated 28 August 2000, para. 3.28 ff.

[49] Decision by the Arbitrator, *Canada – Export Credits and Loan Guarantees for Regional Aircraft*, Recourse to Arbitration by Canada under Article 22.6 of the DSU and Article 4.11 of the SCM Agreement, WT/DS222/ARB, circulated 17 February 2003, para. 3.3 ff.

elimination of all subsidies that contribute to overfishing and overcapacity. In a novel approach on the regulation on fisheries subsidies under Art. 20.16(5) of the CPTPP, the text provides:

> [...] no Party shall grant or maintain any of the following subsidies within the meaning of Article 1.1 of the SCM Agreement that are specific within the meaning of Article 2 of the SCM Agreement:
> (a) subsidies for fishing that negatively affect fish stocks that are in an overfished condition.[50]

This approach is noteworthy for at least three reasons. First, the CPTPP approach regulates subsidies for fishing (*i.e.* the activity) instead of fish (*i.e.* the product), contrary to the approach of the ASCM which regulates subsidies on trade in goods (*i.e.* production or export of goods or products).[51] Second, Art. 20.16(5) CPTPP does not redress injury suffered by the domestic industry of a WTO Member following subsidisation of another WTO Member, but rather seeks to redress injury to the fish stocks in overfished condition.[52] This means that the injury is not competitive in nature but rather that environmental harm underlies the disciplines. In fact, the text does not even require proof that the subsidies affect trade or investment at all. Third, the injury Art. 20.16(5) seeks to redress does not even need to take place within the jurisdiction of the Contracting Parties: The aggrieved fish stock does not need to be located in the territorial waters or the exclusive economic zone of the Contracting Parties.[53]

The difficulty with redefining the injury from competitive harm to environmental harm is that no quantifiable injury to the domestic industry could be calculated by the (fisheries) subsidies, thus rendering the traditional conception of the ASCM inapplicable. This problem arises for both a multilateral and a unilateral track solution in fisheries subsidies negotiations. In CPTPP, only a dispute resolution procedure similar to the multilateral track under the ASCM is available in Chapter 28 of the CPTPP. This track, however, does not provide an adequate means of remedy for a violation of Art. 20.16(5) CPTPP. The unilateral track of countervailing measures is not foreseen in the CPTPP, but the quantification of the injury margin to the domestic industry arises equally. Against that background, *Jung/Jung* propose a more adequate calculation of the injury in case of pure environmental obligations in RTAs, on the basis of two complementary parameters: The injury to the environment itself and the benefit to the responding party.[54] The authors leave discretion to a tribunal that could authorise the complaining Party to take appropriate countermeasures.[55]

---

[50] Art. 20.16(5) CPTPP.

[51] Jung and Jung (2019), p. 1011.

[52] *Ibid*, p. 1012.

[53] *Ibid*.

[54] *Ibid*, pp. 1015 ff.

[55] *Ibid*.

Also in other regional agreements, fisheries subsidies have been tackled, but not as comprehensively as in the CPTPP. They do not include the possibility to impose CVDs or related other unilateral remedies to offer relief in a similar manner as trade remedies.

8.3.2.2 Fossil Fuel Subsidies

Fossil fuel subsidies influence both trade and environmental protection. Whereas their effect on trade brings the issue to the WTO, it is the environmental effect which drives the quest for reform of the WTO rules. One type of fossil fuel subsidies are 'anti-Pigouvian subsidies' which are defined as a failure to impose taxes to account for the social cost of carbon.[56] Designing appropriate remedies against fossil fuel subsidies requires taking into account the environmental objectives underlying fossil fuel subsidies reform. The prime remedy will be the withdrawal of the state's subsidy to fulfil the carbon emissions reduction goal. An immediate phase-out and prohibition of subsidies on fossil fuel and other resource-depleting subsidies should be the main goal of fossil fuel subsidy reforms.[57]

Although other remedies—most notably the retraction of the environmentally harmful subsidy—would be more appropriate and in line with the environmental protection goal, the option to impose unilateral CVDs could be retained for those imports that do cause trade injury besides environmental injury. As *Trachtman* points out, when disciplining fossil fuel subsidies, the remedy of CVDs is largely inappropriate because the disciplining is underlined by environmental effects and not trade effects as the CVD seeks to countervail.[58] CVDs have the advantage that they are a readily available remedy, which is fast and can be applied without multilateral authorisation. Should CVDs nonetheless be available more broadly, a trade-based injury test as a condition for actionability is not apposite to a carbon emission reduction purpose, as opposed to a competitive injury purpose.[59] In such cases, the calculation methodologies would need to be modified to reflect the environmental cost in the assessment of the injury to the domestic industry.

8.3.2.3 Agricultural Subsidies

Agricultural subsidies are part of the WTO Agreement on Agriculture (AoA). Subsidies disciplines in the agricultural sector have also been driven by environmental considerations. Some biofuels (e.g. bioethanol) fall under the Amber Box disciplines of the AoA, which foresee a progressive phase-out of the support

---

[56] Trachtman (2019), p. 3.

[57] Horlick and Clarke (2017), p. 684.

[58] Trachtman (2019), p. 15.

[59] *Ibid*, p. 14.

schemes rather than a total prohibition. Therefore, the classification of other types of biofuels (e.g. biodiesel) as agricultural products would result in permitted subsidies under the AoA.[60] To that extent, the WTO contributed to the SDG 2.

8.3.3 Rebalancing Measures in the EU-UK TCA

Another significant development is the EU-UK Trade and Cooperation Agreement (TCA), where innovative treaty drafting led to the explicit link between the goals of sustainable development, environmental protection and climate change mitigation to level playing field considerations.[61] The EU-UK TCA established a new tariff-free and quota-free trade relationship between the UK and the EU and is a front-runner on trade and sustainable development. In line with this commitment, the TCA confirms that international trade and development contributes to the objective of sustainable development.[62] Through the possibility to impose so-called "rebalancing measures", these objectives are included in the level playing field chapter.

The Parties acknowledge that significant divergences in policies and priorities with respect to environmental and climate protection may impact trade between Parties in a manner that changes the circumstances at the time of the conclusion of the TCA.[63] Art. 9.4.2 of the TCA foresees that:

> If <u>material impacts</u> on trade or investment between the Parties are arising as a result of <u>significant divergences between the Parties in the areas referred to in paragraph 1</u>, either Party may take appropriate <u>rebalancing measures</u> to address the situation. Such measures shall be <u>restricted with respect to their scope and duration to what is strictly necessary and proportionate</u> in order to remedy the situation. Priority shall be given to such measures as will <u>least disturb the functioning of this Agreement</u>. A Party's assessment of these impacts shall be based on <u>reliable evidence</u> and not merely on conjecture or remote possibility.[64]

Thus, rebalancing measures can be imposed when either of the trade partners significantly lowers its environmental protection standards. This is seen as a successful way to defend the European interests and values: Rebalancing measures will be applicable if the UK attempts to diverge from European regulations to such an extent as to have a significant impact on internal market.[65] Hailed by some for being an improvement on TSD chapters in EU FTAs which lacked firm enforcement and dispute resolution mechanisms, it is to be awaited how rebalancing will work in the

---

[60] Decision of the Ministerial Conference, Export Competition, WT/MIN(15)/45, 19 December 2015. See Farah and Cima (2015), p. 528.

[61] EU-UK TCA, Title XI: Level Playing Field for Open and Fair Competition and Sustainable Development.

[62] *Ibid*, Art. 1.1.

[63] *Ibid*, Art. 9.4.1.

[64] *Ibid*, Art. 9.4.2.

[65] Fabry (2021).

future—particularly where it comes to the definition of "significant divergences" and the exact scope of "rebalancing measures".[66]

The measures that may be imposed may likely be additional tariffs—although the text of the provision does not display a limitation to duties alone. The unilateral nature of the measures confirms the similarity to trade remedy duties. A difference is, however, that the procedures for applying rebalancing measures are shorter and simpler than the elaborate investigation to be carried out by the Commission under the trade remedy agreements.[67] Nonetheless, it can be expected that a certain administrative, quasi-judicial proceeding will have to be established—perhaps modelled after and executed by the trade remedy authorities.[68] Art. 9.4.2 of the EU-UK TCA includes restrictions and limitations: necessity, proportionality, and choosing the least disturbing measures.

8.3.4 Proposals for Social Safeguard Measures

Another proposal is to design a trade mechanism to ensure protection against social dumping—by extension, this proposal can be considered as an instrument against environmental dumping, too. Legitimisation for trade measures may be found in the transboundary characteristic of environmental harm, particularly in relation to carbon emissions and climate change. Against the discussions to broaden the scope of safeguards measures,[69] *Shaffer* designed a 'Social Dumping Agreement' designed to challenge social dumping by forming an agreement which is a hybrid form between the SGA and ADA.[70] The proposal includes a substantive law trigger based on labour rights violations and a safeguard remedy based on increased imports of products.[71] Procedures would be borrowed from the existing ADA (and/or ASCM). These could include the provisions on 'Initiation and Subsequent Investigation', 'Evidence', 'Duration', 'Public Notice and Explanation of Determinations', 'Judicial Review', amongst others.

The proposal identifies the challenge to determine the amount of tariff that may be imposed on the dumped goods. In the case of social dumping, *Shaffer* suggests applying the duties on the level that would offset the injury that the increased imports from the country in question cause or threaten to cause to the domestic industry.[72] This would also save transactional costs and be more reliable than calculating the exact duty level. The proposal does not include new approaches to injury

---

[66] Luyten (2021). See also Sect. 8.4.1.2 below.

[67] EU-UK TCA, Art. 9.4.3.

[68] Lester (2020).

[69] See Sect. 7.3 above.

[70] Shaffer (2019), pp. 34 ff.

[71] *Ibid*, p. 37.

[72] *Ibid*, p. 36.

and argues that the existing rules provide enough guidance.[73] In addition, he suggests removing the requirement to prove a causal link between the violations and the increased imports, arguing that the establishment of a correlation would suffice.[74]

The anti-dumping and anti-subsidy structures are in place in many countries and provide an adequate framework for ensuring procedural fairness and safeguards to ensure the participation of all interested parties. For instance, a system where the importing company can be relieved by showing that it adheres to sufficient environmental standards can be used and exists as a mechanism in anti-dumping NME methodologies already.[75]

8.4   Designing Trade Remedy Calculation Methods to Remove Environmental Injury

If trade remedy measures would provide a means of recourse against environmental harm caused by the production process, the notion of injury should be reconceptualised to focus on environmental rather than economic harm. This could be achieved through the creation of a trade remedy-like instrument which remedies environmental injury independently from the occurrence of economic harm. Such instrument would sanction imports of countries which do not adhere to sufficient legal standards.

A calculation method would need to be designed to reflect environmental cost externalisation in the assessment of the injury to the domestic injury. Various thorny issues arise, including determining an acceptable standard of environmental injury (Sect. 8.4.1), questions of determining a violation of that standard as well as of proof and evidence (Sect. 8.4.2) and questions of enforcement (Sect. 8.4.3).

8.4.1   Applicable Environmental Standard

A first question is what the applicable environmental standard will be to determine a violation thereof warranting the inclusion of environmental costs in the calculation of trade remedy duties. Two options could be pursued: an absolute standard (an international minimum standard) or a relative standard (an individual standard based on the current level of environmental protection of each trade partner).

---

[73] Shaffer (2019), p. 35.

[74] *Ibid*, pp. 36–37.

[75] Westin (1997); Lothe (2001), p. 201.

8.4.1.1   An International Minimum Standard?

An internationally agreed minimum standard for environmental protection does not exist. Contrary to for instance the eight core ILO labour rights conventions, which are considered the international minimum standard of social protection,[76] there is no single international organisation that can take the lead on defining the core environmental standards. Similarly, contrary to human rights law, where a baseline set of human rights is considered customary international law,[77] such consensus does not exist for environmental protection.[78] Therefore, if countries want to apply a minimum standard for trade measures, a list of relevant MEAs shall be agreed upon by the contracting Members.

The WTO CTE and CTESS maintain and update a list of MEAs with trade-related measures (notably requirements or restrictions on imported or exported products).[79] About 15 of these MEAs include provisions to control trade in order to prevent damage to the environment (see Table 8.1). Besides the trade-related nature of the MEAs, *Žvelc* defines two additional relevant criteria for MEAs that could be used to define the international standard: (1) universal (or at least broad) membership, and (2) the presence of monitoring bodies in the MEAs.[80]

Regarding universal membership, the assessment is not as straightforward as one might think. Membership can be judged based on a purely numerical threshold.[81]

---

[76] The ILO Governing Body has identified eight "fundamental" Conventions, covering subjects that are considered to be fundamental principles and rights at work including freedom of association and the effective recognition of the right to collective bargaining; the elimination of all forms of forced or compulsory labour; the effective abolition of child labour; and the elimination of discrimination in respect of employment and occupation. See ILO Declaration on Fundamental Principles and Rights at Work and its Follow-up, Adopted by the International Labour Conference at its Eighty-sixth Session, Geneva, 18 June 1998 (Annex revised 15 June 2010). All WTO Members committed to these ILO Conventions. At the 1996 Singapore Ministerial Conference, Members identified the ILO as the competent body to negotiate labour standards. See WTO Ministerial Conference, Singapore Ministerial Declaration, WT/MIN(96)/DEC, 18 December 1996, para. 4.

[77] The UN Declaration of Human Rights of 1948 and the Civil/Political Rights and ECOSOC Rights Covenants of 1966 for the so-called "International Bill of Rights" in human rights law. See UNGA Res. 217 A (III), Universal Declaration of Human Rights, U.N. Doc A/810 at 71 (1948). Although UN human rights bodies have not declared an international minimum standard, the UN Declaration of Human Rights of 1948 is generally agreed to constitute binding international law. See Zagel (2004), p. 141.

[78] However, in October 2021, the Human Rights Council recognised, for the first time, that having a clean, healthy and sustainable environment is a human right. See *UN News*, Access to a healthy environment, declared a human right by UN rights council, 8 October 2021, available at https://news.un.org/en/story/2021/10/1102582 (last accessed 22 June 2023).

[79] WTO CTE/CTESS, Matrix on Trade-related Measures Pursuant to Selected Multilateral Environmental Agreements, Note by the Secretariat, WT/CTE/W/160/Rev.9, TN/TE/S/5/Rev.7, 19 March 2021.

[80] Žvelc (2012), p. 180.

[81] For instance, 160, 1890 or 190 Contracting Parties could be taken as a threshold. The WTO has 164 Members since 29 July 2016.

Table 8.1 WTO matrix on trade-related measures pursuant to selected multilateral environmental agreements (MEAs)

Multilateral environmental agreement	Criteria		
	Parties (of which WTO Members)	Monitoring body	Trade measures
Convention on International Trade in Endangered Species of Wild Fauna and Flora (CITES)	183 (160)	Standing Committee (annual reports)	Yes
United Nations Fish Stocks Agreement (UNFSA)	91 (80)	Obligations for the flag state and port state	Yes
Agreement on Port State Measures to prevent, deter and eliminate illegal, unreported, and unregulated fishing (PSMA)	68 (62)	FAO (regular and systematic monitoring)	Yes
International Tropical Timber Agreement (ITTA)	74 (74)	/	Yes
International Plant Protection Convention (IPPC)	184 (158)	/	Yes
Convention on Biological Diversity (CBD)	196 (160)	Members (self-reporting system)	Yes
– Nagoya Protocol on Access to Genetic Resources and the Fair and Equitable Sharing of Benefits Arising from their Utilization to the Convention on Biological Diversity	129 (113)	Compliance Committee (no reporting)	Yes
– Cartagena Protocol on Biosafety to the Convention on Biological Diversity	173 (147)	Compliance Committee (no reporting)	Yes
– Nagoya – Kuala Lumpur Supplementary Protocol on Liability and Redress to the Cartagena Protocol on Biosafety	48 (46)	Members (self-reporting system) reviewed by Compliance Committee	Yes
Montreal Protocol and the Vienna Convention on Substances that Deplete the Ozone Layer, Montreal Protocol on Substances that Deplete the Ozone Layer	198 (161), 198 (161)	Implementation Committee (no reporting)	Yes
United Nations Framework Convention on Climate Change (UNFCCC) – Kyoto Protocol – Paris Agreement	197 (162), 192 (159), 191 (159)	Self-reporting + Multilateral Consultative Committee, Compliance Committee (enforcement branch), committee	Yes
Basel Convention on the Control of Transboundary Movements of Hazardous Wastes and their Disposal	188 (156)	Mechanism for Promoting Implementation and Compliance administered by a Committee	Yes

(continued)

Table 8.1 (continued)

| Multilateral environmental agreement | Criteria | | |
	Parties (of which WTO Members)	Monitoring body	Trade measures
Rotterdam Convention on the Prior Informed Consent Procedure for Certain Hazardous Chemicals and Pesticides in International Trade	164 (145)	Non-compliance procedures and mechanisms	Yes
Stockholm Convention on Persistent Organic Pollutants	184 (154)	Reporting mechanism	Yes
Minamata Convention on Mercury	127 (114)	Implementation and Compliance Committee	Yes

Source: Based on WTO CTE/CTESS, matrix on trade-related measures pursuant to selected multilateral environmental agreements, note by the secretariat, WT/CTE/W/160/Rev.9, TN/TE/S/5/Rev.7, 19 March 2021

Accordingly, some of the most prominent MEAs are the Basel Convention (187 signatories), the Stockholm Convention (183 signatories), the UNFCC (192 State Parties). However, other factors can play a role, including consideration whether Contracting Parties have ratified the MEA, whether they comply with the obligations of the MEA, whether they systematically violate the obligations, etc. Moreover, the absence of a particularly impactful country could also be considered. For instance, the US notably has signed but not ratified the Basel Convention and the Stockholm Convention, which each have a quasi-universal membership. In the framework of climate change cooperation, the UNFCC Paris Agreement has a very high ratification level.

Regarding the presence of an (active) monitoring body, this criterion makes sure there are effective implementation measures in place, rendering the MEA effective in practice. This has advantages regarding the speed, the standard, the difficulty, the conduct of individual non-compliance proceedings and the identification of the critical date.[82] For instance, the Montreal Protocol has a body which can suspend privileges and the Kyoto Protocol has a non-compliance mechanism.

Based on these three criteria, CITES, CBD, the Cartagena Protocol, Montreal Protocol, the UNFCCC Conventions, the Basel Convention, and the Stockholm Convention could be considered most suitable to be part of an agreed upon environmental minimum protection standard. These MEAs could form the basis to judge an adequate level of environmental protection in the framework of trade remedy agreements or a new trade remedy-like instrument. The EU has not included an explicit list in its modernised anti-dumping legal framework. However, it has included such lists containing these core MEAs in other comparable instruments.[83]

---

[82] Žvelc (2012), p. 182.

[83] See, for instance, the relevant MEAs in the GSP Regulation, slightly different in the EU Public Procurement Directive.

However, the problem with setting multilateral standards is that, by allowing CVDs, it encroaches on the regulatory sovereignty over natural resources of trade partners. This spurred the search for an approach overcomes this objection.

8.4.1.2   An Individual Standard?

Setting an individual environmental standard for each of the trade partners in a bilateral or multi-party agreement would respect the regulatory autonomy of each country. The trade agreement would then include a non-regression obligation setting an individual standard for each of the trade partners. Non-regression clauses prevent activities or norms that have the effect of reducing the global level of environmental protection guaranteed by standards at the time of conclusion of the agreement.[84]

The EU-UK TCA includes such a non-regression provision, according to which none of the parties may raise or reduce their level of environmental protection to gain a competitive advantage. In the treaty language, the substantive trigger for rebalancing measures is "significant divergences", *i.e.* changes in environmental regulation. The starting point is a recognition of the right to regulate and to set out the own priorities and policies. It works in two directions: it may entail an increase or decrease in the level of protection, which will impact the costs of production and hence the competitive advantage balance between the EU and the UK. This cannot be used for the lax enforcement in practice. First debates on the regression of environmental regulation in the UK emerged in the European Parliament regarding the announcement of the UK's intention to deregulate gene editing and the emergency authorisation in the UK of pesticides dangerous to bee colonies.[85] Moreover, the changes in the regulatory standard must materially impact trade and investment. This means that the criterion only leaves room for grave damage cases, following a *de minimis* rule of neglectable damage, without excluding potential or foreseeably risk of harm to fulfil the standard.[86] The provision foresees that these impacts shall be evidenced and may not be merely relying on conjecture of remote possibility of material impact.

A similar approach has been discussed in relation to the US environmental CVD proposal. In that regard, *Cima/Mbengue* see a renewed potential for debate on non-regression clauses in international trade law in the same way as it has become standard practice in international investment law.[87] It would set an acceptable standard

---

[84] See, for instance, Art. 1 Stockholm Declaration.

[85] See Meeting of the Committee on Environment, Public Health and Food Safety, 14 January 2021, available at https://multimedia.europarl.europa.eu/en/committee-on-environment-public-health-and-food-safety_20210114-1645-COMMITTEE-ENVI-1_vd (last accessed 22 June 2023).

[86] Gupta (2021).

[87] Cima and Mbengue (2021), p. 7.

of environmental protection that can be used to measure compliance with WTO rules.[88]

This relative approach may be especially useful where two trade partners discuss non-regression clauses in RTA negotiations, which can be used as the starting point for a bilaterally defined environmental protection standard.

8.4.2   Violation and Evidence

Besides defining the applicable environmental standard, further rules are necessary on the determination of a violation, the burden of proof and the evidentiary standard. The threshold for a violation of the environmental standard should not be occasional, but rather a display of systematic violations.[89] Only sustained violations can lead to the imposition of remedies.

To determine whether a violation of the environmental standard has occurred, in the social safeguards proposal—and by analogy in an environmental safeguards proposal—*Rodrik* replaces the 'serious injury' test of the SGA with the need to demonstrate broad domestic support for an increased tariff for goods that violate environmental standards—a sort of public interest test.[90] The legitimacy of raising tariffs on low-priced imports that can be traced back to environmental violations would be determined through public debate. As such, the safeguard mechanism can be used as a tool to safeguard the social contract within a country. For many people, sustained environmental harm raises moral concerns and would find support by the public to close the markets for products that exploit the environment in a detrimental manner.

However, similar to the ADA and ASCM, a bias in favour of the domestic groups competing with the imports may exist in the examination of the public interest.[91] Therefore, a danger exists that the public interest discussion may still be overshadowed by domestic interests, but that does not mean that consequences in foreign countries would be entirely overlooked.[92] As such, to assess the relevance of hindering low-priced imports from countries with a weak environmental track record, it would be important to make sure a broad spectrum of interested parties is involved, including consumer groups and other public interest groups.[93] To ensure the broadest possible spectrum, interested parties include domestic and foreign producers, domestic importers exporting WTO Members (whose exporters would be affected

---

[88] *Ibid.*

[89] Per analogy, Shaffer (2019), p. 35.

[90] *Ibid*, p. 4.

[91] See Sects. 3.2.3.5 and 4.4.2.10 above.

[92] *Ibid*, p. 5, referring to Howse (2000), p. 2357.

[93] *Ibid*, p. 4.

by the imposition of safeguard measures[94]), but could possibly also include industry associations, unions and consumer organisations.[95] To remove any nationalistic bias, a WTO tribunal could be set up to carry out an international review procedure on increased imports, serious injury and causation.[96] This could rebalance the position of the WTO regarding domestic protectionism, explicitly granting the possibility in warranted cases, rather than being the organisation that always thwarts such measures.[97]

A concern is that these mechanisms would in practice constitute MEA enforcement mechanisms outside the MEAs. This objection has been raised in relation the social safeguard discussion proposal formulated by *Shaffer*. His proposal does not rest directly on the ILO Conventions but envisages cooperation with ILO officials and reliance on ILO reports.[98] This raises the concern that an environmental safeguard would essentially amount to the enforcement of ILO obligations in a forum outside the ILO. In the same vein, *Davis* has opined that a labour agreement would not fall in the WTO's sphere of work.[99] Similarly, the danger exists also in relation to environmental obligations in MEAs.

This discussion also exists in relation to recent jurisprudence on violations of environmental obligations in FTAs. A first dispute is the CAFTA-DR dispute between the US and Guatemala, which was decided in 2017. In 2021, the publication of the report of the Panel of Experts in the proceedings constituted under Art. 13.15 of the EU-Korea FTA followed.[100] The Panel scrutinised the meaning of the labour chapter in the FTA, which incorporates fundamental social rights through reference to core ILO Conventions. Criticised for taking the role of ILO enforcers,[101] the Panel in effect enforced ILO obligations. Indeed, the ILO supervisory body does not have the 'teeth' to enforce—which is extra apparent in relation to South Korea—but it is questionable whether trade agreements should take over this role. In effect, the EU-Korea labour dispute enforced the ILO obligations. In a first dispute of its kind,[102] the report illustrates how FTAs can be used to indirectly enforce sustainable development obligations. It is important to underline that not the ILO obligation

---

[94] See also Panel report, *Ukraine – Definitive Safeguard Measures on Certain Passenger Cars*, WT/DS468/R, adopted 20 July 2015, para. 7.403.

[95] Rios Herran and Poretti (2008), Art. 3 SGA, para. 11–12.

[96] Gnutzmann-Mkrtchyan and Lester (2017), p. 249.

[97] Cosbey et al. (2017), p. 79.

[98] Shaffer (2019), p. 35.

[99] Davis (2019), pp. 17–18.

[100] See Report of the Panel of Experts, Panel of Experts Proceeding Constituted Under Article 13.15 of the EU-Korea Free Trade Agreement, 20 January 2021.

[101] LeClercq (2021).

[102] The EU requested arbitration proceedings under the EU-Ukraine Association Agreement concerning export restrictions on timber and unsawn wood. That dispute regarded disciplines equivalent to Art. XI and XX GATT. See Dolle and Medina (2020).

was enforced, but the FTA commitment.[103] Although not binding, this report will not only be influential for the future, but also craft the discussions on environmental obligations in FTA jurisprudence.

In sum, the threshold for violation should be one representing a significant violation rather than any violation and should not amount to an extra-MEA mechanism of MEA obligations. Moreover, the determination of a violation should take due account of developing countries' comparative advantage in producing goods with different levels of environmental regulation.

8.4.3 Remedies

Trade remedy duties are the most frequently used remedies against findings of dumping or specific subsidies. The quantification of the cost of adherence to social and environmental standards is a difficult task which comes with a lot of transaction costs. *Brown Weiss* sees difficulties in gathering enforcement data which is time-consuming and expensive and not many countries would want their environmental efforts to be subject to the scrutiny of other ministries around the world.[104] It would nonetheless be necessary to determine the level of duty to ensure cost internalisation.[105]

Whether it is feasible to agree on monetary remedies for insufficient levels of environmental regulation is questionable. As discussed above, it is unlikely that the Fisheries Subsidies Agreement, the first multilateral rules against environmentally unfriendly subsidy practices, will include the unilateral remedy. WTO Members and negotiators currently prefer a mechanism of dialogue which would possibly lead to the removal of the injurious subsidy. By contrast, the EU-UK TCA rebalancing measures are expected to take the form of monetary measures.

Furthermore, the trade remedy agreements contain several other possible remedies. For instance, the ASCM allows WTO Members to initiate a multilateral challenge of subsidies before the DSB.[106] Another possible 'remedy' exists in prohibiting certain types of environmentally harmful subsidies.[107] Furthermore, price undertakings are alternatives to the imposition of anti-dumping duties.[108] Finally, the SGA

---

[103] Report of the Panel of Experts, Panel of Experts Proceeding Constituted Under Article 13.15 of the EU-Korea Free Trade Agreement, 20 January 2021, para. 107, 109–110.

[104] Brown Weiss (1992), pp. 733–734.

[105] Chapters 5 and 6 will ways in which environmental costs of production could be included in the calculation of environmental costs in the dumping margin and the amount of subsidy.

[106] See Art. 3–4, 5–6, 17, 18 and 19 ASCM.

[107] Horlick and Clarke (2017), pp. 681 ff.

[108] Art. 8 ADA; Art. 18 ASCM.

contains a more open system of remedies, where safeguards measures can take the form of duties, Tariff Rate Quotas (TRQs), quotas and other measures.[109]

8.4.4   Enforcement Mechanisms

A decision to impose a trade remedy measure is a decision made by a national administrative body. As outlined above, a nationalistic tendency could arise there, leading to proposals to eliminate procedural bias in favour of the domestic industry.[110] Therefore, also supervision mechanisms over the decisions of the domestic agency by the judicial branch should be foreseen.

Shaffer proposes a three-fold option for enforcement for the social safeguard agreement: a specifically designed complementary review mechanism such as the NAFTA Chapter 19 Tribunals, WTO dispute settlement and review at the WTO.[111] A similar rule to Art. 17.6 ADA should be replicated in the new agreement, where Panels may only review whether the relevant standards of procedure have been met, but not make a judgement on the decision itself.[112] This could lead to condemnations of investigating authorities that failed to take into account evidence of the views of parties, but not for investigating authorities not giving any weight to evidence or views of interested parties.[113] Constant monitoring on the standard created and maintained under a new agreement is necessary. The WTO already carries out a monitoring and surveillance role in the TPRM mechanism. These reports should hence also include an analysis of the measures notified and challenged under the new agreement. *Shaffer* proposes the creation of a special monitoring sub-committee at the WTO Committee on Anti-Dumping Practices.

For an alternative in the framework of a bilateral trade relationship, an example of enforcement procedures is included in the EU-UK TCA for the application of rebalancing measures.[114] Contrary to FTA chapters on trade remedies as well as environmental protection, there is a binding dispute resolution mechanism included in the form of arbitration, which may confirm the imposition of measures in an expedited manner. This is a complementary mechanism to the dispute settlement provisions of the agreement.[115] The arbitral proceedings are very expeditious, with timeframes including 14 days for negotiations, five days for the imposition of the

---

[109] Art. XIX GATT nor the SGA specify the form of a safeguard measures (except for provisional safeguards, Art. 6 SGA). See Piérola (2014), pp. 307 ff.

[110] See Sect. 4.4.2.10 above.

[111] Shaffer (2019), pp. 37–38.

[112] See Sect. 3.2.3.5 above.

[113] Rodrik (2018), p. 5.

[114] See Art. 9.4(3)(b) ff. and Art. INST.14 EU-UK TCA.

[115] The TCA also explicitly includes an obligation for the parties not to invoke the WTO Agreement or any other international agreement to prevent the other party from taking rebalancing measures. See Art. 9.4.3(g) EU-UK TCA.

measures, 30 days for the delivery of the final award by the tribunal. This is a significant difference compared to a challenge at the WTO, which can take several months or years to complete.

8.5 Chapter Summary

The WTO trade remedy agreements include strict injury and causation requirements, obliging investigating authorities to carry out economic assessments of the impact of imports on the domestic industry. Under the current injury rules, environmental harm can only be considered when linked to injury to the domestic industry. The consideration of environmental costs borne by the domestic industry, for instance in the form of extra costs for compliance with stringent environmental legislation, into the injury margin level would lift the trade remedy burden. In line with this, the EU has implemented new rules that consider environmental costs of the domestic injury in the calculation of the injury margin upon application of the LDR.

Although traditional remedies in trade remedy procedures do not capture environmental harm, new rulemaking on trade remedies and related fields is increasingly motivated by environmental considerations rather than competitive considerations. These developments affect ADA, ASCM and domestic calculation methods to reflect environmental cost externalisation in the assessment of the injury to the domestic injury. New approaches are discussed and adopted, notably in the EU-UK TCA, the fisheries subsidies negotiations and beyond. Especially an application of the rebalancing measures in the EU-UK TCA will display for the first time a quantification of environmental costs and environmental obligations in the form of a trade remedy-like duty. In addition, the proposed Social Safeguards Agreement could serve as an example towards an Eco-Dumping Agreement which is vested on an expanded safeguards notion, crossed with procedural and substantive provisions of the ADA.

If trade remedy calculation methods were to serve as a model for an instrument remedying environmental harm, an appropriate environmental standard should be a relative, individualised standard for each trade partner. Appropriate provisions for determining a violation and appropriate enforcement measures are necessary, too. These can be based on the current procedural framework of the ADA or ASCM.

References

Barceló JJ III (1980) Subsidies, Countervailing Duties and Antidumping After the Tokyo Round. Cornell Int Law Rev 13(2):257–288

Bigdeli SZ (2008) Will the "friends of climate" emerge in the WTO? The prospects of applying the "fisheries subsidies" model to energy subsidies. Carbon Climate Change Law Rev 08(1):78–88

Brown Weiss E (1992) Environment and trade as partners in sustainable development: a commentary. Am J Int Law 86(4):728–735

Cho Y (2015) Revisiting WTO fisheries subsidies negotiations. Beijing Law Rev 6(1):9–15

Choi H, Lee SH (2017) Using modified anti-dumping mechanisms for sustainable development: the case of the Chinese Iron and Steel Industry. ASAN Report

Cima E, Mbengue MM (2021) 'Kind of Green'. The U.S. proposal to advance sustainability through trade rules and the future of the WTO. ESIL Reflect 10(1):1–9

Cosbey A, Wooders P, Bridle R, Casier L (2017) In with the good, out with the bad: phasing out polluting sectors as green industrial policy. In: Altenburg T, Assmann C (eds) Green industrial policy: concept, policies, country experiences. UNEP/DIE, Geneva/Bonn, pp 69–86

Davis WJ (2019) Comment on Shaffer, retooling trade agreements for social inclusion. Univ Ill Law Rev Online 19:17–21

De Baere P, du Parc C, Van Damme I (2021) The WTO anti-dumping agreement. A detailed commentary. Cambridge University Press, Cambridge

Dolle T, Medina L (2020) The EU's request for arbitration under the EU-Ukraine Association Agreement. Global Trade Cust J 15(2):104–110

Fabry E (2021) Using the "Barnier Method" to deal with China. Institut Jacques Delors Blog Post

Farah PD, Cima E (2015) The World Trade Organization, renewable energy subsidies, and the case of feed-in tariffs: time for reform toward sustainable development. Georgetown Int Environ Law Rev 27(4):515–537

Fletcher CR (1996) Greening World Trade: reconciling GATT and multilateral environmental agreements within the existing world trade regime. J Transnatl Law Policy 5(2):341–372

Gnutzmann-Mkrtchyan A, Lester S (2017) Does safeguards need saving? Lessons from the *Ukraine – Passenger Cars* Dispute. World Trade Rev 16(2):227–251

Gupta A (2021) Analysis of environmental dispute resolution mechanisms in the EU-UK trade deal. Kluwer Arbitration Blog. http://arbitrationblog.kluwerarbitration.com/2021/08/10/analysis-of-environmental-dispute-resolution-mechanisms-in-the-eu-uk-trade-deal/. Accessed 22 June 2023

Horlick G, Clarke PA (2017) Rethinking subsidy disciplines for the future: policy options for reform. J Int Econ Law 20(3):673–703

Howse R (2000) Democracy, science, and free trade: risk regulation on trial at the World Trade Organization. Mich Law Rev 98(7):2329–2357

Jung H, Jung NR (2019) Enforcing 'purely' environmental obligations through international trade law: a case of the CPTPP's fisheries subsidies. J World Trade 53(6):1001–1020

Komoroski KS (1988) The failure of governments to regulate industry: a subsidy under the GATT. Houst J Int Law 10(2):189–209

LeClercq D (2021) The panel report under the EU-Korea Trade Agreement concerning labor practices: what are the purposes of trade agreements as they relate to the ILO's fundamental labor rights? IELP Blog. https://ielp.worldtradelaw.net/2021/02/guest-post-the-panel-report-under-the-eu-korea-trade-agreement-concerning-labor-practices-what-are-t.html. Accessed 22 June 2023

Lester S (2020) A few quick thoughts on the "rebalancing" provisions in the "level playing field" section of the UK-EU trade agreement. IELP Blog. https://ielp.worldtradelaw.net/2020/12/a--few-quick-thoughts-on-the-rebalancing-provisions-on-the-level-playing-field-in-uk-eu-trade-agreeme.html. Accessed 22 June 2023

Lothe S (2001) Contradictions between WTO and sustainable development? The case of environmental dumping. Sustain Dev 9:197–203

Luyten AE (2021) The EU-UK TCA: a front-runner in trade and sustainable development. Trade Experettes. https://www.tradexperettes.org/blog/articles/the-eu-uk-tca-a-front-runner-in-trade-and-sustainable-development. Accessed 22 June 2023

Natens B (2020) Belangrijkste wijzigingen aan de Europese antidumpingregelgeving: Het pad naar (nog) meer onzekerheid. Tijdschrift voor Europees en economisch recht 20(3):106–115

Nedumpara JJ (2016) Injury and causation in trade remedy law. A study of WTO law and country practices. Springer, Singapore

Piérola F (2014) The challenge of safeguards in the WTO. Cambridge University Press, Cambridge

Prost O, Berthelot E (2008) Art. 4 SGA. In: Wolfrum R, Stoll PT, Koebele M (eds) Max Planck commentaries on trade law – trade remedies. Brill, Leiden

Rios Herran R, Poretti P (2008) Art. 3 SGA. In: Wolfrum R, Stoll PT, Koebele M (eds) Max Planck commentaries on trade law – trade remedies. Brill, Leiden

Rodrik D (2018) Towards a more inclusive globalization: an anti-social dumping scheme. ECONFIP Research Brief

Schoenbaum T (1992) Free international trade and protection of the environment: irreconcilable conflict? Am J Int Law 86(4):700–727

Shaffer G (2019) Retooling trade agreements for social inclusion. Univ Ill Law Rev 19(1):1–44

Tipping A, Irschlinger T (2020) WTO negotiations on fisheries subsidies: what's the state of play? GSI Policy Brief

Trachtman J (2019) Functionalism, fragmentation, and the future of international (trade) law, The 2018 Robert E. Hudec Lecture in International Economic Law. J World Invest Trade 20(1):15–31

Vermulst E (2005) The WTO anti-dumping agreement. Oxford University Press, Oxford

Vermulst E, Sud JD (2018) The new rules adopted by the European Union to address "significant distortions" in the anti-dumping context. In: Bungenberg M, Hahn M, Herrmann C, Müller-Ibold T (eds) The future of trade defence instruments. Global policy trends and legal challenges. Springer, Cham, pp 63–87

Westin RA (1997) Environmental tax initiatives and multilateral trade agreements: dangerous collisions. Kluwer Law International, Alphen aan den Rijn

Zagel G (2004) The WTO and trade-related human rights measures: trade sanctions vs. trade incentives. Austrian Rev Int Eur Law 9(1):119–160

Žvelc R (2012) Environmental integration in the EU trade policy: the generalised system of preferences, trade sustainability impact assessments and free trade agreements. In: Morgera E (ed) The external environmental policy of the European Union, EU and international law perspectives. Cambridge University Press, Cambridge, pp 174–203

Chapter 9
Concluding Remarks

9.1 A Dual Role for Trade Remedies in Greening World Trade

Trade remedies traditionally do not take a prominent position in the debate on reconciling world trade and environmental objectives. Within the WTO, much of the discussions and jurisprudence of the last years has centred around the environmental exceptions to the central trade disciplines of the GATT. Trade remedies are historically vested on economic considerations and has not sparked much debate on including environmental or sustainability objectives. Nevertheless, the recent rise of green industrial policy introduced trade remedies—ADDs, CVDs and even SMs—as a central instrument of trade policy in the service of environmental protection and sustainable development. Most notably, challenges of trade remedy duties have been a strategic industrial policy instrument in green industry sectors.

As any WTO instrument, trade remedies are subject to the commitment to sustainable development and environmental protection expressed in the first recital of the Preamble to the WTO Agreement. Trade remedies can play two roles as border instruments in the achievement of these sustainability goals:

- First, the reduction of the additional burden of trade remedies on environmentally friendly goods may be a tool to promote green industries with positive spillovers. Trade remedies are frequently applied in various renewable energy sectors, which creates a heavy burden on the industry. A limitation on the use of trade remedies, governments may relieve these green goods industries from the trade restriction and advance competitive development of the market and the positive spill-over effects it creates.
- Second, trade remedies may be considered as a level playing field instrument to internalise environmental costs of production which have not been reflected in

P. Van Vaerenbergh, *Greening Trade Remedies*, EYIEL Monographs - Studies in European and International Economic Law 31, https://doi.org/10.1007/978-3-031-38172-0_9

the price of internationally traded goods. The non-internalisation of environmental costs creates a competitive advantage for goods produced in countries with low environmental standards. The application of trade remedies may equal out this difference and restore the environmental level playing field. However, the debate on incorporation of environmental costs into the price of a good through border measures is thus one that needs to consider the balance between the climate ambition of developed WTO Members and the aim for economic development of developing countries.

In these two manners, trade remedies may contribute to advancing environmental protection, mitigate the effects of climate change and thereby contribute to the attainment of the SDGs. Although the legal framework on trade remedies does not include the consideration of non-trade aspects, there are flexibilities and remaining options to exert policy space, which can be used by domestic legislators and investigating authorities in WTO Members across the globe. Accordingly, green policy goals may be advanced within the boundaries of the applicable WTO rules on trade remedies.

9.2   Limiting the Use of Trade Remedies on Green Goods

The observation that the renewable energy sector became a prime target for the imposition of sometimes very high trade remedy duties has led to the consideration that trade remedies create an obstacle for the renewable energy sector to become a worthy competitor of fossil fuel energy. Thus, some restrictions on the use of such trade remedies would be an appropriate policy standpoint for WTO Members to establish. Various policy options are available to WTO Members that prevent or restrict the imposition of trade remedies on environmental goods.

The ideal solution would be for trade remedies not to be imposed at all on environmental goods. Absent trade remedies, environmental goods do not face additional trade hurdles and can be fully subject to free trade market forces. However, trade partners are reluctant to abolish the possibility to resort to contingent protection measures in trade negotiations. Short of a total ban on trade remedies, exploiting so-called 'procedural weaknesses' in the trade remedy agreements in favour of environmental protection is more feasible. Possibilities range from reducing the amount of duty, limitations on the duration, level, or scope of the measure to adding additional procedural steps to the investigation. Amongst others, a focus on a mandatory environmental LDR and shorter time limits for imposition of trade remedies for environmental goods are recommended. In addition, due consideration of environmental stakeholders, not only in the application of an environmental public interest test, but throughout the investigation procedure should also lead to policy decisions by investigating authorities in favour of environmental protection. The core idea is to urge investigating authorities to rethink, ameliorate or mitigate the impact of trade remedy measures on green goods.

As to the implementation, multilateral, plurilateral, sectoral (most notably the EGA initiative) and bilateral options exist between willing trade partners. Some of the options for disciplining trade remedy action can also become self-imposed behavioural reforms implemented by WTO Members within their existing domestic legal framework or trade remedy practice. As discussed above, the EU has taken a forefront position by including some environmental considerations in its legal framework. One remaining question is whether this example will move other countries to commit to similar or additional trade remedies restrictions.

9.3 Calculating Environmental Costs of Production in Trade Remedy Calculations

To answer to charges of unfair trade and eco-dumping, *i.e.* the critique by certain countries to situations where the environmental impact of producing a good is not reflected in the price of that good on the global market, calculating environmental costs of production in trade remedy duties could provide a strong policy response. Including such costs in the duty level may internalise environmental externalities and is considered in line with the polluter-pays principle. However, the underlying concepts of subsidisation, dumping and safeguards are not designed to challenge low-priced goods that have been produced under poor environmental conditions. The basic trade remedy agreements are vested on economic criteria and technical requirements. Nonetheless, environmental policies have been considered in the notion of subsidy and in safeguards investigations. Two main lessons may be drawn in this regard.

First, low environmental standards in a country of production cannot be considered as a situation of dumping, subsidisation or be a reason to impose safeguard measures. Qualifying insufficient environmental regulation as countervailable subsidies can, however, be considered in light of the ASCM disciplines. Subsidies in the form of low environmental standards undoubtedly confer a benefit to producers, but qualification as a subsidy under the ASCM is problematic, particularly on account of the criterion of a financial contribution and the specificity requirement. To sustain such argument successfully, the subsidy notion would need to be stretched to include regulatory failure subsidies, such as absence or lax enforcement of environmental standards. In the case of dual pricing schemes, additional legal hurdles arise relating to the financial contribution, government criterion for public bodies and benefit pass-through. It is unlikely that a strong argument can be made under the current rules. Thus, legislative amendments would be necessary to broaden the subsidy concept to any kind of regulatory (in)action by a government, or to include specific exceptions for instance related to environmental cost internalisation or specifically for the renewable energy sector.

Similarly, environmental policies and measures have been considered in the framework of safeguard investigations in the examination whether "unforeseen developments" exist. Notably, both foreign policies as well as domestic policies have been brought about by investigating authorities. In some instances, countries directly referred to foreign policies causing an increase in imports mandating protective measures because they caused serious injury on the domestic market.

Second, environmental costs may not be calculated in the benchmark prices for comparison, as the benchmarks are oriented to costs and prices in the country of production, where environmental standards are not applied in the first place. Only when an out-of-country benchmark is used, environmental costs may be calculated (partially) in the duty level. However, even in such cases, the benchmark is to reflect as close as possible the situation of the country of production. This conclusion can be drawn from anti-dumping and anti-subsidy jurisprudence alike.

In relation to subsidies, the benchmarking techniques developed by several WTO Members have been curtailed by the Appellate Body to resemble as closely as possible the situation on the market in the country of production. Even though the jurisprudence has accepted several techniques of alternative benchmarks—including out-of-country benchmarks—the ultimate aim is to reconstruct as closely as possible the domestic market benchmark in the country of production. Moreover, should reliance on world prices be allowed, this may not provide a sufficient solution in case of dual pricing schemes, absent internationally accepted prices for oil, natural gas, and electricity, for instance.

In relation to dumping, arguing that insufficient environmental government policies which fail to provide a minimum standard of environmental protection or fail to ensure a proper internalisation of negative environmental externalities may be considered in two phases of the investigation. First, it may be argued to constitute a ground to disregard domestic prices in the sense of Art. 2.2 ADA. Second, in the alternative calculation methodologies, investigating authorities could make use of their discretionary powers to consider environmental costs of production. In particular, NME methodologies in anti-dumping law are in essence meant to be used to address general distortions in the market, not environmental regulation as a standalone government policy. A too liberal application of this methodology would be out of the scope of the rules.

It is therefore hard to sustain an argument based on the current rules of the WTO trade remedy rules and jurisprudence to calculate environmental costs in the level of duty. Legislative amendments to the basic trade remedy rules would be required. For goods produced in China, a largely unexplored legal basis exists to rely on out-of-country prices in anti-subsidy procedure can be found in the accession protocol to the WTO. Despite these shortcomings, it cannot be overseen that the concept of dumping as well as the procedural framework could have potential as an instrument to counter eco-dumping. Thus, trade remedies can be used as an inspiration to design a mechanism to address environmental injury.

9.4   Designing an Instrument to Remedy Environmental Injury Based on Trade Remedy Calculation Methods

The WTO trade remedy agreements include strict injury and causation requirements, obliging investigating authorities to carry out economic assessments of the impact of imports on the domestic industry. Under the current injury rules, environmental harm can only be considered when linked to injury to the domestic industry. The consideration of environmental costs borne by the domestic industry, for instance in the form of extra costs for compliance with stringent environmental legislation, into the injury margin level would lift the trade remedy burden. Accordingly, the EU has developed a first mechanism to consider not only actual but also future costs for environmental compliance in its recent modernisation of the trade remedy rules. Whether this approach will be followed by other countries is doubtful.

Recently, new rulemaking on trade remedies and trade-remedy like mechanisms is increasingly motivated by environmental considerations rather than competitive considerations. These welcome developments may inspire ADA, ASCM and domestic calculation methods to reflect environmental cost externalisation in the assessment of the injury to the domestic injury. Multilateral amendments would be difficult, so ASCM and ADA negotiations are not recommended. Novel approaches to subsidies disciplines outside the ASCM have been proven to be possible, as illustrated by the Fisheries Subsidies Agreement. In bilateral relations between treaty partners, bilateral or regional/multi-party agreements may offer an even broader freedom to design novel instruments and procedures. The EU-UK TCA sets an example how environmental and climate change objectives can be embedded in a level playing field chapter. The 'rebalancing measures' are close to a mechanism trade remedy procedure but with the aim to remedy environmental rather than competitive harm. The application of the rebalancing measures in practice will display for the first time a quantification of environmental costs and environmental obligations in the form of a trade remedy-like duty.

Such trade remedy or trade remedy-like mechanism may be incorporated in the framework of an Eco-Dumping Agreement. Drawing parallels with the discussed Social Safeguards Agreement, an Eco-Dumping Agreement can be vested on an expanded safeguards notion, crossed with procedural and substantive provisions of the ADA. If trade remedy calculation methods were to serve as a model for an instrument remedying environmental harm, an appropriate environmental standard should be a relative, individualised standard for each trade partner. Appropriate provisions for determining a violation and appropriate enforcement measures are necessary, too. These can be based on the current procedural framework of the ADA or ASCM.

Cited Case Law

GATT

GATT Panel report, *Spain – Tariff Treatment of Unroasted Coffee*, L/5135, BISD 28S/102, adopted 11 June 1981.

GATT Panel report, *United States – Prohibition of Imports of Tuna and Tuna Products from Canada*, L/5198-29S/91, adopted 22 February 1982.

GATT Panel report, *Canada – Measures Affecting Exports of Unprocessed Salmon and Herring*, L/6268-35S/98, adopted 22 March 1988.

Canada/Japan – Tariff on Imports of Spruce, Pine, Fir (SPF) Dimension Lumber, L/6470, BISD 36S/167, adopted 19 July 1989.

GATT Panel report, *United States – Restrictions on the Importation of Sugar and Sugar-Containing Products Applied Under the 1955 Waiver and Under the Headnote to the Schedule of Tariff Concessions*, BISD 36S/331, adopted 7 November 1990.

GATT Panel report, *United States – Countervailing Duties on Fresh, Chilled and Frozen Pork from Canada*, DS7/R, adopted 11 July 1991, BISD 38S/30.

GATT Panel Report, *United States – Restrictions on Imports of Tuna*, 3 September 1991, unadopted, BISD 39S/155.

GATT Panel Report, *United States – Restrictions on Imports of Tuna*, DS29/R, 16 June 1994, unadopted.

GATT Panel report, *European Economic Community – Imposition of Anti-Dumping Duties on Imports of Cotton Yarn from Brazil*, BISD 42S/17, adopted 30 October 1995.

© The Author(s), under exclusive license to Springer Nature Switzerland AG 2023
P. Van Vaerenbergh, *Greening Trade Remedies*, EYIEL Monographs - Studies in European and International Economic Law 31,
https://doi.org/10.1007/978-3-031-38172-0

WTO

Appellate Body report, *United States – Standards for Reformulated and Conventional Gasoline*, WT/DS2/AB/R, adopted 20 May 1996.

Appellate Body report, *Japan – Taxes on Alcoholic Beverages*, WT/DS8/AB/R, WT/DS10/AB/R, WT/DS11/AB/R, adopted 1 November 1996.

Appellate Body report, *European Communities – Regime for the Importation, Sale and Distribution of Bananas*, WT/DS27/AB/R, adopted 25 September 1997.

Appellate Body report, *United States – Import Prohibition of Certain Shrimp and Shrimp Products*, WT/DS58/AB/R, 12 October 1998.

Panel report, *European Communities – Measures Affecting Importation of Certain Poultry Products*, WT/DS69/R, adopted 23 July 1998.

Panel report, *United States – Anti-Dumping Duty on Dynamic Random Access Memory Semiconductors (DRAMS) of One Megabit or Above from Korea*, WT/DS99/R, adopted 19 March 1999.

Panel report, *Australia – Subsidies Provided to Producers and Exporters of Automotive Leather*, WT/DS126/R, adopted 16 June 1999.

Panel report, *Brazil – Export Financing Programme for Aircraft*, WT/DS46/R, adopted 20 August 1999.

Panel report, *Canada – Measures Affecting the Export of Civilian Aircraft*, WT/DS70/R, adopted 20 August 1999.

Appellate Body report, *Turkey – Restrictions on Imports of Textile and Clothing Products*, WT/DS34/AB/R, adopted 19 November 1999.

Appellate Body report, *Argentina – Safeguard Measures on Imports of Footwear*, WT/DS121/AB/R, adopted 12 January 2000.

Appellate Body report, *United States – Tax Treatment for "Foreign Sales Corporations"*, WT/DS108/AB/R, adopted 20 March 2000.

Appellate Body report, *European Communities – Imposition of Countervailing Duties on Certain Hot-Rolled Lead and Bismuth Carbon Steel Products Originating in the United Kingdom*, WT/DS138/AB/R, adopted 7 June 2000.

Appellate Body Report, *Canada – Certain Measures Affecting the Automotive Industry*, WT/DS139/AB/R, adopted 19 June 2000.

Decision by the Arbitrators, *Brazil – Export Financing Programme for Aircraft*, Recourse to Arbitration by Brazil under Article 22.6 of the DSU and Article 4.11 of the SCM Agreement, WT/DS46/ARB, circulated 28 August 2000.

Appellate Body report, *United States – Anti-Dumping Act of 1916*, WT/DS136/AB/R, adopted 26 September 2000.

Appellate Body report, *United States – Definitive Safeguard Measures on Imports of Wheat Gluten from the European Communities*, WT/DS166/AB/R, adopted 19 January 2001.

Panel report, *European Communities – Anti-Dumping Duties on Imports of Cotton-type Bed Linen from India*, WT/DS141/R, adopted 12 March 2001.

Panel report, *Thailand – Anti-Dumping Duties on Angles, Shapes and Sections of Iron or Non-Alloy Steel and H Beams from Poland*, WT/DS122/R, adopted 5 April 2001.

Appellate Body report, *European Communities – Measures Affecting Asbestos and Products Containing Asbestos*, WT/DS135/AB/R, adopted 5 April 2001.

Appellate Body, *United States – Safeguard Measures on Imports of Fresh, Chilled or Frozen Lamb from New Zealand*, WT/DS177/AB/R, adopted 16 May 2001.

Panel report, *Brazil – Export Financing Programme for Aircraft – Second Recourse to Art. 21.5 DSU by Canada*, WT/DS46/RW2, adopted 23 August 2001.

Appellate Body report, *United States – Anti-Dumping Measures on Certain Hot-Rolled Steel Products from Japan*, WT/DS184/AB/R, adopted 23 August 2001.

Panel report, *United States – Measures Treating Export Restraints as Subsidies*, WT/DS194/R, adopted 23 August 2001.

Panel report, *Argentina – Definitive Anti-Dumping Measures on Carton-Board Imports from Germany and Definitive Anti-Dumping Measures on Imports of Ceramic Tiles from Italy*, WT/DS189/R, adopted 5 November 2001.

Appellate Body Report, *United States – Tax Treatment for 'Foreign Sales Corporations' (Article 21.5 – EC)*, WT/DS108/AB/RW, adopted 29 January 2002.

Panel report, *Canada – Export Credits and Loan Guarantees for Regional Aircraft*, WT/DS222/R, adopted 19 February 2002.

Appellate Body report, *United States – Definitive Safeguard Measures on Imports of Circular Welded Carbon Quality Line Pipe from Korea*, WT/DS202/AB/R, adopted 8 March 2002.

Panel report, *Egypt – Definitive Anti-Dumping Measures on Steel Rebar from Turkey*, WT/DS211/R, adopted 1 October 2002.

Panel report, *United States – Preliminary Determinations with Respect to Certain Softwood Lumber from Canada*, WT/DS236/R, adopted 1 November 2002.

Appellate Body report, *United States – Countervailing Measures Concerning Certain Products from the European Communities*, WT/DS212/AB/R, adopted 8 January 2003.

Panel report, *United States – Continued Dumping and Subsidy Offset Act of 2000*, WT/DS217/R, adopted 27 January 2003.

Decision by the Arbitrator, *Canada – Export Credits and Loan Guarantees for Regional Aircraft*, Recourse to Arbitration by Canada under Article 22.6 of the DSU and Article 4.11 of the SCM Agreement, WT/DS222/ARB, circulated 17 February 2003.

Panel report, *Argentina – Definitive Safeguard Measure on Imports of Preserved Peaches*, WT/DS238/R, adopted 15 April 2003.

Panel report, *Argentina – Definitive Anti-Dumping Duties on Poultry from Brazil*, WT/DS241/R, adopted 19 May 2003.

Panel report, *European Communities – Anti-Dumping Duties on Malleable Cast Iron Tube or Pipe Fittings from Brazil*, WT/DS219/R, adopted 18 August 2003.

Appellate Body report, *European Communities – Conditions for the Granting of Tariff Preferences to Developing Countries*, WT/DS246/AB/R, adopted 1 December 2003.

Appellate Body report, *United States – Definitive Safeguard Measures on Imports of Certain Steel Products*, WT/DS248, 249, 253, 258/AB/R, adopted 10 December 2003.

Panel report, *United States – Final Countervailing Duty Determination with Respect to Certain Softwood Lumber from Canada*, WT/DS257/R, adopted 17 February 2004.

Appellate Body report, *United States – Final Countervailing Duty Determination with respect to certain Softwood Lumber from Canada*, WT/DS257/AB/R, adopted 17 February 2004.

Panel report, *United States – Final Dumping Determination on Softwood Lumber from Canada*, WT/DS264/R, adopted 31 August 2004.

Panel report, *United States – Subsidies on Upland Cotton*, WT/DS267/R, adopted 21 March 2005.

Panel report, *Korea – Measures Affecting Trade in Commercial Vessels*, WT/DS273/R, adopted 11 April 2005.

Appellate Body report, *United States – Countervailing Duty Investigation on Dynamic Random Access Memory Semiconductors (DRAMS) from Korea*, WT/DS296/AB/R, adopted 20 July 2005.

Panel report, *European Communities – Countervailing Measures on Dynamic Random Access Memory Chips from Korea*, WT/DS299/R, circulated 3 August 2005.

Appellate Body report, *European Communities – Customs Classification of Frozen Boneless Chicken Cuts*, WT/DS269/AB/R, adopted 12 September 2005.

Panel report, *United States – Final Dumping Determination on Softwood Lumber from Canada*, Recourse by Canada to Art. 21.5 of the DSU, WT/DS257/RW, adopted 20 December 2005.

Panel report, *United States – Laws, Regulations and Methodology for Calculating Dumping Margins (Zeroing)*, WT/DS294/R, adopted 9 May 2006.

Appellate Body report, *Japan – Countervailing Duties on Dynamic Random Access Memories from Korea*, WT/DS336/AB/R, adopted 17 November 2007.

Appellate Body report, *Brazil – Measures Affecting Imports of Retreaded Tyres*, WT/DS332/AB/R, adopted 17 December 2007.

Panel report, *European Communities – Anti-Dumping Measure on Farmed Salmon from Norway*, WT/DS337/R, adopted 15 January 2008.

Panel report, *Mexico – Definitive Countervailing Measures on Olive Oil from the European Communities*, WT/DS341, adopted 21 October 2008.

Appellate Body report, *China – Measures Affecting Trading Rights and Distribution Services for Certain Publications and Audiovisual Entertainment Products*, WT/DS363/AB/R, adopted 19 January 2010.

Panel report, *United States – Definitive Anti-Dumping and Countervailing Duties on Certain Products from China*, WT/DS379/R, adopted 25 March 2011.

Appellate Body report, *United States – Anti-Dumping and Countervailing Duties (China Definitive Anti-Dumping and Countervailing Duties on Certain Products from China*, WT/DS379/AB/R, adopted 25 March 2011.

Panel report, *United States – Measures Affecting Trade in Large Civil Aircraft – Second Complaint*, WT/DS353/R, adopted 31 March 2011.

Appellate Body report, *European Communities and Certain Member States – Measures Affecting Trade in Large Civil Aircraft*, WT/DS316/AB/R, adopted 1 June 2011.

Panel report, *European Communities – Definitive Anti-Dumping Measures on Certain Iron or Steel Fasteners from China*, WT/DS397/R, adopted 28 July 2011.

Appellate Body report, *European Communities – Definitive Anti-Dumping Measures on Certain Iron or Steel Fasteners from China*, WT/DS397/AB/R, adopted 28 July 2011.

Appellate Body report, *United States – Measures Affecting Imports of Certain Passenger Vehicle and Light Truck Tyres from China*, WT/DS399/AB/R, adopted 5 October 2011.

Panel report, *European Union – Anti-Dumping Measures on Certain Footwear from China*, WT/DS405/R, adopted 28 October 201.

Panel report, *China – Measures related to the Exportation of Various Raw Materials*, WT/DS394/AB/R, WT/DS395/AB/R, WT/DS398/AB/R, adopted 22 February 2012.

Appellate Body report, *China – Measures related to the Exportation of Various Raw Materials*, WT/DS394/AB/R, WT/DS395/AB/R, WT/DS398/AB/R, adopted 22 February 2012.

Panel report, *European Union – Anti-Dumping Measures on Certain Footwear from China*, WT/DS405/R, adopted 22 February 2012.

Panel report, *United States – Measures Affecting Trade in Large Civil Aircraft – Second Complaint*, WT/DS353/RW, adopted 23 March 2012.

Panel report, *United States – Measures Concerning the Importation, Marketing and Sale of Tuna and Tuna Products*, WT/DS381/R, adopted 13 June 2012.

Appellate Body report, *United States – Measures Concerning the Importation, Marketing and Sale of Tuna and Tuna Products*, WT/DS381/AB/R, adopted 13 June 2012.

Panel report, *China – Countervailing and Anti-Dumping Duties on Grain-Oriented Flat-Rolled Electrical Steel from the United States*, WT/DS414/R, adopted 16 November 2012.

Appellate Body report, *China – Countervailing and Anti-Dumping Duties on Grain Oriented Flat-rolled Electrical Steel from the United States*, WT/DS414/AB/R, adopted 16 November 2012.

Appellate Body report, *Canada – Certain Measures Affecting the Renewable Energy Generation Sector*, WT/DS412/AB/R, adopted 24 May 2013.

Panel Report, *Dominican Republic – Safeguard Measures on Imports of Polypropylene Bags and Tubular Fabric*, WT/DS417/R, adopted 22 February 2012.

Appellate Body report, *Canada – Certain Measures Affecting the Renewable Energy Generation Sector*, WT/DS412/AB/R, adopted 24 May 2013.

Appellate Body report, *Canada – Measures Relating to the Feed-In Tariff Program*, WT/DS426/AB/R, adopted 24 May 2013.

Panel report, *China – Anti-Dumping and Countervailing Duty Measures on Broiler Products from the United States*, WT/DS427/R, adopted 25 September 2013.

Appellate Body report, *European Communities – Measures Prohibiting the Importation and Marketing of Seal Products*, WT/DS401/AB/R, adopted 22 May 2014.

Appellate Body report, *European Communities – Measures Prohibiting the Importation and Marketing of Seal Products*, WT/DS400/AB/R and WT/DS401/AB/R, adopted 16 June 2014.

Panel report, *China – Measures Related to the Exportation of Rare Earths, Tungsten and Molybdenum*, WT/DS431/R, adopted 29 August 2014.

Appellate Body report, *China – Measures related to the Exportation of Rare Earths, Tungsten, and Molybdenum*, WT/DS431/AB/R, WT/DS432/AB/R, WT/DS433/AB/R, adopted 29 August 2014.

Appellate Body report, *United States – Countervailing Measures on Certain Hot-Rolled Carbon Steel Flat Products from India*, WT/DS436/AB/R, adopted 19 December 2014.

Appellate Body report, *United States – Countervailing Duty Measures on Certain Products from China*, WT/DS437/AB/R, adopted 16 January 2015.

Panel report, *Ukraine – Definitive Safeguard Measures on Certain Passenger Cars*, WT/DS468/R, adopted 20 July 2015.

Panel report, *United States – Measures Concerning the Importation, Marketing and Sale of Tuna and Tuna Products, Recourse to Article 21.5 by Mexico*, WT/DS381/RW, adopted 3 December 2015.

Appellate Body Report, *European Communities – Definitive Anti-Dumping Measures on Certain Iron or Steel Fasteners from China (Recourse to Article 21.5 of the DSU by China)*, WT/DS397/AB/RW, adopted 12 February 2016.

Appellate Body report, *Argentina – Measures Relating to Trade in Goods and Services*, WT/DS453/AB/R, adopted 9 May 2016.

Panel report, *European Union – Anti-Dumping Measures on Biodiesel from Argentina*, WT/DS473/R, adopted 26 October 2016.

Appellate Body report, *European Union – Anti-Dumping Measures on Biodiesel from Argentina*, WT/DS473/AB/R, adopted 6 October 2016.

Appellate Body report, *India – Certain Measures Relating to Solar Cells and Solar Modules*, WT/DS456/AB/R, adopted 14 October 2016.

Panel report, *United States – Anti-Dumping Measures on Certain Oil Country Tubular Goods from Korea*, WT/DS488/R, adopted 12 January 2018.

Panel report, *European Union – Anti-Dumping Measures on Biodiesel from Indonesia*, WT/DS480/R, adopted 25 January 2018.

Panel report, *China – Anti-Dumping and Countervailing Duty Measures on Broiler Products from the United States, Recourse to Art. 21.5 of the DSU by the United States*, WT/DS427/RW, adopted 28 February 2018.

Appellate Body report, *Appellate Body report, United States – Countervailing Measures on Certain Products from China, Recourse to Article 21.5 of the DSU by China*, WT/DS437/AB/RW, adopted 15 August 2019.

Panel Report, *Ukraine – Anti-Dumping Measures on Ammonium Nitrate*, WT/DS493/R, adopted 30 September 2019.

Appellate Body report, *Ukraine – Anti-Dumping Measures on Ammonium Nitrate*, WT/DS493/AB/R, adopted 30 September 2019.

Panel report, *Australia – Anti-Dumping Measures on A4 Copy Paper*, WT/DS529/R, adopted 4 December 2019.

Appellate Body report, *United States – Countervailing Measures on Certain Hot-Rolled Carbon Steel Flat Products from* India, WT/DS436/AB/R, adopted 19 December 2019.

Panel report, *Morocco – Anti-Dumping Measures on Certain Hot-Rolled Steel from Turkey*, WT/DS513/R, adopted 8 January 2020.

Panel report, *European Union – Cost Adjustment Methodologies and Certain Anti-Dumping Measures on Imports from Russia – (Second complaint)*, WT/DS494/R, circulated 24 July 2020.

Panel report, *United States – Countervailing Measures on Softwood Lumber from Canada*, WT/DS533/R, circulated 23 August 2020.

Panel report, *United States – Safeguard Measure on Imports of Crystalline Silicon Photovoltaic Products*, WT/DS562/R, circulated 2 September 2021.

EU

ECJ, *Daiber v. Hauptzollamt Reutlingen*, Case 200/84, judgment of 10 October 1985, ECLI:EU:C:1985:403.

ECJ, *Nakajima All Precision Co Ltd v Council*, case C-69/89, judgment of 7 May 1991, ECLI:EU:C:1991:186.

ECJ, *T.KUP SAS v Belgium*, case C-349/16, judgment of 15 June 2017, ECLI:EU:C:2017:469.

General Court, *VTZ OAO and Others v Council*, T-432/12, Order of 17 May 2017, ECLI:EU:T:2017:397.

General Court, *Shanxi Taigang Stainless Steel Co Ltd v European Commission*, case C-436/18 P, judgment of 29 July 2019, ECLI:EU:C:2019:643.

Other

Report of the Panel of Experts, Panel of Experts Proceeding Constituted Under Article 13.15 of the EU-Korea Free Trade Agreement, 20 January 2021.

Printed by Printforce, the Netherlands